Local
Area
Networking

Other McGraw-Hill Communications Books of Interest

Subscription information to BYTE Magazine:
Call 1-800-257-9402 or write Circulation Dept.,
One Phoenix Mill Lane, Peterborough, NH 03458.

Local
Area
Networking

Matthew G. Naugle

3Com Corporation
Vienna, Virginia

McGraw-Hill, Inc.

New York   St. Louis   San Francisco   Auckland   Bogotá
Caracas   Hamburg   Lisbon   London   Madrid   Mexico
Milan   Montreal   New Delhi   Paris
San Juan   São Paulo   Singapore
Sydney   Tokyo   Toronto

This book is dedicated to my supportive wife, Regina.

*Special thanks to John Covert, Donna Kirstukas,
Tom Gillman, Dean Murray, and Chip Redden.
Also, special thanks to 3Com Corporation.*

Library of Congress Catalog Card Number: 91-16716

1 2 3 4 5 6 7 8 9 0   DOC/DOC   9 8 7 6 5 4 3 2 1

ISBN   0-07-046455-3

*The sponsoring editor for this book was Neil Levine, the editing
supervisor was Joseph Bertuna, and the production supervisor was
Pamela A. Pelton. It was set in Century Schoolbook by McGraw-Hill's
Professional Book Group composition unit.*

Printed and bound by R. R. Donnelley & Sons Company.

Several trademarks appear in this book. The companies listed here
are the owners of their trademarks: DELNI, DEMPR, and LAT are
trademarks of Digital Equipment Corp.; 3090, 3270, and 3274 are
trademarks of International Business Machines; NB2000 is a
trademark of 3Com Corp.; XNS is a trademark of Xerox Corp.

Contents

Preface

Just ten years ago, it was hard to imagine the strategic dominance of the local area network in today's data communications environments. Before local area networks (LANs), the mainframe was the centerpiece of any computing environment. Peripheral devices such as terminals, printers, and even modems were connected directly to this computer. The user was connected to the mainframe with the terminal and was able to share data, send messages, and communicate via electronic mail. Although this type of computing seemed to be all that businesses wanted, it did have many disadvantages, but at the time, it was the only way commercial business knew how to compute.

The first network computing devices started to enter the commercial marketplace around 1981. Even though LANs were being extensively used in the scientific and engineering communities, the acceptance of LANs was limited until they entered the commercial business community.

With the advent of LANs, the demands grew from simple terminal-host connectivity to complex personal computer file servers, print servers, terminal servers, protocol interconnectivity, and the ability to share data remotely.

With the advent of the personal computer, mainframe applications were now on the desktop. Users enjoyed having the whole computing environment on their desktops. Within a couple of years all the programs that were available on the mainframe were now available on the desktop.

The combination of LANs and personal computers became an essential business tool. The advantages were too great for anyone to ignore. With one LAN system, users could access one mainframe or many mainframes. They had the ability to share data more easily. The first network computing devices were terminal servers that enabled terminals to connect to hosts through the use of one cable system. Today, with the personal computer, the user has the capability to accomplish work on the personal computer, access the mainframe when needed, and easily share data with other users on the network when needed. The devices on the network enabled users in geographically dispersed areas to share data as if these users were in the same room.

The intent of this book is to show where LANs started and where they are today. This book gives many examples of actual products, as well as their operation and interoperation. From LAN cabling schemes to Ethernet and Token Ring access methods to wide area networking, all the devices used are explained.

This book takes an approach which is favorable to most readers. Some readers are interested in the intricacies of LANs; others are not. The detailed chapters of the book are divided into two sections, one section for the nontechnically oriented reader and another section for the technically oriented reader. Each chapter presents material that is completely appropriate for each type of reader.

The book was designed with one goal in mind: to teach LAN concepts in a way that everyone can understand. There is nothing complex in learning about LANs.

Matthew G. Naugle

1

Networking Basics

Background

During the initial rampup of the computer environment in the mid-1960s, the computer environment consisted of large mainframes with terminals attached directly to the mainframe itself. The large computers resided in environmentally controlled computer rooms which were expensive to build and required specially trained personnel to maintain the computer system. In the business community, this was the only method of user-computer interface until around 1980, when the first personal computers were introduced on the market.

Referring to Figure 1.1, you will see that the early method of computing had many disadvantages as well as advantages. The computing environment allowed for multiple users on one computer; these users had access to the same applications and files, some capability of messaging (i.e., transmitting and receiving mail electronically), and equal access to the associated peripheral devices such as printers and modems. For system administrators, this allowed for centralized management of the computer. All management—whether for user accounts, the file system, or the mainframe itself—was done in one room by specialized individuals.

The disadvantages were extreme. For example, the cost of running individual cables for user terminals represented the second most expensive aspect of installing a computer; the first was the cost of the computer itself.

This environment was known as *centralized computing*. If the mainframe or minicomputer went down, all users were affected and would remain idle until the computer became operational. This also represented a tremendous cost, for the users were unproductive until the computer was operational.

The user's terminals were usually "dumb" terminals, that is, termi-

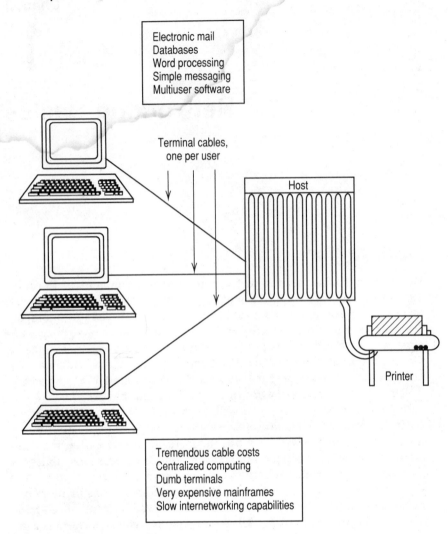

Figure 1.1 Original computing.

nals having very little intelligence, as most of the host-terminal interface processing was done on the mainframe.

Multiple-host connections were limited. When users wanted to connect to a host other than the one that they were directly connected to via their terminal cable, they had limited choices. They could connect their terminal to an A-B switch which would allow connection to another host by simply moving the switch to the next position. But this would require more cable and therefore would drive the cost up once again. The user could also use a device known as a *modulator-demodulator* (modem) to dial up another computer. Modems, at that time, were expensive and required attachment to the host end also, thus tying up a host port that could be used by a terminal. During the 1970s a device known as a *digital private branch exchange* (DPBX) was installed to provide for this capability (DPBXs are explained in Appendix G).

This centralized computing environment was effective at the time, but increasing demands were placed on it and few alternatives were available. In 1981 IBM introduced the personal computer (the IBM PC), and the computing environment was changed forever. A personal computing system is shown in Figure 1.2.

The personal computer gave the user much more freedom. In effect, the personal computer brought the mainframe functionality to the desktop. It did not bring the power of the mainframe to the desktop, but it did not need to for there was only one user working on only one application at any given time. It did eliminate the disadvantages of a mainframe. Gone were the disadvantages of a centralized computer, extreme cabling costs, environmentally controlled computer rooms, expensive maintenance costs, and so forth.

Users had complete control over their computing environments and enjoyed having personal-application software that would run on their

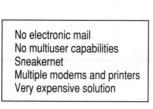

Mainframe power brought to the desktop
Terminal emulation
Individual word processing
Individual database applications
Graphics
Spreadsheet
Decentralized computing

PC   PC   PC

No electronic mail
No multiuser capabilities
Sneakernet
Multiple modems and printers
Very expensive solution

Figure 1.2   Personal computing.

individual computers. A user would run an application program, enter the required data, and print out a report on a local printer attached to the PC. But there were no multiple-user applications, multiple-user printer queues, messaging capabilities, and multiple-host support. The original mainframe-PC connectivity was still accomplished using the original terminal cable. The PC was attached to the mainframe with this cable, and a terminal emulation software program was run on the PC to emulate the original dumb terminal.

For file transfer between the mainframe and the PC, the terminal emulation software usually included some support for file transfer, but at very slow speeds. Obviously, this new freedom introduced some new disadvantages.

An interim fix was applied in the form of a network known as *Sneakernet*. Sneakernet accomplishes exactly what the name implies: a network based on sneakers. For example, a user would perform some work on their PC and would save the work. The data would then be copied to a floppy disk and transported by literally walking to someone else's computer and giving them the floppy. A remote office was supported by saving the data to a floppy, tape, or printout and then shipped by air freight to the other site. This represents an extreme waste of valuable time, not to mention money.

About the same time as the introduction of the personal computer, the local area networks (LAN) were introduced into the market. A LAN allowed not only connection from the host-terminal environment but also complete interconnection with the personal computer (see Fig. 1.3). All devices and associated peripherals could be shared across a *single* cabling scheme. At first, LANs were usually confined to the scientific and engineering communities, but it did not take long for networks to spread to the commercial community.

The advantages of a LAN were so great that they tended to overshadow the disadvantages. The disadvantages that the personal computer introduced were now eliminated. Not only did a network allow personal computers to work with each other; the mainframe or minicomputer was now integrated with the personal computer without the use of a terminal cable.

The disadvantages were equally complemented by advantages. For example, a new cabling scheme was employed for LANs, and this new cable had to be run throughout the building. Cable costs? Sure, the initial cable cost was high, but once this cable was installed, a company seldom had to run any more cable. This new cable, coupled with LAN hardware and software, would handle any type of device. The only other cable costs would be the short cable runs for terminals to attach to the network device or the personal computer LAN cable to the network cable. On small- and medium-size networks, these cables

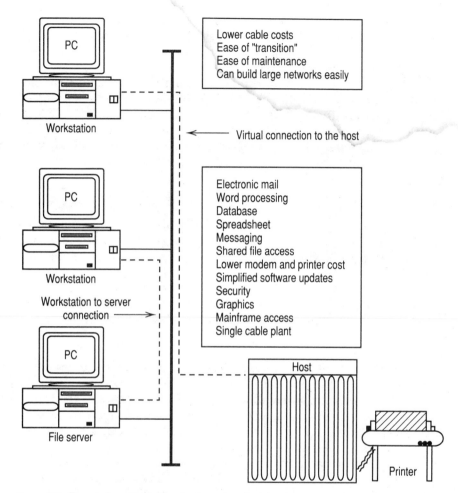

Figure 1.3 Personal computer local area network.

could be installed by the network administrator or even the user. No longer did the network administrator call the cable company when the new device was to be added to the system.

Networks usually transmit and receive in megabits per second (Mbps). This is much faster than the 9600 or 19,200 bits per second (bps) that the terminal-host interface supported.

Maintenance costs seemed to increase with the introduction of LANs. In the beginning that was true. These devices were new, and few people knew how to install and maintain them. Installation of networking equipment usually could be done only by the company who supplied that equipment.

More internal (local company) employees are now trained in the intricacies of the equipment. Companies usually have their own employees administer the network. On-site maintenance is usually reserved for only very large networks.

Today, networks are well established; networking equipment has become stable. That is, the networking equipment has been designed and used for a sufficiently long period that most of the bugs have been worked out, causing a longer mean time between failures (MTBF) rating. For example, 3Com Corporation offers a lifetime warranty on their entire Ethernet controller card product line.

Overview

To define exactly what a LAN provides in one sentence should seem impossible. The network provides many capabilities, and so much is involved. The following definition sums it up: *Local area networking permits information and peripherals to be shared efficiently and economically.* That's really what networking is all about—sharing information and peripheral devices, efficiently and economically. The current concept of centralized computing is drilled into everyone's head. Networking and network theory are slowly abolishing this philosophy.

It is difficult to establish clear advantages and disadvantages of one type of network over another. The choice of a network depends on the particular needs of the installation; therefore, advantages tend to be site-specific. The cabling, transmission method, and access method for Ethernet (3Com Corp.) and Token Ring (IBM) networks are listed and described on the following pages.

The advantages and disadvantages of centralized and network computing have been presented here. Networks have been called "decentralized" or "distributed" computing, and for good reason. The networking equipment is not one large piece of equipment and rarely is located in the computer room. The networking equipment is located wherever the users are located. The computing power is distributed. Centralized computing is on the decline, but that does not mean that mainframes are also on the decline.

Mainframes and LANs coexist peacefully. It is important to note that the original methods for accessing the mainframe were not replaced, per se; only the method of physical connection to the mainframe was replaced. A terminal was connected to the mainframe, and applications were run on the mainframe, with input and output data being displayed on the user's terminal. With LANs and personal computers, the interface connection between the user and the host was replaced. Users still access the mainframe computer and are able to run the same applications as if they were directly connected to the mainframe with a terminal. Networks, in this case, simply replace the terminal cable. But LANs offer much more than the simple terminal-host access.

Another example of mainframe access is on-line transaction processing software (OLTP), a type of software application that runs time-critical large applications such as an airline reservation system or a bank computer. This software application is in its infancy in the networking environment and still runs on large mainframes. There are many other applications that run efficiently on the mainframe. Networks, personal computers, and the software that runs them operate efficiently and are cost-effective. The user will have the best of both worlds by integrating both the centralized computer system with the network computing system.

The mainframe can be accessed through personal computers and can also be used for communication between personal computers. The network interface cards (for personal computers) are available from scores of companies, which has driven the cost down. (For a total listing of the vendors, see the vendor listing in Appendix C.) Networking software, internetworking (the ability for a network to traverse geographically dispersed areas), and networking applications have led to a whole new generation of computing.

When I first started to investigate the local area networking environment, few people knew what a network was, and few books, training classes, or other study methods were available. I learned by buying books from the standards committees and staying late at work experimenting with the equipment to comprehend networking.

Today, there are more books, training classes, seminars, and a host of other methods for networks training. With the proper education, networks are neither difficult to understand nor difficult to maintain. Networks are not mysterious devices known to only a few people. Education cannot be stressed enough. Most networking companies offer specialized networking classes, and many universities and colleges are now offering accredited data communication classes.

One area of education that is quick, easy, and inexpensive is the continuing or community education courses taught at universities and colleges. The author personally teaches a networking course at a local community college in northern Virginia. With the education classes that are available today, there is no reason to be "uneducated" about a network.

2

The Physical Layer

The International Standards Organization Model

The standards association known as the International Standards Organization (for a full explanation refer to Appendix E) developed an architectural model known as the ISO reference model for open-systems interconnection. It will be a model discussed time and time again. In all lectures on local area networks (LANs), the first item that is introduced is this model. What makes this model so important?

The model divides a local area network system into seven processing layers. Each layer performs specific functions as part of the overall task of allowing application programs, on different systems, located anywhere in the world, to communicate with each other as if the programs resided in the same system.

The ISO model is an architectural model based on modularity. The model is not specific to software or hardware. ISO has defined what each of the seven modules consists of but does not write the code or design the hardware that implements this model. This model's ultimate goal is for interoperability between multiple vendors' communication products.

Any communications equipment may be designed after this model. Although mentioned more often in terms of LANs, many data and telephone communications are designed with it in mind. Local area networking software (protocol suites) of Xerox Network Systems (XNS), Transport Control Protocol/Internet Protocol (TCP/IP), Netbios, and hardware protocol suites such as Ethernet, Token Ring, CCITT X.25, and a multitude of other protocols were designed using this model. These protocols may be intermixed completely in the model. For example, you may have XNS defined at the network and transport layers with Ethernet and its appropriate cabling system at the second and first layers—or maybe TCP/IP at the transport and network layers with X.25 defined at the second and first layers. How is all this accomplished without total chaos as the final result? The ISO model design as well as the way it has been established and mandated allows for all this. Let's take a closer look at this model and see how it is done.

There are seven and only seven modules (layers) in this model. (Within context of this text, layers and modules will mean the same thing.) The layers, in order, are the physical, data-link, network, transport, session, presentation, and application layers (see Fig. 2.1.) The ISO model has been drawn in many different ways, with boxes attached to the side and dotted line boxes on top, indicating an eighth layer and so forth. But the ISO model design comprises only seven layers.

Each layer has a specific purpose and functions independently of the other layers. However, each layer is "aware" of its immediate upper and lower layer (module).

Modularity was paramount in the ISO model design. Each individual module may be replaced with a module of a different protocol. The only stipulation is that the new module provide the same functionality

Layer	Function
Application	Specialized functions such as file transfer, virtual terminal, electronic mail
Presentation	Data formatting and character code conversion
Session	Negotiation and establishment of a connection with another node
Transport	Provision for end-to-end delivery
Network	Routing of packets of information across multiple networks
Data Link	Transfer of units of information, frames, and error checking
Physical	Transmission of binary data over a communications channel

Figure 2.1   ISO reference model: open-system interconnect.

as the module it replaced. This is accomplished without any interruption in the function of the other layers.

For example, as we study the wiring systems for the Ethernet and Token Ring, you will notice that many types of wiring systems may be incorporated with these access methods. Is a new model built each time the wiring system is replaced? The answer is "No." Only that one particular module was replaced with another specification at the same module. The other six modules were never redefined and can be reused with the new wiring module.

This approach has many advantages. First, it acts as a catalyst for technology enhancements. If changing one layer entailed changing the other six, the amount of work involved would be a deterrent to developing new and more efficient or elaborate protocols. Second, it allows for multiple-vendor operation. If one company operates with one ISO model design and another operates with another design, the two vendors would never interoperate, and when they wanted to, the radical changes in their original designs would become a deterrent.

Each chapter in this book basically discusses each layer in the ISO model in turn. By learning and/or memorizing the functions performed at each layer of the ISO model, you will be able to learn not only about networks but also anticipate the different types of hardware and software needed when you install or enhance your current network.

Referring to Figure 2.1, let's go through each of the layers and define them.

Physical layer—the first layer. This layer defines the methods used to transmit and receive data on the network. It consists of the wiring, devices that are used to connect a station's network interface controller to the wiring, the signaling involved to transmit and receive data on the network, and so forth.

Data-link layer—the second layer. This layer synchronizes transmission and handles packet error control and recovery so that information can be transmitted over the physical layer. The MAC frame formatting and CRC (cyclic redundancy check, which could be regarded as a fancy parity checker to check for errors in the data) are accomplished at this layer. This layer defines the network access methods known as *Ethernet* and *Token Ring.*

Network layer—the third layer. This layer controls the forwarding of messages between stations. On the basis of certain information, this layer will allow data to flow sequentially between two stations in the most economical path both logically and physically. This layer allows packets to be transmitted over special devices known as *routers.*

Transport layer—the fourth layer. This layer provides end-to-end (originating station to destination station) transmission of the data. This layer is responsible for the reliable transmission of data between two communicating stations.

Session layer—the fifth layer. This layer establishes, maintains, and disconnects the communications link between two stations. This layer is also responsible for the station name–physical address translation. (This is analogous to knowing a person's name but being unable to talk to that person on the phone until you dial the phone number; this phenomenon is fully explained in Chap. 6.) If there is a naming scheme on your network, it is the session layer that interfaces to it.

Presentation layer—the sixth layer. This layer is responsible for data translation (format of the data) and data encryption (scrambling the data before it is transmitted on the network). It is not always implemented.

Application layer—the seventh layer. This layer is used for those applications that were specifically written to run over the network. Applications such as file transfer, terminal emulation, and Netbios-based applications are examples.

And that is it! That was the ISO model. Defining these layers is a lot easier than implementing them, which we will accomplish over the next few chapters.

The advantages of this model should be clear. Each layer has its particular place and role. It provides structure. You should be able to understand that the placement of each layer is static. A layer cannot be moved to replace another layer above or below it; this would defeat the purpose of this model.

The last point to bring out is that by studying each layer of this model, you should be able to grasp the fundamentals of a network, both theoretically and practically.

Figure 2.2 shows the ISO model with specific network protocol suites added to it.

Topologies

Before we study the following chapter on wiring systems, it is important to understand topologies. There are three basic types: star, ring and bus. (These topology names will be used throughout this book.) There are variations of these types but these three are the fundamental topologies used in LANs.

Topologies are architectural drawings representing the cable layout

	TCP	XNS
Application	Telnet, FTP, SMPT DNS, time server	MS DOS Redirector server
Presentation		SMB
Session	VT	Courier or Netbios
Transport	TCP/UDP	SPP
Network	IP ARP ICMP	IDP PEP
Data link	Ethernet, Token 802.3	Ethernet, Token 802.3
Physical	Cabling system	Cabling system

802.2	= IEEE 802.2		802.2	= IEEE 802.2	
IP	= internet protocol		IDP	= internet	
TCP	= transport control protocol			= datagram protocol	
VT	= virtual terminal		PEP	= packet exchange	
FTP	= file transfer protocol			= protocol sequence packet	
DNS	= domain name server		SPP	= protocol	

Figure 2.2 ISO model protocol suite implementation.

for the LAN. Topologies can be hardware dependent, i.e., when a particular LAN is chosen, a specific topology must be followed for the implementation of that LAN. Some LANs have the capability of representing many types of topologies. Let's take a further look into the topologies.

Star topology

The *star topology* is probably the oldest topology used for data communications. It was first used with analog and digital switching devices known as Private Branch Exchanges (PBXs, the digital version is known as DPBX).

In the star topology all stations are attached to one common point. As shown in Figure 2.3, this common point is usually a wiring hub with all stations attached via cables that extend from it. Since the net-

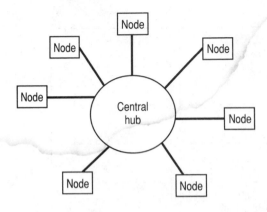

Figure 2.3 Star topology.

work stations are on a point-to-point link with the central wiring hub, the cost and the amount of cable may increase. Considering the type of cable implemented, however, the overall cost is about equal to that of other topologies.

There are two important advantages to this topology. First, there is no cabling single-point of failure that would effect the whole network. If one of the cables should develop a problem, only the station that is attached to the disabled cable will be effected. All other stations will remain operational. Second, the star topology allows for better management of the network (network management is discussed in Appendix D).

With the advent of a new wiring system for Ethernet networks, known as unshielded twisted pair, the star topology is now the most common topology used for Ethernet networks—replacing the bus topology as the most common topology for Ethernet networks.

A combination of the star topology and the ring topology is used for the cabling system of Token Ring. The Token Ring topology is commonly known as the star wired ring. More examples of these topologies will be given in the chapters for Ethernet and Token Ring wiring systems.

Ring topology

In the *ring topology,* as shown in Figure 2.4, all stations are considered repeaters and are enclosed in a loop. There are no end points to this cable topology as in the bus topology. The repeater, for our purposes, is the controller board in the station that is attached to the LAN.

Each station will receive a transmission on one end of the repeater and repeat the transmission, bit by bit with no buffering, on the other end of the repeater. Data is transmitted in one direction only and received by the next repeater in the loop.

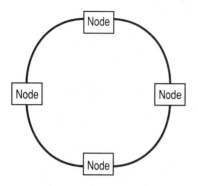

Figure 2.4   Ring topology.

Since each network station is a repeater, each station would repeat any signal that is on the network whether the signal is destined for that particular station or not. Therefore, in a ring topology, there is a possibility that could have a disastrous effect on the ring. If for any reason a repeater should break and quit repeating, this could bring the whole network down. Although the chances of this occurring are slim, the possibility does exist.

The most common cable design for this topology is the star-wired ring. The LAN that best represents it is the Token Ring. A further example of this topology will be presented in the Token Ring wiring chapter.

Bus and tree topologies

The *bus topology* is sometimes known as the *linear-bus* topology. It is a simple design as shown in Figure 2.5. It uses a single length of cable (also known as the medium) with network stations attached, to this cable. All stations share this single cable, and transmissions from the stations can be received by any station attached to the cable (broadcast medium). There are endpoints to the cable segment commonly known as terminating points.

Given the simplicity of this topology, the cost of implementing it is usually low. The single cable can lead to a major problem, however. It

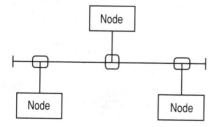

Figure 2.5   Bus topology.

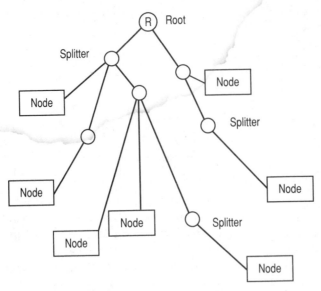

Figure 2.6   Tree topology.

contains a single point of failure. If the cable breaks, then no station will have the ability to transmit. The LAN that best represents this topology is the Ethernet network.

The *tree topology*, as shown in Figure 2.6, is a generalization of the bus topology. The cable plant is known as a branching tree with all stations attached to it. Only one station may transmit at a time, and the transmission can be received by all stations on the cable plant (also a broadcast medium). The network that best represents this topology is broadband Ethernet.

The topologies presented above are the most common topologies used in LANs. Remember that topologies only represent the cabling technique used in a LAN.

Today, there is not a specific topology to any one LAN, and topologies are commonly intermixed. There are some instances where Token Ring and Ethernet networks are found at the same site. Mixing Ethernet and Token Ring is not uncommon, and network stations on one network can communicate with network stations on another network. Topologies that are intermixed do (for the most part) peacefully co-exist.

Wiring Systems

The physical layer is the lowest layer of the ISO model. This does not mean that it is "the low man on a totem pole!" The role of the physical

's to allow transmission and reception of raw data over the com-
tions medium (cable plant). This means that all data being
itted and received for the network will pass through this layer.
~ve a very important role.

  e four main types of wiring systems for Ethernet networks
  ; wiring systems will be discussed later in the chapter):

  ~oaxial cable

2. Thin coaxial cable

3. Unshielded twisted pair

4. Fiber

These four wiring types are also known by many different names,
which will be used interchangeably throughout this text. The column
headings in Table 2.1 are the commonly used names. The different
names are listed in the table and will be explained as they are used in
the following text.

Only the first three types of wiring will be discussed here; the fiber-
optic standard (known as 10BASEF) is not yet standardized for
Ethernet from the IEEE 802.3 standards body.

Before we get started it should be noted that throughout the
changes in wiring, the access method specification as defined for
Ethernet remains unchanged—that is, the access method, defined at
layer 2 of the ISO model (to be discussed in Chap. 3) has not been revised. The only thing that changes is the wiring methodology, layer 1
of the ISO model, itself. This is a perfect example of why data communications systems rely on the ISO model for architecture. We can
change the physical layer of the model with something different and
the remainder of the layers remain untouched.

There can be confusion on which cabling system to use and how to
intermix these cables. Each type of cable for Ethernet and for Token
Ring will be discussed next.

TABLE 2.1   Commonly Used Names for Ethernet Cable

Thick coaxial cable	Thin coaxial cable	Unshielded twisted pair	Fiber
RG-8	RG-58 A/U or C/U	22–26 AWG phone wire	62.5/125 μ
10BASE5	10BASE2	10BASET	10BASEF (not for-mally adopted)
IEEE 802.3	Cheapernet	UTP	
	IEEE 802.3a	IEEE 802.3i	

NOTE: AWG = American Wire Gauge

Ethernet physical layer components

Wiring and its associated devices used for attachment vary widely among the different cable types.

The considerations for installing cable for Ethernet and IEEE 802.3 systems are:

1. Type of wire to be used (thick, thin, unshielded twisted pair).

2. Transceivers (for thick coaxial cable).

3. Transceiver cables (for thick coaxial cable).

4. T connectors (for thin coaxial cable)

5. Twisted-pair repeater modules (10BASET).

6. Repeaters (wiring concentrators).

7. Terminators (for 10BASE5 and 10BASE2).

8. Wiring closets (punchdown blocks, etc.).

9. Distance limitations.

The components needed for each type of wiring scheme are listed below. Notice that throughout the evolution of wiring systems for Ethernet, the components list has shortened.

1. Thick coaxial cable components—standardized in 1980
   a. Thick coaxial cable (characteristic of RG 8)
   b. Transceivers
   c. Transceiver cables
   d. 50-Ω (terminators)
   e. Coring tool
   f. Wiring concentrators, repeaters (not always required—depends on size of network)
2. Thin coaxial cable components—standardized in 1985
   a. RG-58 A/U cable
   b. T connectors
   c. 50-Ω terminators
   d. Wiring concentrators, repeaters (not always required—depends on size of network)
3. Unshielded twisted-pair components—standardized in 1990
   a. 22–26 AWG (American Wire Gauge) cable (telephone cable)
   b. Repeater modules and wiring concentrator (always required)
   c. RJ-45 connectors

Although any of the four (including fiber) cabling schemes may be combined with each other, their individual components may not. For example, the 10BASE2 (thin coaxial) network interface card does not require an external transceiver but the 10BASE5 (thick coaxial) network interface card does.

The cable schemes themselves may be combined or intermixed. For example, in a multifloor building, thick coaxial cable may be used for a backbone cable (i.e., a cable used in the riser of the building). Then on each floor in the building, a thin coaxial cable would be run and attached at one point to the thick cable. However, there are some restrictions on how the different types of cable may be intermixed.

Thick coaxial cable. This cabling scheme is representative of a bus topology. Thick coaxial cable is characteristic of type RG-8 (RG = radio-grade) cable and was the original cabling scheme used when Ethernet was standardized in 1980. This cable is used on 10BASE5 networks. 10BASE5 is the standard term applied by the standards body of IEEE (Institute of Electrical and Electronics Engineers). It represents the primary characteristics of the cabling scheme, using a kind of shorthand. The 10 represents 10 Mbps, the BASE stands for the type of signaling used (baseband), and the 5 represents the longest cable segment that can be run without a repeater (500 m). (Refer to Fig. 2.7).

This cable consists of a center conductor of tin-plated solid copper wire surrounded by thin foil bonded to insulation. This is surrounded by a thin braided shield, followed by foil, followed by a thick braided shield. Figure 2.8 portrays this configuration; compare this with the configuration for thin coaxial cable shown in Figure 2.9. The cable jacket is usually yellow, with the special version of Teflon (used in air plenum for fire regulations) as orange. However, the color scheme is not universal and does vary. Many installations with multiple thick coaxial cable runs use a different color to signify that each cable has a different color. For most applications the color of the jacket is yellow.

The cable is marked in black at 2.5-m intervals to show the placement for a device known as a *transceiver* (explained in the following paragraph). Transceivers may not be placed any closer than 2.5 m apart. Attaching the transceivers any closer to each other may cause excessive reflections on the network, which may, in turn, lead any transceiver to incorrectly report an error on the network. A network station is attached to the cable through an Ethernet controller. The Ethernet controller is attached to this cable through the use of a transceiver and transceiver cable. The Ethernet controller by itself cannot transmit data onto the cable plant without the transceiver and the transceiver cable. The transceiver is the device that will take the data stored on the network controller and transform it into electrical signals for transmission on the cable plant.

A *transceiver* (transmitter-receiver) is the intermediate device that transmits and receives the data from the Ethernet controller onto or from the cable plant. The transceiver couples the station to the cable and is the most important part of the transmission system. The

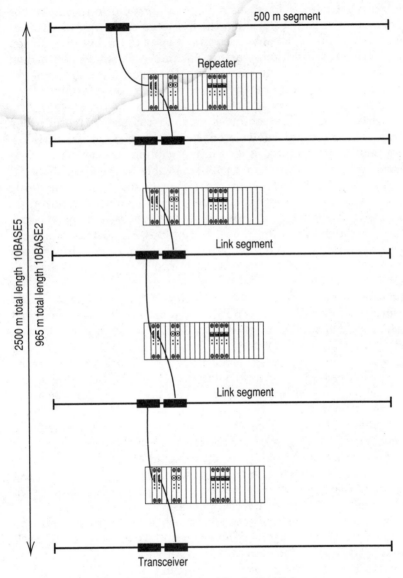

Figure 2.7   Thick coaxial cable segments with repeater link.

controller–transmission system interface (transceiver) is very simple and has not changed functionally throughout its standardization process. The transceiver is also known as the Media Access Unit (MAU). It performs four functions:

1. Transferring transmit data from the controller to the transmission system

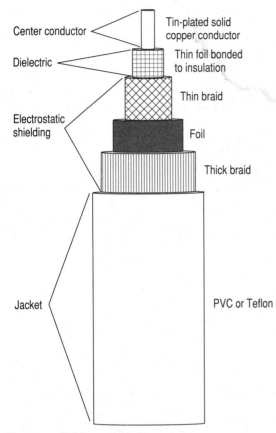

Center conductor — Tin-plated solid copper conductor

Dielectric — Thin foil bonded to insulation

Thin braid

Electrostatic shielding

Foil

Thick braid

Jacket — PVC or Teflon

Figure 2.8 Thick coaxial cable makeup.

2. Transferring receiver data from the transmission system to the controller

3. Indicating to the controller that a collision is taking place

4. Providing power to the transmission system

The transceiver cable is the cable that connects external transceivers to the Ethernet controller itself. It is not a coaxial cable of any type. The cable contains nine individual wires used to carry signals to and from the Ethernet controller. This cable may be up to 50 m (165 ft) in length extending from the Ethernet controller to the transceiver. Refer to Figure 2.10, top diagram.

Before the transceiver is physically attached to the cable, the site on the cable must be prepared for its use. A small hole must be cored into the cable to expose the center conductor. This is done with the use of a

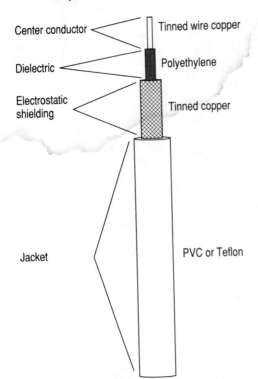

Center conductor — Tinned wire copper

Dielectric — Polyethylene

Electrostatic shielding — Tinned copper

Jacket — PVC or Teflon

Figure 2.9 Thin coaxial cable makeup.

piercing tool. This piercing tool is simply a small drill bit placed in a large handle.

How is all this accomplished? Referring to Figure 2.11, all 10BASE5 transceivers contain two parts: the tap and the transceiver unit itself. The tap (also known as a *clamp*) is placed on the thick coaxial cable. The piercing tool is then inserted into this clamp and twisted to core a hole into the cable. The transceiver is then placed on this clamp and tightened down. The transceiver cable is then placed between this transceiver and the Ethernet controller. The transceiver cable and connectors are also known as the Attachment Unit Interface (AUI).

To accomplish all this it may seem to be a very tedious process, and it is. Normal and careful installation of these transceivers may take up to 5 min each.

One last note, although piercing the cable is allowed when the cable is active (i.e., users are active on this network), problems can arise if any of the foil or shielding that surrounds the conductor of the cable is allowed to come in contact with the center conductor. This will cause what is known as a "short" (short circuit) between the center conductor and the shield and will bring the whole network down. With the introduction of the other two types of cabling (thin coaxial cable and

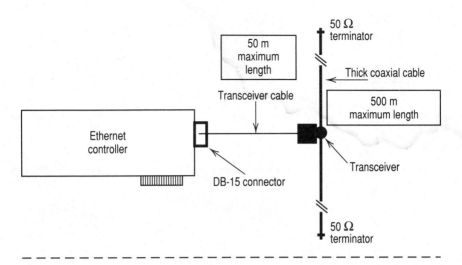

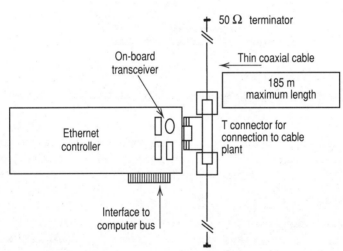

Figure 2.10 Thick coaxial hardware and connection (top); thin coaxial hardware and connection (bottom).

unshielded twisted pair), this cable, for the most part, is now generally used as backbone cable.

External transceivers are available in many different types. Although all transceivers are functionally equivalent, their methods for connection are not. If your current network controller board supports only thick Ethernet (has a DB-15 connector shell on the end of the controller board) and if the wiring in the building changes from thick

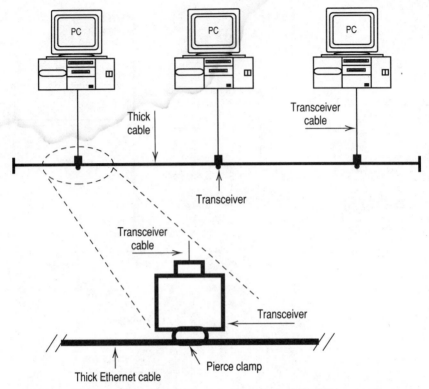

Figure 2.11   Thick coaxial cable wiring and attachment: 10BASE5 bus topology.

coaxial Ethernet to another type, this will not disable the current Ethernet network controller boards that you have purchased. There is a transceiver to connect between the DB-15 connector and the new wiring.

External transceivers are usually found on 10BASE5 networks. There are instances where an external 10BASE2 transceiver would be necessary: if the network device only supports the 10BASE5 connector (the DB-15). So, if your network cable plant is thin coaxial and the network device you wish to add is for thick coaxial only, this special transceiver would be needed. The following are the types of external transceivers currently available:

10BASE2 transceiver for thick coaxial connection on 10BASE2 cable

10BASET transceiver for thick coaxial connection on 10BASET cable

10BASE5 transceiver for thick coaxial connection on 10BASE5 cable.

The point to emphasize here is that if your cabling scheme does not match the connector type on the Ethernet network controller board, do not change the board. There is always a transceiver-type connection to meet any specific cable.

Despite the apparent disadvantages of this cabling scheme, there are many advantages. Each cable segment is allowed to extend up to 500 m. Up to five cable segments may be connected together through the use of 4 repeaters (to be discussed in the section on wiring concentrators later in this chapter).

The total length for a thick coaxial cable plant is 2500 m. This is accomplished using five 500 m cable segments and 4 repeaters as shown in Figure 2.7. Note that the path of the two communicating stations must not transverse more than 4 repeaters, no matter which Ethernet cabling type is used. Figure 2.7 shows a thick coaxial cable; it could also be thin coaxial cable segments (1000 m maximum network cable length). A pink segment is a cable segment without any attachments.

The other advantage of this cabling scheme is the ability to shield from electromagnetic interference (EMI). One example of EMI is when you turn on an electrical device such as the vacuum and your television screen becomes snowy or the radio emits cracking noises. It is electrical interference from an exterior source. You can imagine what this type of EMI could do to the signals that travel on the cable plant. Because of the amount of shielding on this cable it is not as susceptible to EMI as are the other cabling schemes. This can be a factor if you want to run this cable in certain environments that have a lot of EMI (e.g., in factories). Finally, the total amount of stations per physical network is 1024. But this is true for any cabling scheme for Ethernet.

The last piece of physical equipment is the terminator. Terminators are placed at each end of the total physical cable plant (see Fig. 2.10, top panel). For each physical cable segment not separated by a wiring concentrator or repeater, there are no more than two terminators.

Thin coaxial cable. This cabling scheme also represents a bus topology. Thin coaxial cabling (used on 10BASE2 networks) was standardized in 1985. Besides being lower in cost, this cabling scheme offers many advantages over the thick coaxial cabling scheme. A major advantage is that this cable does not have to be pierced in order to place the transceiver on the cable plant. The transceiver was moved from being external to the Ethernet controller to being physically located on the Ethernet controller. Each time you buy a thin coaxial Ethernet card, the transceiver comes with it! Depending on your LAN supplier, this can represent a savings of at least $200.00 or more per station attachment.

Stations are attached to this cable through the use of BNC connectors and T connectors. Each cable segment endpoint contains a male BNC connector. These connectors attach to a T connector. This T connector is placed on the Ethernet card itself. The cable is simply twisted together to form a cable plant (see Fig. 2.12).

There are also limitations—not disadvantages—to this cabling scheme. The number of stations on a single cable segment is reduced from 100 (a single thick coaxial segment) to 30, with the longest cable segment length being 185 m. Stations may be placed no closer than 0.5 m from each other. See Fig. 2.10, bottom diagram.

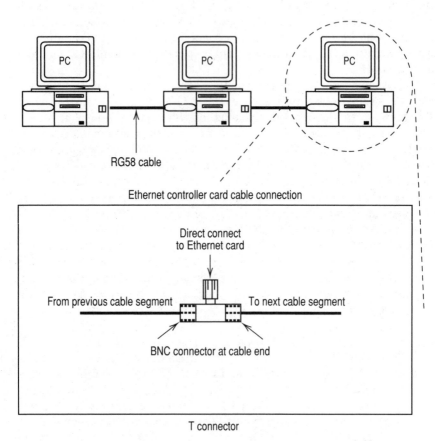

Figure 2.12 Thin coaxial cable wiring and attachment: 10BASE2 bus topology.

The amount of shielding is not as extreme as in thick coaxial cable, but if properly grounded, it is quite adequate for most installations.

The advantages far outweigh the limitations. The restriction on cable segment length is really negligible for use in conjunction with repeaters (repeaters are fully explained in the section on wiring concentrators, below). Just as many stations may be connected on one physical cable plant as 10BASE5 (1024 per physical network).

Unshielded twisted pair. Until this cabling system was devised, thin coaxial cable ruled the Ethernet cabling world. Unshielded twisted pair (used on 10BASET networks) was standardized by IEEE in October 1990. The advantages of this cabling scheme are many, and it has become the most popular cabling scheme for Ethernet networks.

Unshielded twisted pair (UTP) for Ethernet was first introduced by the Xerox Palo Alto Research Center (PARC) spinoff company known as Synoptics. Other vendors quickly followed with their own implementations. The problem that soon arose was that each vendor's implementation was proprietary and these vendors would not interoperate.

In late 1987, the IEEE committee, 10BASET task force, first met and began work on establishing a standard to allow the Ethernet or IEEE 802.3 specification to operate over UTP.

Unlike the coaxial cabling systems mentioned above, UTP is a point-to-point cabling scheme, and its topology represents a star. The cable is not a coaxial cable. It consists of four strands of 22–26 AWG wire (standard telephone wire) and may be run for 100 m between the Ethernet controller and the repeater hub. (Repeater hubs are fully discussed in the section on wiring concentrators, below; see also Fig. 2.13.)

With this cabling scheme, the transceiver is still physically located on the Ethernet card, just as are thin coaxial Ethernet controllers. The only thing that changed was the wiring, the interface and the connector for that wiring. Stations are no longer concatenated with each other as with the 10BASE2. Each station is directly connected into a repeater unit (see Fig. 2.14).

The popularity of this cable scheme is due to the extremely low cost and vast availability of the cable as well as network management tools available to manage this type of cabling scheme. UTP is recommended to use 24-AWG telephone cable. It has been in use for decades and is extremely low in cost.

A network that utilizes UTP is far more manageable than the bus methodologies mentioned above. For example, if the cable that links a station with its repeater hub (see Fig. 2.13) is damaged in any way, only that station will shut down. With thick or thin coaxial cable, if

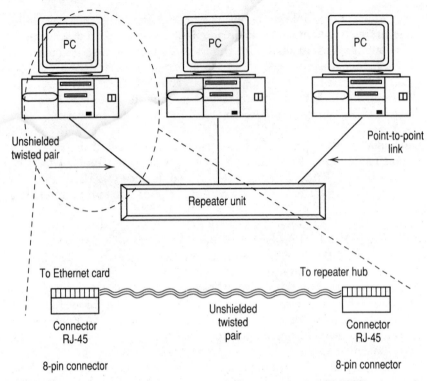

Figure 2.13   Unshielded twisted-pair wiring with repeater unit (10BASET, star topology, using 24-AWG common telephone wire).

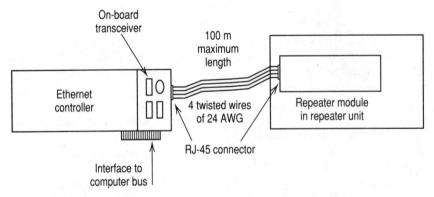

Figure 2.14   Unshielded twisted-pair wiring and connection (10BASET, point-to-point connections).

anything happens to that single cable all stations attached to the cable will be inhibited.

Another example is the *link status monitor*. The link status monitor is part of the IEEE 10BASET standard only. It has to be built into the repeater module, or that particular vendor's implementation will not follow the IEEE standard.

The link status monitor is used for transmitting a signal between the repeater module and the Ethernet controller to test the link. If the link is deemed improper, the repeater module will shut that link down. But instead of the whole network shutting down, this will be the only station that is affected and the rest of the network will continue to operate. The repeater will continuously retest the link, and when it becomes stable (viable), it will reattach the station with the rest of the network. All of this is accomplished without user intervention.

The point-to-point topology is very effective. Using wiring concentrators, you could run a point-to-point link using the thin coaxial scheme. Now that UTP is formally adopted by the IEEE 802.3 working group, this would represent poor design and would also be cost-prohibitive.

Review and installation guidelines. As each new cabling scheme is devised for Ethernet, the cost and amount of physical equipment needed has been reduced, representing a significant savings to the customer. This only adds to the popularity of Ethernet networks and has allowed Ethernet to become as widespread as it is.

Let's review these cabling schemes with the help of the following lists (and Fig. 2.8 to 2.14, again). The advantages and disadvantages of each wiring system in the physical layer are as follows.

1. Thick coaxial cable is thick and inflexible, is difficult to install, requires transceiver tap for connection to node, uses 50-Ω-impedance terminators, is used for backbones (risers), has 500-m segment limitation, is known as 10BASE5, and can be used in high-EMI areas because of the shielding.

2. Thin coaxial cable is thin and flexible, is easy to install, requires the use of a T connector and uses 50-Ω terminators, extends to 185-m runs and is known as 10BASE2, and is used for floor installation.

3. Twisted-pair cable is very inexpensive, is thin and flexible, is available in shielded and unshielded versions, uses point-to-point connections, uses 22-, 24-, or 26-AWG wire, extends to 100-m runs and is known as 10BASET, and can use existing telephone wire. Wire that is 24-AWG is recommended.

4. Fiber is expensive (although its cost is declining), is very flexible,

has a high bandwidth, extends to very long runs, has low emanations, and is used for future 10BASEF standards.

A further look into the 10BASET standards reveals the following.

1. Star Topologies mandated
   a. Point-to-point connections desktop to wiring hub
   b. Centralized connection point
2. Inexpensive cable used as media
   a. Widely accepted media
   b. Structured wiring systems
3. Media decision can be independent of Token Ring versus Ethernet
4. Standardized, interoperable products allowed
5. Centralized management and control
6. Simplified service and support
7. Lower cost of ownership

Twisted-pair and coaxial cables are briefly compared in Table 2.2.

Other considerations are expected growth, installed base of products, and existing media (see Table 2.3). Note: 10BASET cable is the same cable used in UTP for Token Ring.

Preinstallation guidelines for coaxial cable are as follows. Because of the number of components in coaxial cable, special considerations are required before and during installation. The following list is a composite of information the author has accumulated over the past 10 years; these recommendations should be applied only for thick and thin coaxial cable installations. Before beginning the actual installation, consider the following issues:

- *Cable length.* For 10BASE5 networks, the maximum length of a single cable segment containing no repeaters is 500 m (1640 ft). If the cable is segmented, section lengths of 23.4 m (76.8 ft), 70.2 m (230.3 ft), and 117 m (383.3 ft) produce the minimum signal reflection. These signals are further reduced when all segments of the cable are obtained from the same manufacturer. For 10BASE2, the

TABLE 2.2   Recommendations for Coaxial versus Twisted-Pair Cable

Cable type	Application	Media
Coaxial	Small networks (<50 stations)	Thin coaxial cable
	Building backbones	Fiber, thick coaxial cable
Twisted pair	Larger networks (>50 nodes)	Twisted-pair cable
	Building to building	Fiber

TABLE 2.3   Physical-Layer Media Specifications

< speed in Mbps >< signaling technique >< * 100 m)	
Parameter	Value or specification
10BASE5	
Cable type	Thick coaxial cable (impedance 50 Ω)
Signaling techniques	Baseband (Manchester)
Data rate	10 Mbps
Maximum cable segment length	500 m
Maximum network length (with repeaters)	2500 m
Attachments per segment	100
Attachments spacing	2.5 m
Connector type	DB-15 connector
Topology	Linear bus
Maximum number of stations per network	1024
10BASE2	
Cable type	Thin coaxial (impedance 50 Ω)
Signaling techniques	Baseband (Manchester)
Data rate	10 Mbps
Maximum cable segment length	185 m
Maximum network length (with repeaters)	925 m
Attachments per segment	30 (29 with a repeater)
Attachments spacing	0.5 m
Connector type	BNC
Topology	Linear bus
Maximum number of stations per network	1024
10BASET	
Cable type	Twisted pair (85–110 Ω impedance)
Signaling techniques	Baseband (Manchester)
Data rate	10 Mbps
Maximum segment length	100 m
Maximum network length (with repeaters)	2500 m
Attachments per segment	1
Cable size	24 AWG
Connector type	RJ 45 (8 pin)
Topology	Star-wired bus
Maximum number of stations per network	1024

maximum segment length is 185 m. A connection from one physical node (attachment) to another should go through no more than four repeaters (802.3 specification). In networks built to Ethernet specification version 1.0 or 2.0, the connection should go through no more than two repeaters (see Fig. 2.7).

- *Transceiver placement.* Most Ethernet coaxial cable is marked at 2.5 m (8.2-ft) intervals for 10BASE5. Place transceivers at these marks to minimize reflection effects. If the cable is not marked, measure the distance between transceivers. The recommended maximum number of taps per 500-m (1640-ft) cable segment is 100.

- *10BASE5 cable bend radius.* This represents the bending of the cable. Do not exceed the minimum bend radius (6 in) of the cable as specified by the manufacturer.

Observe the following guidelines when installing coaxial cable.

1. *Do not twist the cable or exceed the maximum recommended pulling force of the cable.* You should be able to tug on any of the connectors used in cabling for Ethernet. If the connectors come off, call the cable installer and have the connectors replaced. There is nothing wrong with giving the cables a tug. If the connector was incorrectly installed, you could spend days tracking a problem down or have intermittent errors occur on the network. Intermittent errors are often impossible to track.

2. *Route cables to allow easy access for when stations need to be added, moved, or serviced.*

3. *Ensure that nothing strikes or dents the cable during installation and that the routing of the cable is such that it will not be physically degraded during service.*

4. *Install the cable as a logically continuous length, with no branches.* Remember that 10BASE5 networks do not use T connectors. If you must segment the network, connect the segments with barrel connectors for flexibility and ease of fault isolation (troubleshooting).

5. *In 10BASE2 networks, the T connector attaches directly to the Ethernet controller.* Do not run a piece of thin coaxial cable from the Ethernet controller to the associated T connector. This may work, but the network will tend to be very unstable and unreliable.

6. *Firmly attach all transceivers to the building*; transceivers must not rely on the cable for physical support. Some facilities install protective brackets around each transceiver. You may use a side-mount transceiver to facilitate attachment to the building. You may place the transceiver in a retainer or attach it to a bracket if necessary. Do not allow the cable tapping clamp to be grounded. Where the cable does not run through supportive raceways or conduits, support it every 4.5 m (15 ft). Ensure that the supporting clamps do not pinch, dent, or deform the cable.

7. *For 10BASE5 and 10BASE2 networks, terminate cable ends*

with a 50-Ω(-impedance) terminator. Install terminators midway between two 2.5-m (8.2-ft) markings on 10BASE5 networks.

8. *Measure and mark this measurement on the cable as you install it, about every 5 ft.* These markings will assist you in troubleshooting a cable problem when your test equipment indicates an open circuit on the cable 114 ft down the cable. If you marked the cable, this will be an easy task; otherwise you could guess for hours.

9. *Ground the cable to ensure reliable communications and prevent safety hazards during installation and maintenance.* This, by far, is the most important guideline that you should follow. Nongrounded or improperly grounded cable will cause the most illogical problems that you have ever seen. *Cables that are not grounded or that are grounded at more than one point may appear to function, but problems occur as network size and traffic increase.* To ground the cable, connect the electrostatic shield to a reliable earth ground, for instance, at one of the terminators.

10. *All elements connected to the shield such as transceiver tap block, segment connection, barrels, and terminators, must be electrically isolated to ensure that the cable is grounded at one point only.* In other words, do not let any metal object come into contact with any metal part of the cable plant, with the exception of the ground connector.

11. *If the cable is divided by repeaters* (unless otherwise specified by a manufacturer), *you must ground each segment of the cable individually.* Grounding does not pass through the transceivers that attach each cable segment to the repeater.

Token Ring physical layer components

All the considerations and components used in a Token Ring network can be briefly summarized as follows.

1. Type of wire to be used (shielded or unshielded twisted pair)

2. Wiring concentrators

3. Connectors (hermaphroditic, DB-9, RJ-11)

4. Patch panels

5. Faceplates

6. Token Ring controllers

Cable. The cabling scheme used for Token Ring networks is commonly known as the *IBM cabling scheme for Token Ring networks.*[1] It has been designed to provide a structured wiring system that will work with all IBM communicating devices, including Token Ring networks. It is the intent of the cabling system to replace the ad hoc wiring system which has occurred in the past with a new, medium- to low-cost, flexible wiring scheme.

A device is connected to the cabling system as follows (see also Fig. 2.15).

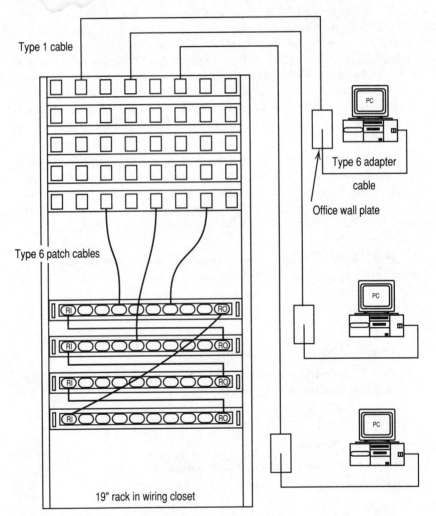

Figure 2.15 Token Ring connectivity.

---

[1]Portions of the following were reprinted with permission from *Inside the Token Ring* by J. Scott Haugdahl, Architecture Technology Corporation.

A wire runs between the office and the central wiring closet. The wire end in the office has a data connector attached to it that is mounted into a faceplate (either wall mount or surface mount). The cable in the wiring closet also has a data connector attached and is mounted on a distribution panel. The distribution panel is mounted on a distribution rack above the media access units (MAUs). Patch cables link the data connectors on the distribution panel to the MAUs, creating the physical link between the cables. In the case of a small office network, with less than eight stations, the cables can be connected directly to a single MAU which may be wall-mounted.

A Token Ring cable plant differs from Ethernet in the fact that Token Ring uses only shielded and unshielded twisted-pair cable. Although Token Ring is allowed to run on coaxial cable, it is not designed for use with coaxial cable, either thick or thin coaxial cable. The IBM cabling scheme for Token Ring does implement fiber, but to be used only with repeater (according to IBM). Let's take a closer look at each of the cable types used in Token Ring. Two simple rules are defined:

Stations attach directly to one of six copper cable types: type 1, 2, 3, 6, 8, or 9.

Type 5, fiber-optic cable, can be used only with the fiber-optic repeater.

These types of cable are defined as follows:

Type 1 is an overall, shielded data-grade cable, with two solid twisted-pair 22-AWG wires. It is available as an indoor version with a braided shield or as an outdoor version with a corrugated metallic shield that is suitable for aerial installation or underground conduit. Type 1 indoor is also available in nonplenum or plenum versions.

Type 2 is a type 1 indoor cable with four solid twisted pairs of telephone-grade (26-AWG) wire added around the outside of the shield. Type 2 is not available in an outdoor version. Type 1 cable is used exclusively for outdoor and indoor use.

Type 3 wire can be used where existing, unused or used phone wire is already in place. A special jumper cable, consisting of type 6 wire, a filter, and a data connector must be used to connect type 3 wire to a MAU. A type 66 connection block (or "punchdown block") is used to connect the type 3 wire to the jumper.

Type 5 is a 100- or 140-μm cable (which contrasts with the FDDI standard of 62.5/125-μm) that can be used with a pair of 8219 fiber-optic repeaters. The repeater essentially bridges together data-grade twisted-pair wire to fiber.

Type 6 is a data-grade wire of stranded 26 AWG used for short runs in patch cables. Type 6 is often used to connect a device to a faceplate which, in turn, connects to a type 1 or 2 cable. In small systems, type 6 can also be used to directly attach a device to a MAU. Patch cables manufactured with type 6 cable are available in lengths of 8, 30, 75, or 150 ft. The 8-ft length is used to connect a device adapter to a faceplate.

Type 8 wire is a 26-AWG twisted-pair data-grade wire with a plastic ramp cover for use in subcarpet installation. It can run half the distance of type 1.

Type 9 wire is a 26-AWG shielded twisted-pair wire in a plenum jacket. It is designed for use in environments where stringent fire codes are to be met, such as in plenums. Type 9 is a lower-cost version of type 1 plenum with a distance rating two-thirds that of type 1.

The maximum cable run for Type 1 is 300 m from a wiring closet to a work area and 200 m between wiring closets. These are absolute maximum distances that become shorter as the physical ring wiring becomes larger (i.e., more wiring closets, MAUs, station wiring, and devices are added). Because type 3 consists of small-diameter unshielded copper wire, it is subjected to many restrictions when used with the 4-Mbps Token Ring network. The distance and number of devices it can serve are about a third of those for data-grade wire. Types 1 and 2 cable are also guaranteed by IBM to support bit rates up to 16 Mbps, whereas type 3 is not. Type 3 cable cannot be mixed with data-grade wire (except when connecting two wiring closets in which type 1 is used).

A special device is needed when type 3 cable is used for Token Ring networks. Since this cable type is very susceptible to interference to externally generated noise, a filter is used on the Token Ring controller card to filter out any noise that may have entered the cable plant. Some networking vendors have designed the network interface cards with this filter built in. The 3Com Corporation is one vendor that implements this. Other vendors require you to buy this filter separately. Always ask! When using type 3 wire, be careful to avoid intercoms, fluorescent lighting, power cable, arc welding equipment, heating equipment, electric motors, or any high-voltage equipment.

Up to 260 stations (250 on IEEE 802.5 networks) can be attached to a single wiring system configured for the Token Ring, provided type 3 wire is not used; if type 3 cable is used, the limit is 72 devices. Limitations are not dependent on the token protocol or capacity (loading) of the system; instead they result from an electrical phenomenon known as jitter. The amount of jitter depends on the number of devices passed through by the data signal in the ring, as well as the length and quality of the wire.

IBM's support of type 3 wire was first speculated as a competitive measure against AT&T's popular Premises Distribution System (PDS). Many of IBM's customers already had miles of type 3 wire installed in their buildings and wanted to make use of the unused wire. Type 3 support was designed as a temporary measure to a migratory path to the data-grade wire. If type 3 wire is not already installed, IBM strongly recommends the use of type 1, 2, 5, and 9.

Data connector. The data connector is the plug which terminates all twisted-pair wire. Two data connectors can mate together by a 180° rotation of one (hermaphroditic, i.e., genderless) connector. When two connectors are used, one of the connections is contained in a faceplate. Faceplates containing RJ-11 jacks, necessary for connection of a telephone to the type 2 cable, are available. (An RJ-11 jack is a connector. This connector is the same as that used in home telephones.)

There are three types of connectors used on a Token Ring network: hermaphroditic, DB-9, and RJ-11. The hermaphroditic connector is used to connect a network station to a MAU. (It is physically located on the MAU end of the cable connection.) The connector that attaches to the network station is the DB-9 connector. Those connectors are for shielded twisted pair type 1 and type 2 cables. For an unshielded pair cable, the connector used is the RJ-11 on both ends of the cable.

Token Ring cabling scheme recommendations are listed in Table 2.4.

Copper and fiber repeaters. The *copper repeater* extends the allowable distance between MAUs up to 750 m (2500 ft). Operating in pairs, the repeaters regenerate electrical signals on both the main ring path and backup path. Two patch cables are required for each pair of repeaters. An individual repeater amplifies and reclocks data transmission signals along the ring. Typically, these units are installed in a standard 19-in rack (as shown in Fig. 2.15) or are attached to flat surfaces such as walls or shelves. Copper repeaters can operate in a Token Ring environment which has type 3 media installed. The repeaters are not supported for use on lobe wiring (i.e., the wire that attaches from the MAU to the physical device). In this environment, two data-grade me-

TABLE 2.4   Token Ring Cabling Scheme Recommendations

Recommended uses	Type of wire
Interconnection of terminal devices (located in work areas) and distributed panels (located in wiring closets)	Type 1, type 1 plenum, type 2, type 2 plenum
Data communication between wiring closets	Type 1, type 1 plenum, type 5
Data communication only	Type 1, type 1 outdoor, type 1 plenum, type 5, 6, 8
Data and telephone communication	Type 2, type 2 plenum
Outdoor aerial and dry underground conduit installation	Type 1 outdoor, type 5
Patch and extension cables for use in work areas and wiring closets	Type 6
Installation inside conduit or enclosed wireways	Type 1, type 2, type 5
Installation (without conduit) in plenums, ducts, and other areas used for environmental air	Type 1 plenum, type 2 plenum (check local ordinances)
Optical fiber communication	Type 5
Data communication, user-carpeted floor	Type 8
Unused telephone wire for connection to stations	Type 3 (requires type 3 media filter)

dia to type 3 filters are required where the repeaters are used between two MAUs and type 3-specified media is installed from the office to the wiring closet.

The *fiber repeater* extends the allowable distance between MAUs up to 2000 m (6600 ft). These repeaters operate in pairs to convert data signals from electrical to optical. By operating in pairs, one repeater converts the electrical signal to an optical (light) signal and transmits the signal over the fiber-optic cable which is received by the other fiber-optic repeater. This repeater converts in the input light signal to an electrical signal and sends the electrical signal onto the ring. Individually the repeaters can convert and redrive the signal on either the main path or the backup path. These repeaters cannot be used for lobe wiring. If fiber repeaters are used with type 3 wiring, each repeater must be fitted with a type 3 media filter. Also, these repeaters may be used with fiber-optic cable other than that specified by IBM (type 5). These sizes are 62.5 or 125 μm (FDDI standard and AT&T), 50 or 125 μm and 85 or 125 μm.

Multistation access units.   The MAU is a wiring concentrator that connects up to eight stations to the ring via drop cables called "lobe cables." The physical topology of the fiber used in MAU networks is termed "star" wired ring topology. On either side of the MAU are the "ring-in" and "ring-out" ports. These ports are used to concatenate MAUs. The ring-in port from one MAU is connected to the ring-out port of another MAU. Refer to Figure 2.16.

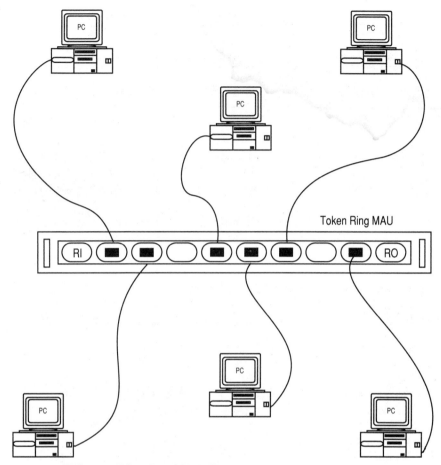

Figure 2.16   Eight-port Token Ring MAU [RI = ring in (from another MAU); RO = ring out (to another MAU)].

As shown in Figures 2.16, 2.17, and 2.18 there are many ways to connect Token Rings together. By attaching one MAU to another, this does not create two distinct rings. Only a special device known as a "bridge" has that capability (bridges are discussed in Chap. 4). You can concatenate up to 33 MAUs together for a total limit of 260 devices on the ring without having a bridge (assuming that the wire installed is type 1—shielded twisted pair). If the ring installed is using type 3 wire, the amount of nodes able to attach to one particular ring is 72, because of the limitations of the type 3 wire.

The attached network device (node) is responsible for activating a relay within the MAU to enable the token to come out to the node. This is accomplished by initiating and maintaining a phantom voltage

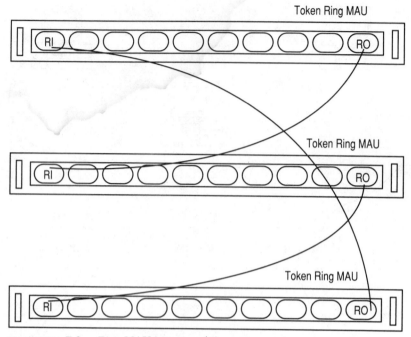

Figure 2.17   Token Ring MAU interconnection.

on the lobe (station-to-MAU) cable (see Fig. 2.16). This phantom voltage is much less than the voltage applied for transmitting data or repeating the token. When this phantom voltage is detected at the MAU, a relay is then switched open, allowing the token to come out to the node. When this relay is switched from one position to another (open to close or vice versa), enough noise is generated on the line that the token will be lost. But the algorithm devised to create a new token on the network will work quickly enough that this will not be noticed by a user or administrator (see Chap. 3). It will be reported to the monitor. This is not important because once a node is powered on, it will not be powered on and off during the day, causing the token to be lost that many times. (See Figs. 2.18 and 2.19.)

When investigating different MAU's, you will observe differences. For example, Proteon has developed a MAU that incorporates out-of-band diagnostics. This means that even though the Token Ring cable plant cannot be accessed by any station, the MAUs may still be accessed through a different cable in the back of the MAU. This type of MAU is called an "intelligent" MAU. Their diagnostic software also enables the administrator to remotely (via electronic signals) deacti-

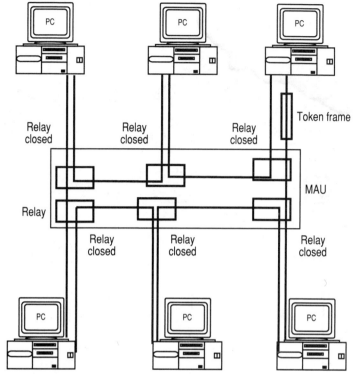

Figure 2.18 Token Ring path with all stations active.

vate a particular node (flip the relay). Some vendors also have LED (light-emitting diode) indicators on the front of their MAUs to show power, node insertion, and any faults that have been detected.

Wiring Concentrators

The last piece of equipment that plays a major role in the Ethernet physical layer is the wiring concentrator (see Figs. 2.20 and 2.21). The concentrators presented here are specialized concentrators specifically developed for the Ethernet and IEEE 802.3 networks. The Token Ring wiring concentrator, the MAU, was presented in the previous section.

There are three types of concentrators or repeater units: *Multiport transceiver units* (MTUs) for thick coaxial cable; *multiport repeater units* for thin coaxial cable, and a *wiring concentrator,* a type of concentrator that combines the cabling systems of thick coaxial, thin co-

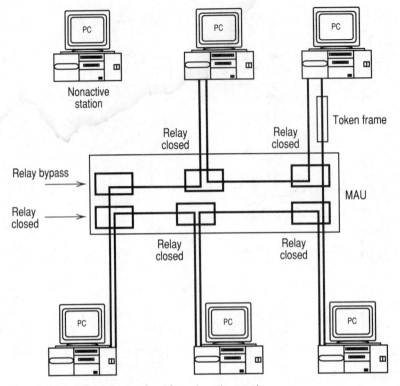

Figure 2.19 Token ring path with an inactive station.

axial, and unshielded twisted-pair cable; these are specialized wiring concentrators.

Multiport repeater and transceiver units and wiring hubs (concentrators)

These devices do not have to conform to any size or module-specific sizes (form factors) or even a common name; nor do they conform to the number of modules that may be inserted in one device. Each vendor's implementation can be (and usually is) different. Minimally, they do have to conform to the repeater specification specified in the IEEE 802.3c document and to the attachment unit interface of the IEEE 802.3 specification. They are merely a convenient way of concentrating an endpoint for the wiring to enlarge a network and make it more manageable.

Three types of repeaters:

Multiport repeater unit (10BASE2)

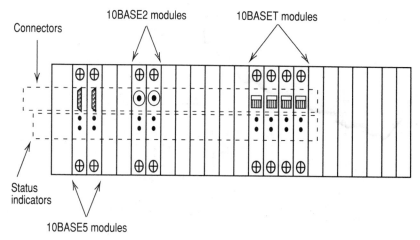

Figure 2.20   Example of a wiring concentrator.

Multiport transceiver unit (10BASE5)

Wiring concentrator (10BASE2, 10BASE5, 10BASET)

The wiring concentrator has capabilities that exceed the specification requirements. For example, the original Ethernet and IEEE 802.3 repeater units, based on the IEEE 802.3c document, were bit-repeater units. That is, any signal on one cable was automatically repeated to the other cable. This created a substantial problem, for any signaling-type errors that occurred on one cable plant were automatically repeated to all the other cable plants.

The wiring concentrator contains intelligence to know when an error is occurring on the physical part of the network. Therefore, they will not repeat these errors to any of the other cable plants that they are connected to. For example, in the next chapter we will study the Ethernet specification. There is an inherent error that will occasionally occur; this is called a "collision." This error occurs when two stations try to transmit on the same cable plant at the same time. This collision will cause the original packet to become fragmented. With the original (older) repeaters, these collision fragments would be transmitted to *all* other attached cable plants, causing an unnecessary interruption and transmission delays. The wiring concentrators described here will detect the collision fragment and will not transmit the fragments to all other cable plants attached to the repeater.

Another feature of the wiring concentrator is fault isolation. For example, if a module in the repeater unit counts too many collisions, an open circuit on its cable segment, or even a short circuit on its cable, the module in the repeater unit will deinsert itself from the network

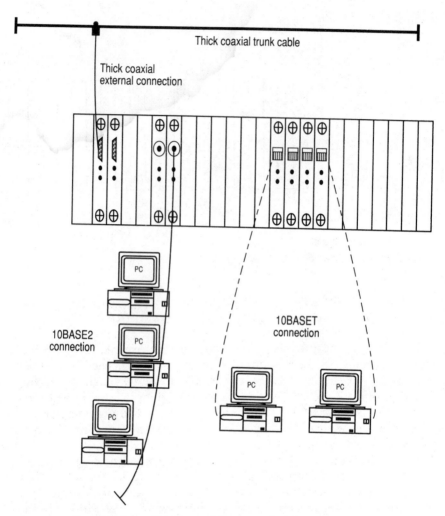

Figure 2.21 Backbone connection for a wiring concentrator.

(remove itself from the physical cable plant). This will not affect any of the other modules of the repeater unit. All other stations attached to different modules of the repeater unit representing different cable runs will operate normally. The module will then repeatedly try to determine whether the problem has been fixed and if so it will automatically reinsert itself back onto the cable plant. All this is accomplished automatically and is completely transparent to the users of the network, with the exception of that one user attached to the faulty repeater module.

For network administrators, there are usually multiple indicators, in the form of LEDs (lights), that are labeled as to network activity

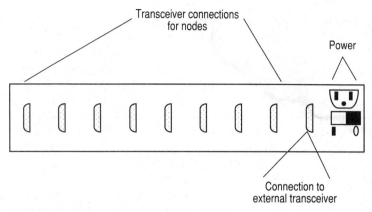

Figure 2.22   Multiport transceiver unit.

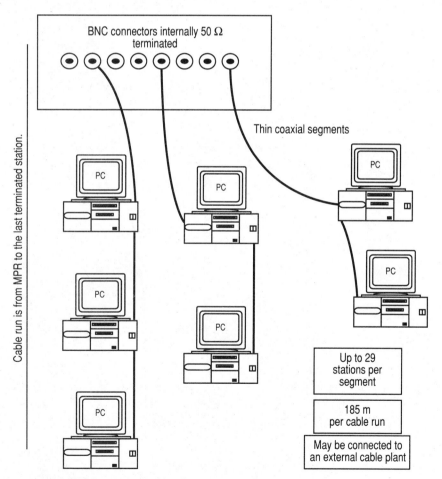

Figure 2.23   Multiport repeater for thin coaxial cable.

(normal operation), collisions occurring, or instances where the repeater card has removed itself from the network. These indicators are physically located on each repeater card and are used for determining faults. Some vendors even supply network management software for these concentrators, so that a network administrator may manage the device remotely or gain statistical information remotely from it.

The other two types of repeater units are the multiport transceiver unit (MTU) and the multiport repeater unit. (These terms may differ according to the vendor.) These concentrators are used in 10BASE5 (thick coaxial) and 10BASE2 (thin coaxial) networks. These devices originated before UTP was even conceived of. The most notable one is the DELNI (Digital Equipment Local Network Interconnect) and the DEMPR (Digital Equipment Multiport Repeater) from Digital Equipment Corporation. Refer to Figures 2.22 to 2.26.

Each respective repeater may be used only on one or the other type

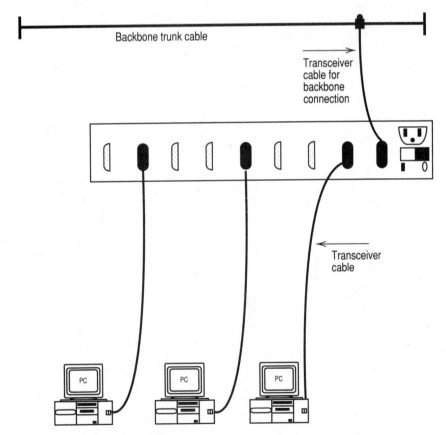

Figure 2.24 Backbone cable connection for a multiport transceiver unit (MTU).

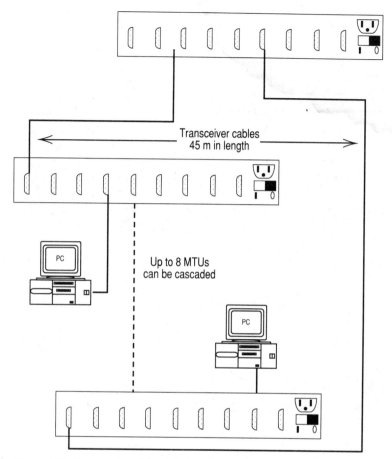

Figure 2.25 Cascaded multiport transceiver units (up to 64 devices may be connected together without a cable plant).

of cabling. These repeater units contain eight connections for attaching each type of cabling. Each repeater unit will also have a connector for attaching a backbone cable.

For the MTU, the unit replaces the external transceivers normally used in this type of wiring scheme. The station's Ethernet controller still attaches to the unit with a transceiver cable. The box contains the circuitry for transceivers. (See Fig. 2.26).

These two types of repeaters may be intermixed on a backbone type of cable. For example, if you have thick coaxial cable as the backbone, each type of repeater may be connected to it (see Figs. 2.27 and 2.28).

When LANs were initially used, most companies had mainframes or minicomputers, not personal computers, located in their office buildings. One way to interconnect these computers without having to run

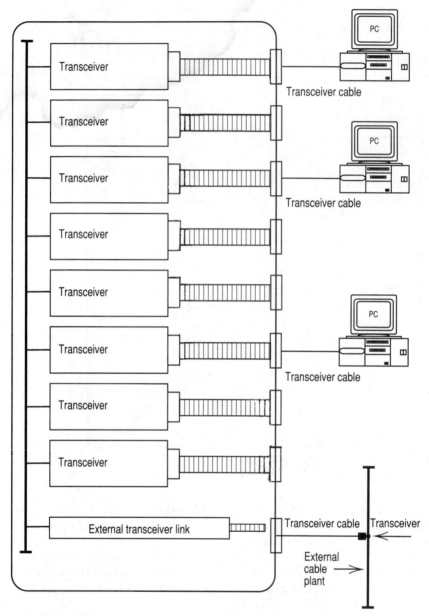

Figure 2.26 Theoretical view of a multiport transceiver unit.

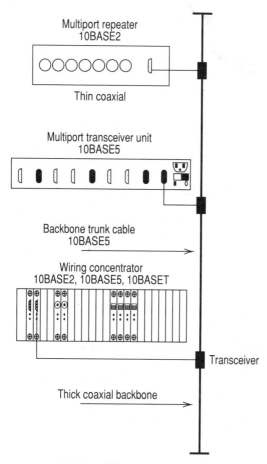

Figure 2.27 Mixing different repeater types.

a cable plant was to use the MTU. This was a self-sufficient device that could interconnect devices without having to use a cable plant. The MTU could be considered as a cable plant in a box. If the network does expand and a cable plant is incorporated, the MTU has a port that is used for external connection to a cable plant (see Figs. 2.22 and 2.24).

Another feature of the multiport transceiver unit is that it can be concatenated. As noted in Figure 2.25, you could have one MTU that acts as a root MTU with secondary MTUs connected off of it. Eight secondary MTUs could be connected to the root, allowing up to 64 devices to be connected without necessitating the use of a cable plant. This scheme somewhat represents a tree topology.

This device (theoretically) contains multiple transceivers combined

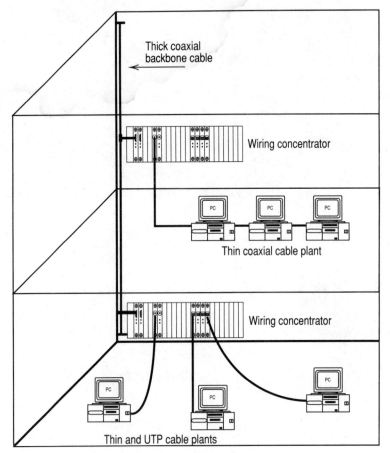

Figure 2.28   Cabling scheme for an office environment.

into one box (see Fig. 2.26). Many vendors currently support this. This type of concentrator is not specified in any of the IEEE 802.3x specifications or the Ethernet V2.0 (Blue Book) specifications. Even without a standard supporting it, most MTUs interoperate not only with each other but operate with most vendors' Ethernet cards.

With this type of box, as with the multiport repeater units, *there is no need to connect them externally with any type of a cable plant.* They are self-terminating devices. All transceiver cables can run the Ethernet controller to the MTU and are terminated at that point. Figures 2.20 to 2.28 show a connection to an external cable plant, but this is only to make the point of the capability and not to impose a requirement.

With the advent of the personal computer and the decreasing cost of the cabling used for Ethernet systems, the MTU scheme is not as popular as it once was.

10BASE2 (multiport repeater units) repeaters connect up to 8 thin coaxial wire runs. This eliminates the deficiency of 30 stations per thin coaxial cable segment. When used with a repeater only 29 stations may connect to a single thin coaxial cable run. Up to 232 stations may connect to one repeater. This repeater may be externally connected to allow more stations on the network. See Fig. 2.23.

Although the 10BASE2 and 10BASE5 concentrators are still used today, many wiring concentrators have evolved; thus, any type of physical cabling scheme may be combined in the same repeater. As shown in Figure 2.28, a wiring concentrator may connect up thin coaxial cable, thick coaxial cable, and UTP all in the same box. These wiring concentrators are also called wiring hubs.

To summarize, there are three types of repeater units:

1. Multiport repeater units (10BASE2 wiring only)
2. Multiport transceiver units (10BASE5 wiring only)
3. Wiring concentrator (will handle all types of wiring schemes)

All three types may be intermixed through the use of a backbone cable plant.

Note: two communicating stations paths may not be separated by more than 4 repeaters.

Remember that, at this (physical) layer, there is very little intelligence in any of these units. Repeater units do not "know" about other repeater units on the network, some boxes are assigned network addresses, for they contain intelligence for network management.

Wiring concentrators (wiring hubs) are special repeater units and are the most commonly found repeater units in use today. Not only do they extend the cable plant, connect multiple wiring types together, and contain certain errors to their respective cable plants, these wiring concentrators contain the intelligence for network management functions.

These network management functions enable a network administrator to query the wiring concentrator from a network management software program, to gather statistics from each of the wiring concentrators repeater modules, enable or disable individual wiring ports, and many other functions.

These hubs are evolving into second generation hubs that will not only house wiring repeater modules but also house devices known as communication servers (Appendix G) bridges and routers (Chap. 4) all in one concentrator. Call any of the hub vendors listed in Appendix B.

Cable matching

The last topic that needs to be discussed for the physical layer is using multiple cable types and how to intermix them. The cable types to be discussed here are not thick or thin coaxial or twisted-pair cable; these types of cable, as discussed previously, may be combined by using a wiring concentrator. There are certain types of cables that were not originally designed for use on Ethernet; examples are the 93-Ω and 75-Ω cables used on IBM systems and broadband systems, respectively.

Think about this situation. You are the network planner in New York City and are in the process of converting some of the applications that currently run on the IBM 3090 to some newly acquired PCs. You also have planned to install a LAN to connect all the PCs together and to tie this network to the mainframe.

Remembering that a large part of the cost for installing a LAN is the cost of manpower or labor to run the cable plant, you naturally are looking for an alternative approach. There may be an alternative solution. Since the previous system was 3270 terminal connectivity, you probably have miles of 3270 coaxial cable running through your building. This cable was used to connect the 3270 terminals to the 3274 cluster controller. Since that cable is already run throughout the building, would it be possible to use it? The answer is "Yes!"

There is a device that almost all cable companies in the world will be happy to provide for you. This is known as a *BALUN,* which is an acronym for BALanced UNbalanced.

This device will enable you to use almost any type of cable on the LAN. A strong point should be made here: *It is not always recommended to use this device.* For example, this device may affect the distance of your individual cable runs. Extreme care and tremendous thought should be taken when this device is used.

This device is also known as an *impedance matcher.* The impedance of a cable is the cable's natural ability (the way it is constructed) to resist current flow. It impedes the cable to allow the signals to flow through it. Impedance is measured in ohms (Ω).

As mentioned before, the cable types used on Ethernet have 50-Ω impedance rating. The impedance of unshielded twisted-pair cable can range anywhere from 73 to 150 Ω. Broadband cabling (CATV) has a characteristic impedance of 75 Ω, and the IBM terminal-host connection cable is measured at 93 Ω.

It should be obvious by now that you cannot just buy a male-female connector and connect two different types of cable together. This is what the BALUN is for. (For more information, contact your local cable company.)

The other type of connector, known as a "barrel" connector, is a simple device that allows you to extend your cable plant without having to splice a new cable. This connector is available for both thick and thin coaxial cable. It is not used all the time but can come in handy when you have two short pieces of coaxial cable and you need a long one or when you simply have to extend the existing coaxial cable. Instead of cutting a new piece of cable, simply attach the barrel connector to the two ends of the coaxial cable, and you will have a longer cable. *Barrel connectors are used only to extend the length of a piece of cable*, but not beyond the standard length specified by the standard.

3

The Data-Link Layer

Nontechnical Report: Ethernet

In a transmitting and receiving communication system, if there is only one cable to use and multiple stations need access to it, there must be a control mechanism in place to allow a fair system for the stations to share the cable plant. In an Ethernet LAN system, the control mechanism is an access method known as Carrier Sense Multiple Access with Collision Detection (CSMA/CD). The name Ethernet defines the algorithm of CSMA/CD. (See the technical sections of this chapter that explain the Ethernet system in more detail.)

The Ethernet access method for LANs follows an algorithm known as *carrier sense multiple access with collision detection* (CSMA/CD). It constitutes the lower two layers of the ISO model (the physical and data-link layers). Diagrams for CSMA/CD are given in Figures 3.1 and 3.2.

The Ethernet access method basically performs three functions: transmitting and receiving data packets, decoding the data packets for transmission or reception, and detecting errors within the data packet or on the network.

CSMA/CD (Ethernet) algorithm

A station wishing to transmit is said to contend for use of the cable until it acquires (access to) the cable; once the cable is acquired, the station uses it to transmit a packet.

To contend for sole use of the cable plant, any station wishing to transmit checks whether the cable plant is busy (i.e., uses *carrier sense*) and defers transmission of their packet until the cable is quiet (no signals on the cable). When the cable is quiet, the deferring station immediately begins to transmit. During this transmission, the trans-

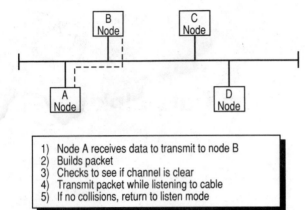

Figure 3.1   CSMA/CD algorithm. Node is any PC, terminal server, host, etc.

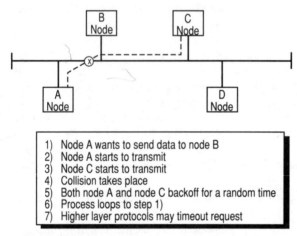

Figure 3.2   CSMA/CD with collision algorithm. Node is any PC, terminal server, host, etc.

mitting station listens for a collision (other stations transmitting at the same time). (Multiple access means multiple stations having access to the same cable.)

The Ethernet network controller transmits its data in groups or blocks called *packets* (or a frame). *A packet is a unit of information.* All data that is transmitted and received on a network is accomplished through the use of *packetization*.

A packet is a unit of information which will contain not only user data but information known as header information. This header information is control information that is applied to the data in the formation of a packet. Each respective layer (network, transport, and session layer) of software that is implemented on the network station will apply its header information into the packet. This information is used by the receiving station; it will take action based on the header (control information). Header information is also considered overhead. Overhead information is anything that is not data from the application program (Wordperfect, Lotus, etc.) that is running on the network station.

For example, the network software residing in a networked PC receives the information from the running application (Lotus, Word Perfect, etc.). The network software will append distinguishable network information to the data frame and then submit the whole frame to the network interface controller to be transmitted to its destination. This whole unit of information, including the appended network information, is called a *packet* and therefore the network is known as a *packet-switched* network.

The basic Ethernet packet contains five fields: the destination address, the source address, the type field, the data field (which may contain more fields appended from the upper-layer protocols of the ISO model or may contain circuit control or user data), and the cyclic redundancy check (CRC) field. The destination and source address indicate where the packet is destined and where the packet came from. The type field indicates what protocol (network protocol suite) submitted the packet. The data field holds user data and the CRC is an error-checking algorithm to ensure the integrity of the packet. See Fig. 3.14.

Collisions

On Ethernet networks, a collision occurs when two stations transmit at the same time. Normally the first station that has data to transmit and senses the cable as clear will immediately attempt to transmit data to the cable. Stations do not indicate to each other that they are transmitting.

In a correctly functioning system, collisions occur only within a short time interval following the start of transmission, since after this interval all stations will detect carrier and defer transmission. This time interval is called the *collision window* or the *collision interval*.

If no collision occurs during this time interval, a station is said to have acquired the cable and continues to transmit the packet until completion. Once a packet is transmitted, the Ethernet controller assumes that the packet was successfully transmitted without error. No acknowledgment is sent from the recipient of the packet to the sender to indicate the status of the frame. It is up to the higher-level protocols to ensure the packet reliability. The Ethernet's responsibility is considered done. It will then defer until more data is to be transmitted or information is to be received from the cable plant.

If a station detects collision, the transmission of the rest of the packet is immediately aborted. *A collision is detected when the signal level on the cable is equal to or exceeds the combined signal level of two stations transmitting.* To ensure that all stations to the collision have properly detected it, any station that detects a collision invokes a jam signal that, appropriately, jams the cable plant. Each station then invokes its respective backoff algorithm and attempts to transmit the packet at a later time. (We're talking a matter of microseconds here!)

Ethernet packet reception and transmission

The receiver function of Ethernet is activated when the controller "sees" the cable become active. A receiver will process an incoming packet in the following way. Since there is no master clock on an Ethernet network, the first 64 bits of information that is transmitted on the network is the preamble. This bit pattern is used to synchronize all active receiving stations with the bit pattern that a station is about to transmit on the network. This preamble is never noticed by the end user. It is only used for station synchronization.

On the receiving station, the preamble (first 64 bits) is first removed. If the end of the frame is detected before the end of the preamble, the controller will assume that it was a collision fragment and will loop to the start of the receive process. See Figure 3.1.

The receiver will then determine whether the packet is addressed to it. There are four conditions in which a controller will accept a packet:

1. The destination address matches the specific address of the station.

2. The destination address is a broadcast address.

3. The destination address is a multicast address.

4. The station has set the controller in a special mode known as the "promiscuous" mode. In the promiscuous mode, the controller will accept all packets, no matter what the destination address is. This is how network protocol analyzers work.

Most Ethernet controllers will check the destination address as it is receiving the packet. If the address is not recognized as its own, the rest of the packet is ignored. (Addressing is fully discussed in the technical section.)

If the destination address was recognized, the receiver will accept the rest of the packet into its buffer space. Some simple checks are accomplished on the packet before the upper-layer software is notified that it has information.

The packet is checked to be of minimum length. At a minimum, the packet has to contain the 6 bytes for each source and destination addresses, the 2-byte type field, a 46-byte data field, and a 4-byte CRC field, giving the minimum of a 64-byte packet. You will hear the minimum size of 72 bytes. This is when the 8-byte preamble is included in the total length of the packet. The controller itself will strip the preamble from the packet and begin the packet count at the destination address. The length must be greater than or equal to 64 bytes. If the length is less than 64 bytes (usually a fragment of a packet), the packet is once again discarded.

For Ethernet transmission, if the information in the data field to be transmitted is less than 46 bytes, the Ethernet controller software will pad the field with zeros to bring the packet up to the minimum 64-byte packet.

The packet is also checked to make sure that the packet received was the one that was transmitted. This check is known as a *cyclic redundancy check* (CRC). This is an error-checking algorithm. If there is an error, the packet is discarded. This error checking is done on the whole packet with the exception of the CRC field itself. The receiving station will not notify the originating station that it discarded the packet. It is the responsibility of the network software, not the Ethernet controller, to timeout and retransmit the data (packet).

It is impossible to guarantee that all packets transmitted will be delivered successfully. For example, a packet may be transmitted to a station that has been powered off. The packet incurred no collisions, or CRC errors; the receiver was just not there to accept the packet. It is up to the higher-layer protocols (ISO layers 3, 4, 5) to ensure proper delivery and what actions to take otherwise.

An analogy

An analogy would be this: suppose you are with a group of people and one of the individuals within this group is talking. The rest of the group should be listening. At one instance, two people begin to talk at the same time. Usually, both will stop and back off for a random time, and then one will try to talk again. During this time that the two people began to talk simultaneously, no one understood what the two were originally trying to say. One of the individuals will usually gain control and resume talking while the other backs off (defers) until that individual is finished talking.

Error detection

The *transceiver* (transmitter-receiver) contains the circuitry necessary to detect collisions on a cable plant. Once a collision is detected, the transceiver sends a signal to the network controller board, indicating that a collision has taken place on the network. The controller will then execute a backoff algorithm (a fancy name meaning defer all future transmissions and back off for a random amount of time). A jam signal will then be transmitted on the cable plant to ensure that all stations on the network have seen the collision.

What is a jam signal? In the standardized Ethernet Version 2.0, it is a random series of data 4 to 6 bytes long transmitted on the cable plant (which is well below the 64-byte minimum packet size for Ethernet) that all controllers will recognize as a jam signal and is used to indicate that a collision has occurred on the network. This signal will force Ethernet controllers to defer transmission for a short (microseconds) period of time and then try to transmit again.

Here in its simplest form, is the Ethernet (CSMA/CD) algorithm. The primary goal of the algorithm is to transmit and receive data with address recognition to and from the cable plant. If an error occurs during this process, it will handle the error and the physical and data link (packet) layer. It is up to the upper layer (network, transport, and session layer) to handle an error internal to the packet. The next section will explain the algorithm in greater detail.

Conclusion

Some final key issues should be discussed here. Ethernet is a relatively simple protocol, but certain stipulations should be noted.

The Ethernet algorithm is implemented by means of hardware. The Ethernet algorithm is invoked via special hardware that is located on the Ethernet controller board. You cannot load up software that will run the Ethernet specification.

Ethernet is a multiple protocol solution. Remembering the ISO model and the fact that it is modular, Ethernet represents the bottom two layers (the physical and data-link layers). The layers that reside on top of Ethernet may be any of the different types of TCP/IP, XNS, Netbios, or even proprietary protocols. (These layers are discussed in Chap. 5.) Any of these protocols may be run on top of Ethernet. In fact, the protocol may change, but it will not affect Ethernet. If one station is working with one type of upper-layer protocol, this does not mean that another type of protocol may not reside on the same physical Ethernet. The upper-layer protocols will decide what to do with the packet. Hence, as many different types of protocols as you possess may run simultaneously on the Ethernet network.

Ethernet controllers do miss packets that are destined for them. Ethernet controllers may be busy doing something else while the packet destined for them is transmitted onto the cable plant. The Ethernet controller does not care, for the upper-layer protocols of the transmitting station will timeout and retransmit the packet. More times than not, the packet will be accepted on its first try.

Ethernet uses a broadcast medium (cable) for packet transmission. What this represents is the fact that all packets are seen by all stations. Ethernet controllers can operate in what is known as the promiscuous mode. This means that the Ethernet card, regardless of its address, will accept all packets and in turn give the packets, minus the CRC, to the upper-layer software for processing. This is how network protocol analyzers work. What is the problem with this? Besides the burden on the upper-layer software, security is gone.

For example, I remember a time when I was working on a problem at a government installation and the problem analysis required the use of a network protocol analyzer. These devices were fairly new at that time, so they allowed me to connect this device to the network. Since the Ethernet controller card on the protocol analyzer was programmed to receive all packets (promiscuous mode) and display them on the screen, I could see all data that was transmitted on the network. What problem arose? I could see all passwords that were on the network at the time. Well, needless to say, that scenario was not to be repeated.

This is not a problem for most Ethernet LANs today. Passwords are usually encrypted, and the data as well is capable of being encrypted.

Ethernet does not guarantee the delivery of the packets that it is transmitting. Do not confuse this with IEEE 802.3 used with IEEE 802.2. This is completely different. We are talking only about the Ethernet specification.

Ethernet's responsibility is to transmit and receive packets in good condition using the CSMA/CD algorithm. Once a packet is received by an Ethernet controller, the receiver does not reply to the originator that it received the packet in good condition ACK (acknowledge) the packet. If a receiver receives a packet with errors, it will discard that packet and mark a status register on its card with the error. It will not send the originator a packet back saying "received in poor condition, please retransmit." It is up to the upper-layer protocols to provide this. This is known as *connectionless-oriented protocol*. Remember, though, Ethernet by itself is connectionless, but the protocols that reside above it may not be; they may be connection-oriented (meaning that a connection is established and maintained before any data is transferred).

A misconception of Ethernet is when cable requirements come into play. *The size of the cable does not impact the speed of Ethernet.* This may sound crazy, but people have mentioned it! Ethernet will run at 10 Mbps regardless of what kind of cable you run on. Nothing will ever affect the speed at which Ethernet will transmit a packet. What does cause the variations on data speed? This is known as *throughput.* Just because Ethernet transmits at 10 Mbps does not mean that the file transfer you initiated will transmit and be received at that rate.

When users initiate a file transfer through a networking protocol such as TCP/IP, the first thing they are bewildered at is the data throughput rate. At the end of a file transfer, the program will display the throughput. With TCP, it is usually 50 to 70K/s (kilobytes per second). The question usually arises as to what happened to 10 Mbps (million bits per second). The answer lies in the upper-layer software. The data may reside on the disk drive, but the data must first travel through the upper-layer software (five layers' worth with TCP/IP) before it finally reaches the Ethernet controller. Also, the network might be extremely busy and the Ethernet controller might not acquire the cable to transmit. Maybe a collision or two happened during the transmit, causing the part of the file to be retransmitted. If the data were to be transferred to the mainframe, maybe the mainframe was busy during some of that time. These and many other possibilities exist.

When using a LAN with Ethernet, the usual determining factor for Ethernet speed is disk access time. Disk access time is the amount of time it takes to retrieve data from the disk once it is requested. Disk access time, which is measured in milliseconds, varies from 16 to 80 ms.

The point here, is that *Ethernet transmits at 10 Mbps, but there are many variables on the network which slow the rate of actual data throughput.*

Finally, back to the issue of Ethernet and IEEE 802.3 protocols. We learned before that both use the CSMA/CD algorithm but that the frame format is different. Most CSMA/CD controllers support both IEEE 802.3 and Ethernet frame formats, but the similarity stops there. What happens after this can be confusing.

Nontechnical Report: Token Ring

Token Ring (deterministic, 4 and 16 Mbps) is probably the oldest ring access technique, originally proposed in 1969.[1] It has become the most

---

[1]Portions have been reprinted from *Inside the Token Ring* with permission from J. Scott Haugdahl, Architecture Technology Corporation.

popular ring access technique in the United States. This technique is the one ring access method selected for standardization by the IEEE 802 committee. IBM's product and those of a number of competitors are compatible with this standard.

Milestones

IBM first entered the Token Ring local area networking world with a series of four papers that it first presented to the IEEE 802 committee in March 1982 and at a conference in Florence, Italy, in April 1982. The IEEE 802 presentation described a new architecture; the Florence presentation described some implementations of that architecture. In August of that same year, at an IBM users' group meeting, IBM presented a fifth paper outlining the wiring. IBM then took the IEEE 802 papers and presented them at an IEEE Computers Society semiannual conference, COMPCON, in Fall 1982.

The next major development was a public demonstration of a Token Ring prototype at Telecom in 1983 in Geneva, Switzerland. This demonstration was a simplified version of today's Token Ring. An attached device gained access to the network by changing the status of a perpetually circulating 1-bit token from "free" to "busy"; the token is in the header of a message frame, and this frame is then filled with all or part of the message itself. The demonstration ring consisted of a wiring concentrator connected to several terminals: 3270 terminals, 8775 display terminals, a 3275 front-end processor, and 8100 distributed processors.

In May 1984, IBM announced the IBM Cabling System that was designed to connect all IBM data communications devices and accommodate the future Token Ring. In October 1985, IBM officially announced the Token Ring and a series of products, all for the IBM PC family. The products were developed by the IBM Telecommunications at Raleigh, North Carolina and were an outgrowth of the research performed by IBM Zurich (also known as the Zurich Ring). IBM felt that 4 Mbps was adequate for departmental and office-automation requirements, that the token passing protocol offers superior (over Ethernet) throughput under heavy loads, and that the protocol is better suited to supporting IBM's synchronous devices.

These product announcements included the multistation access unit (MAU), support for telephone (type 3) wire, and the IBM PC Token Ring adapter, the asynchronous communications server, the Netbios emulation program, enhancements to the 3270 SNA emulation program, and APPC/PC. IBM stated that the IBM PC network program could operate as is but was later released as an upgrade (now called the PC LAN program), along with PC-DOS (disk-operating system) 3.2.

Much criticism and speculation was created over the announcements. Criticism stemmed from the ring supporting only 260 devices (10 more than the IEEE specification of 250) over a limited distance (no bridging or routing). The only physical attachment was for the PC. Later announcements in April to June 1986 specifying enhancements soon quieted the criticism.

IBM has remained distant from the IEEE 802.5 standard with its own proprietary Token Ring standards. When the IEEE 802.5 committee adopted their standard, it was IBM who helped shape their standard. With the IEEE 802.5 standard, the Token Ring access method became an open standard for all who wished to create products for it.

There are many fancy definitions of Token Ring, many fields in the Token Ring frame (which will be discussed in the next section), and many components in the physical layer itself. But what exactly does Token Ring accomplish?

Theory of operation

Operation of the Token Ring access method is completely different from that of the CSMA/CD algorithm for Ethernet. On a Token Ring network a certain bit pattern is continuously transmitted on the ring. This particular bit pattern is called the *token*. Any station that has received this token and has data to transmit may then transmit onto the ring (see Fig. 3.3). All other stations must wait for the token.

Basically, a Token Ring controller may be in one of three states: *repeat mode, transmit mode,* or *copy mode*. When a Token Ring controller does not contain any data that needs to be transmitted onto the network, the controller will stay in a mode known as the *normal repeat mode*. This allows the controller to repeat any signals to the next active station on the network.

When the controller has data that needs to be transmitted on the network, the Token Ring controller must wait until a particular bit pattern called the *token frame* comes around. Once the token is presented, the controller will make sure that the token has not been reserved by another station. If this checks out, the controller will transmit its data without the token onto the network.

When the controller realizes that a packet is destined for itself (packet reception), the controller will copy the frame as it is repeated. The destination station copies only a packet that is destined for it. It will then repeat the packet onto the network. The station that originally submitted the packet is the only station that may take the packet off the ring (with the exception of a special station known as the *active monitor*). A new token will be issued to the network after

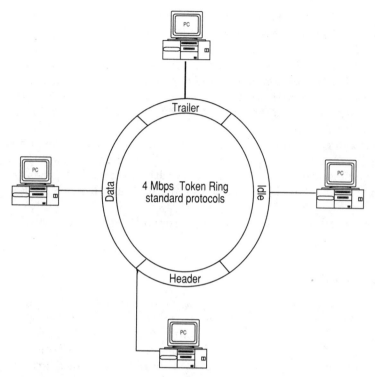

Figure 3.3   Token passing ring.

the originating station "drains" the packet from the network. The token frame will then circulate around the ring for the next station that
has data to transmit.

There is one station on the ring that provides special maintenance
functions. It is known as the active monitor. The active monitor provides the central clocking on the ring, checks for packets that have
circulated the ring more than once, ensures that only one token is allowed on the network, and so forth.

Whereas the Ethernet specification states that the network will op-
erate at 10 Mbps, there is no specification for speed on Token Ring.
Currently IBM is supporting two speeds for its Token Ring network.
These are 4 Mbps and 16 Mbps, commonly known as 4/16. The original
Token Ring network ran at 4 Mbps. In 1989, IBM began to ship the 16
Mbps controllers. The 4/16 controller may operate at either 4 Mbps or
16 Mbps. A 16 Mbps station will not transmit on a 4 Mbps network.
The card will transmit and receive at 4 Mbps. In other words, on any
single physical network you may have controllers operating at 4 Mbps
or 16 Mbps, but not at both speeds. Two networks operating at different speeds may co-exist, but they must be separated by a special de-

vice known as a bridge (bridges are covered in the next chapter). Currently the 16 Mbps is successfully operating on shielded twisted-pair wire. Its operation on unshielded twisted-pair wire is currently having some difficulties, although this is sure to be a short term difficulty.

The last thing to mention about Token Ring is an enhancement that IBM has made to the algorithm. It is known as the *early-release program*. With this, there may be more than one token frame circulating the ring. The early-release program enables a sending station to release the token before its packet has arrived back, thereby allowing a packet and a free token to be on the network at the same time. This allows for efficient use of the cable bandwidth and usually speeds up data transmission. This is now an option on all Token Ring controller boards.

For more detail about the operation of Token Ring see the technical section.

Technical Report: Ethernet

Ethernet was developed at the Xerox Palo Alto Research Center (Xerox PARC) in 1972. It was known as the *experimental Ethernet*. It transmitted at 2.94 Mbps, had a maximum segment length and end-to-end length of 1000 m, used 75-Ω-impedance cable, had a 1-bit preamble, 8-bit address fields, and a host of other differences compared to the standards that Ethernet follows today. Ethernet has changed tremendously in 18 years (see Table 3.1).

Today Ethernet is the most widely used data communications facility, connecting hundreds of thousands of computers together using a variety of host communications protocols.

There are very few computers on the market today that cannot be attached to an Ethernet LAN. Even IBM, which has built the net-

TABLE 3.1 Comparison of Ethernet Systems

Parameter	Experimental Ethernet	Ethernet specification (1980, 1982)
Data rate	2.94 Mpbs	10 Mbps
Maximum end-to-end length	1 km	2.5 km
Maximum segment length	1 km	500 m
Encoding	Manchester	Manchester
Coaxial cable impedance	75 Ω	50 Ω
Coaxial cable signal levels	0 to +3 V	0 to −2 V
Transceiver cable connectors	25- and 15-pin D series	15-pin D series
Length of preamble	1 bit	64 bits
Length of CRC	16 bits	32 bits
Length of address fields	8 bits	48 bits

NOTE: Courtesy IEEE Computer Society

working products around the Token Ring environment, has realized this and offers a variety of options to attach their computers to Ethernet.

It should be noted that there are extreme differences between the IEEE-adopted Ethernet version and the true Ethernet Version 2.0. These differences are described fully in a later section.

With all this, a basic understanding of how an Ethernet works is in order.

Milestones

Ethernet was developed at the Xerox Palo Alto Research Center by 3Com Corporation founder Robert M. Metcalfe and David R. Boggs, starting in 1972. In 1975, "experimental Ethernet" was implemented. In 1980, a cooperative effort involving DEC, Intel, and Xerox produced an updated version of the Ethernet design, generally known as the "Ethernet specification" (the "Blue Book") or Ethernet V1.0. In 1982, the same companies published Version 2.0. The IEEE 802.3 working group developed the IEEE 802.3 standard that was approved by the IEEE Standards Board in 1983, by the American National Standards Institute (ANSI) in 1984, and by the International Organization for Standards (ISO 8802/3) in 1985.

Definition

The Ethernet specification conforms only to the bottom two modules, the physical and data link, of the ISO model presented earlier. It does not pertain to any of the other layers above it and can have multiple protocol modules installed above it. For example, Xerox Network Specifications (XNS), Transmission Control Protocol/Internet Protocol (TCP/IP), Netbios, and a multitude of other protocols may all be installed above Ethernet. All of these protocols will be explained in a later chapter.

Ethernet is a multiaccess, packet-switched communications system for carrying digital data among locally distributed computing systems. The shared-communications channel in Ethernet is a passive broadcast medium with no central control point; packet address recognition in each station is used to take packets from the channel. Access to the channel by stations wishing to transmit is coordinated in a distributed fashion by the stations themselves, using a statistical arbitration scheme (copyright 1982, IEEE Computer Society).

The standards body known as the Institute of Electrical and Electronics Engineers (see Appendix F for a full explanation of the standards bodies), adopted the original Ethernet version and has labeled it

IEEE 802.3. The IEEE standard is based on the CSMA/CD access protocol, mentioned earlier. It is intended to encompass several wiring types and techniques for signal rates from 1 to 20 Mbps; there are multiple editions (versions) to this standard, and the 1985 edition provides the specifications and related parameter values for a 10-Mbps baseband implementation on thick coaxial cable, which has a maximum segment length of 500 m (this specification is also known as *10BASE5*). The IEEE Standards Board approved the 10BASE2 specification for thin coaxial cable in 1986 (10-Mbps baseband at 185 m). The IEEE 802.3i edition (also known as 10BASET, Ethernet, on unshielded twisted pair) was formally adopted in October 1990.

Both the Ethernet and IEEE 802.3 follow the CSMA/CD access method algorithm. The implementation of the algorithm is where the two differ. Except where noted, the terms *IEEE 802.3* and *Ethernet* will be synonymous. The Ethernet specification is the most commonly followed standard.

Theory of operation

The Ethernet access method basically performs three functions: transmitting and receiving packets, decoding and encoding the packets, and detecting errors within the packet or on the network.

A station wishing to transmit is said to contend for use of the shared-communications channel (sometimes called the *Ether*) until it acquires (access to) the channel; once the channel is acquired, the station uses it to transmit a packet.

To contend for sole use of the cable plant, any station wishing to transmit checks whether the cable plant is busy (i.e., uses *carrier sense*) and defers transmission of their packet until the cable is quiet (no signals on the cable). When the cable is quiet, the deferring station immediately begins to transmit. During this transmission, the transmitting station listens for a collision (other stations transmitting at the same time).

What is a packet? *A packet is a unit of information.* All data that is transmitted and received on a network is accomplished through the use of packetization. For example, the network software receives the information from the running application (Lotus, Word Perfect, etc.). The network will append distinguishable network information to the data and then submit the whole unit to the network interface controller to be transmitted to its destination. This whole unit of information, including the appended network information, is called a packet and therefore the network is known as a packet-switched network. Refer to Figure 3.9, later in this chapter.

An Ethernet packet contains five fields: the destination and source addresses, the type field, the data field, and the CRC field. The destination and source addresses indicate where the packet is destined and from where the packet originated. The type field indicates the controller protocol that submitted the packet. The data field holds information, whether control information or user data, and the CRC is an algorithm that ensures the integrity of the packet (an error checker).

Collisions

On Ethernet networks, a collision occurs when two stations transmit at the same time.

In a correctly functioning system, collisions occur only within a short time interval following the start of transmission, since after this interval all stations will detect carrier and defer transmission. This time interval, the collision window or the collision interval, as mentioned earlier, is a function of the end-to-end propagation delay. (This is where the 64-byte minimum packet size was introduced. It takes a minimum of 64 bytes to be transmitted on a cable 2500 m long, including repeaters, to ensure that all stations have seen the packet. If the first 64 bytes is transmitted without collision, the collision interval has passed.)

If no collision occurs during this time interval, a station is said to have acquired the cable and continues to transmit the packet until completion. Once a packet is transmitted, the Ethernet controller assumes that the packet made it without error. No acknowledgment is sent from the recipient of the packet to the sender to indicate the status of the frame. It is up to the higher-level protocols to ensure the packet reliability.

If a station detects collision, the transmission of the rest of the packet is immediately aborted. A collision is detected when the signal level on the cable is equal to or exceeds the combined signal level of two stations transmitting. To ensure that all stations to the collision have properly detected it, any station that detects a collision invokes a jam signal that, appropriately, jams the cable plant. Each station then invokes its respective backoff algorithm and attempts to transmit the packet at a later time. (We're talking a matter of microseconds here!)

The receiver function of Ethernet is activated when the controller sees the cable become active. A receiver will process an incoming packet in the following way. Since there is no master clock on an Ethernet network, the first 64 bits of information transmitted on the network is the preamble. This bit pattern is used to synchronize all active receiving stations with the bit pattern that a station is about to transmit on the network. This preamble is never noticed by the end user.

Ethernet packet reception and transmission

On the receiving station, the preamble (64 bits) is first removed. If the end of the frame is detected before the end of the preamble, the controller will assume that it was a collision fragment and will loop to the start of the receiving process.

The receiver will then determine whether the packet is addressed to it. There are four conditions in which a controller will accept a packet:

1. The destination address matches the specific address of the station.
2. The destination address is a broadcast address.
3. The destination address is a multicast address.
4. The station has set the controller in a special mode known as the promiscuous mode. In the promiscuous mode, the controller will accept all packets, no matter what the destination address is. This is how network protocol analyzers work.

Some Ethernet controllers have been designed to accept the whole packet into its buffer before checking the destination address. This is not efficient, in the sense that if the packet is not addressed to it, it has wasted not only a lot of time receiving the packet, but buffer space is used to receive the whole packet.

Most controllers will check the destination address as it is receiving the packet. If the address is not recognized as its own, the rest of the packet is ignored.

If the destination address was recognized, the receiver will accept the rest of the packet into its buffer space. Some simple checks are accomplished on the packet before the upper-layer software is notified that it has information. The packet is first checked for a 16-bit boundary. Since all data is transferred as 8-bit bytes, this ensures that the packet has not ended abruptly. If there is an error, the packet is simply discarded.

The packet is then checked to be of minimum length. At a minimum, the packet has to contain the 6 bytes for each source and destination addresses, the 2-byte type field, a 46-byte data field, and a 4 byte CRC field, giving the minimum of a 64-byte packet. You will hear the minimum size of 72 bytes. This is when the 8-byte preamble is included in the total length of the packet. The controller itself will strip the preamble from the packet and begin the packet count at the destination address. The length must be greater than or equal to 64 bytes. If the length is less than 64 bytes, the packet is once again discarded.

The packet is also checked to make sure that it is the same packet as the one that was transmitted. That is, the packet is checked for errors. This check, the CRC, is an error-checking algorithm. If there is an error, the packet is discarded. This error checking is done on the whole packet with the exception of the CRC field itself.

It is impossible to guarantee that all packets transmitted will be delivered successfully. For example, a packet may be transmitted to a station that has been powered off. The packet incurred no collisions, or CRC errors, the receiver was just not there to accept the packet. It is up to the higher-layer protocols (ISO layers 3, 4, 5) to ensure proper delivery and what actions to take otherwise.

Error detection

The transceiver (transmitter and receiver) contains the circuitry necessary to detect collisions on a cable plant. Once a collision is detected, the transceiver sends a signal to the network controller board, indicating that a collision has taken place on the network. The controller will then execute the binary exponential backoff algorithm (a fancy name meaning defer all future transmissions and back off for a random amount of time). A jam signal will then be emitted on the cable plant to ensure that all stations on the network have seen the collision.

The amount of time that an Ethernet controller will back off is dependent on many complex factors. Simply stated, a retransmission delay time is selected between 0 and some upper limit (usually the amount of stations that are allowed on the Ethernet, viz., 1024). This number is then multiplied by a second number which is known as the *retransmission slot time*. (The retransmission slot time is just slightly larger than the collision interval time; the collision interval time is the time it takes to transmit a 64-byte packet.) This product, known as the *real-time delay,* is the amount of time that an Ethernet controller will back off before a retransmission. The process is known as the *binary exponential backoff algorithm.*

After the maximum of 16 retries, the transmission is aborted. The backoff time restarts at 0 for transmission of every new packet.

What is a jam signal? In the experimental Ethernet, it was a series of code violations (an incorrect electrical signal). All network controllers would detect this and recognize it as a jam signal. In the standardized Ethernet Version 2.0 it is a random series of data 4 to 6 bytes long (which is well below the 64-byte minimum packet size for Ethernet).

Figures 3.4 and 3.5 summarize Ethernet transmission and reception for data, respectively.

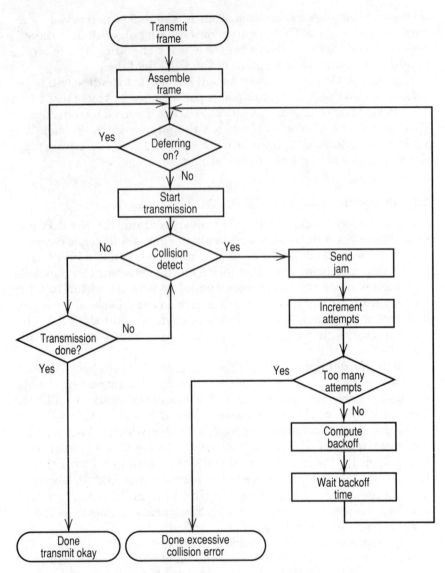

Figure 3.4 Ethernet transmission flowchart. (*Courtesy Xerox Corp.*)

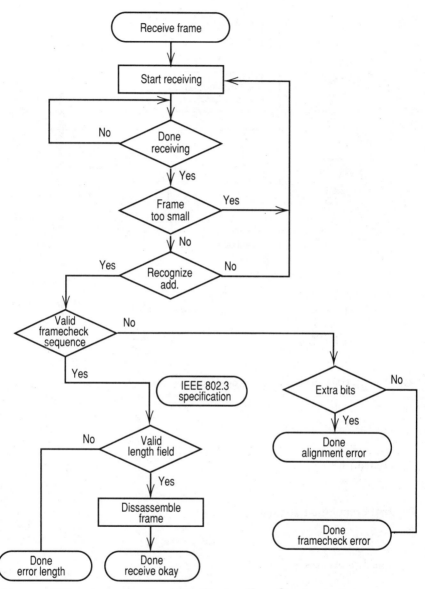

Figure 3.5   Ethernet reception flowchart. (*Courtesy Xerox Corp.*)

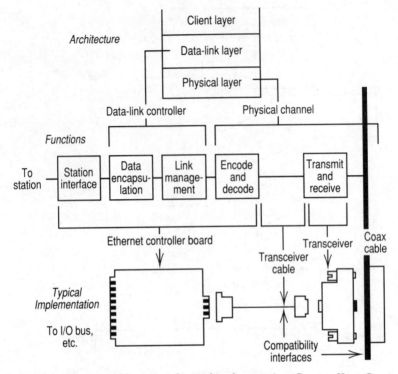

Figure 3.6   Ethernet architecture and typical implementation. (*Courtesy Xerox Corp.*)

Architecture and control

The next flowcharts (**Figures 3.6, 3.7, 3.8**) summarize Ethernet's architecture and control.

Ethernet component summary

Controller

- Preamble recognition
- Address recognition
- Checking of packet integrity (CRC)
- Packet generation
- Parallel-to-serial conversion
- Packet buffering
- Basic CSMA/CD channel management

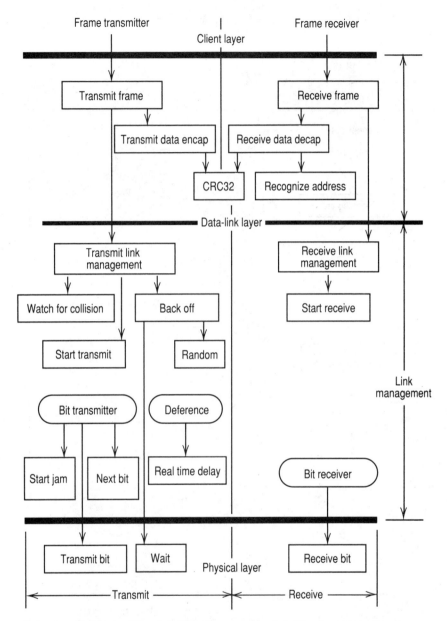

Figure 3.7 Structure of the data-link procedural model. (*Courtesy Xerox Corp.*)

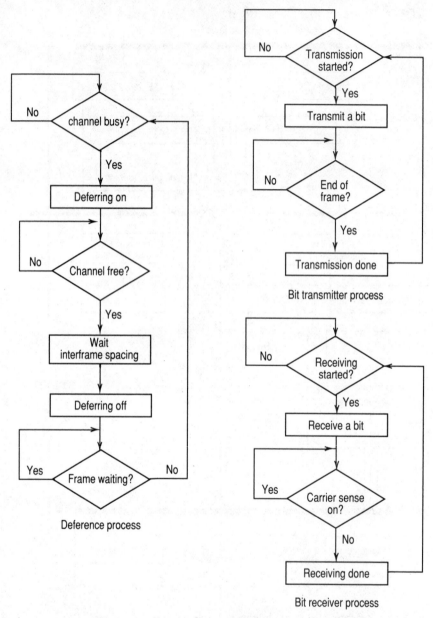

Figure 3.8 Data-link layer processes-control flow summary. (*Courtesy Xerox Corp.*)

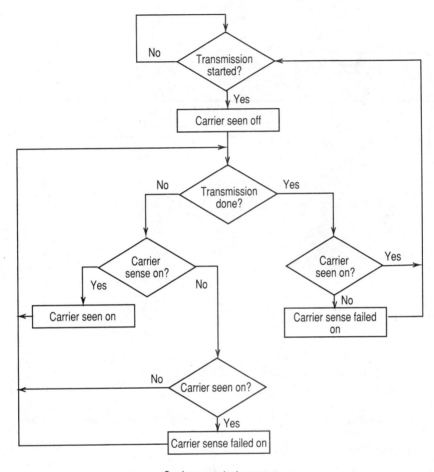

Carrier sense test process

Figure 3.8 (*Continued*).

Transceiver

- Transfers transmit data from the controller to the cable system
- Transfers receive data from the coaxial cable to the controller
- Detects transmission by other stations
- Detects collisions
- "Heartbeat" (Signal Quality Error) tests
- Jabber control
- Provides ground isolation between signals from the controller and signal from the cable plant

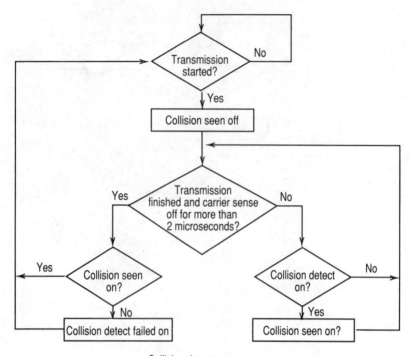

Collision detect test process

Figure 3.8 (*Continued*).

Transceiver Cable (called the attachment unit interface or AUI cable)

- Shielded twisted-pair cable (not UTP)
- Four pairs to transmit, receive, collision, and power
- Male 15-pin D-series connector with lock posts on the controller side, and a female 15-pin D-series connector with a slide lock assembly on the transceiver side

Repeaters

- Extend the length of the transmission system beyond the physical limits imposed by the transmission medium (cable)
- Use two transceivers to connect two different Ethernet segments (thick coax only)
- Combine the segments into one logical channel, amplifying and regenerating signals as they pass through in either direction
- Repeaters are transparent to the rest of the system, and packets

from stations on different segments can still collide (Ethernet collisions)

Ethernet versus IEEE 802.3

The previous discussion was generalized for both the Ethernet and IEEE 802.3 standards for CSMA/CD. There are specific differences between the two standards. Most individuals will exclaim that the difference is in the packet. While this is true, they usually end the discussion there without further explaining *all* the differences between the two.

Since the adoption of Ethernet by the standards bodies, several differences between Ethernet V1.0 (now obsolete), Ethernet V2.0, and IEEE 802.3 have been noted. The terms *Ethernet* and *IEEE 802.3* are synonymous as used below. The major similarities and differences are detailed below.

Electrical functions.   Ethernet V2.0 and 802.3 include a "heartbeat" function. This is a signal sent from the transceiver or MAU to the Ethernet controller immediately after each transmission. This confirms that the transceiver or MAU collision signaling is working and connected to the station. How does the Ethernet controller know this is a test signal and not a real collision? The signal sent is usually much shorter in duration than it would be if a real collision were detected and the proper collision signal was generated. This is also known as the signal-quality-error (SQE) signal. Without this signal, the station is unsure whether the frame was actually sent without a collision or whether a defective MAU failed to properly report a collision. Ethernet V1.0 does not support this function. It must be pointed out here that most Ethernet controllers do not support this function and will misinterpret the signal. It will detect it as a collision. Nothing will be transmitted or received. On most transceivers and MAUs there is a jumper that allows this function to be enabled or disabled. For most uses it is disabled.

Jabber function.   Both 802.3 and Ethernet V2.0 have a "jabber" function. This is a self-interrupt capability that allows a transceiver or MAU to inhibit transmitting data from reaching the cable plant if the transmission occurs for longer than the maximum frame size (1518 bytes). The transceiver does not simply count the number of bytes that it is currently transmitting. It simply invokes a timer and notes the duration of the current transmission. It will invoke the jabber control function within 20 to 150 ms.

Frame format.   The Ethernet V2.0 format differs significantly from the 802.3 format. Figure 3.9 covers the differences. Ethernet does

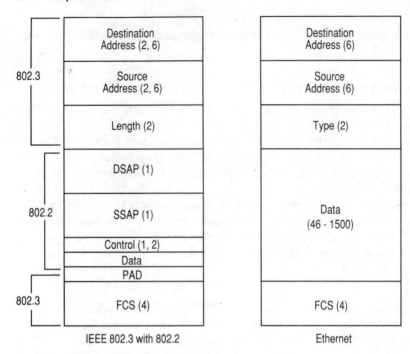

Figure 3.9   IEEE 802.3 and Ethernet frame formats.

not support a length field. (Remember that the minimum packet size for Ethernet is 64 bytes.) The Ethernet-type field is used to determine for which client protocol the frame is intended. This concept is similar to the IEEE 802.2 service access point (SAP). Ethernet provides what amounts to LLC type 1 operation and does not need a control field. (Refer to Fig. 3.9.)

Link control services.   The IEEE 802.3 standard is comprised of two sublayers: the MAC sublayer and the logical link sublayer (LLC is explained later). Ethernet V2.0 combines the link and the MAC functions into a single protocol. Only an unacknowledged connectionless service is provided for Ethernet. (Connectionless-oriented protocol means that all packets are transmitted on a best-effort basis. The packets transmitted are not acknowledged by the recipient.) The IEEE 802.3 standard can use the IEEE 802.2 data-link service, which provides not only connectionless service but also connection-oriented service. (Connection-oriented service providing for guaranteed delivery of the packet, IEEE 802.2, is further explained below.) Very few vendors implement the IEEE 802.3 with IEEE 802.2. Most vendors today are supporting the Ethernet V2.0 standard. Vendors are slowly switching to the IEEE 802.3 standard.

The Ethernet standard mandates a 10-Mbps channel (cable) rate or speed. The IEEE 802.3 standard varies the speed between 1 and 20 Mbps. The AT&T Starlan system is compatible with the CSMA/CD algorithm of IEEE and runs at 1 Mbps on unshielded twisted pair. AT&T recently upgraded their implementation to run at 10 Mbps.

One of several differences between the Ethernet standard and the IEEE 802.3 standard is the address fields. The Ethernet standard mandates only a 6 byte source and destination address field (48 bits each). The IEEE 802.3 standard allows for both a 2 byte (16 bits) or 8 byte source and destination address field. If you are using the 2 byte address, then all stations must be using the 2 byte address.

The destination address for the IEEE 802.3 packet allows for 48 bits of address of which 46 bits may be used for the actual address. Two of the bits are reserved and are known as the Individual/Group (I/G) bit and the Universal/Local (U/L) bit. Thus,

I/G bit = 0 for an individual (unique) address
       = 1 for a group (multicast) address
U/L bit = 0 for universally administered address (IEEE assigned)
       = 1 for locally administered (private networks)

Ethernet reserves only one bit in the destination field for unique/multicast addresses. See Figure 3.17

The source address will always be a unique address and the IEEE 802.3 frame only reserves one bit to indicate this; the I/G bit will always be a 0.

Please remember that throughout all these differences, most CSMA/CD controller cards are able to read both the IEEE 802.3 frames as well as Ethernet frames. Refer to Figures 3.18 and 3.22.

IEEE 802.2 data-link service

The following is also a major difference between IEEE 802.3 packets and Ethernet V2.0 packets. Yes, the length field is the obvious indicator that a packet is of type IEEE 802.3 or Ethernet. If a IEEE 802.3 packet is obtained from the network by an Ethernet controller, the IEEE 802.2 headers will usually be included. Therefore, a discussion of IEEE 802.2 is in order here. This is the preferred data-link protocol suite of the IEEE. It differs tremendously from the Ethernet Version 2.0 specification. This is the only data-link protocol used in IEEE 802.5 Token Ring. IEEE 802.2 services are provided for both IEEE

802.3 and 802.5 standards. It is not provided for use with Ethernet and is rarely used with the IEEE 802.3 standard. The following is just an introduction to the IEEE 802.2 data-link layer. (First a little history; see also Fig. 3.10).

On setting up the IEEE 802 committee, a subcommittee known as the IEEE 802.2 working group was set up to establish a networking standard for the data-link module. The working group decided to split the data-link layer into two distinct sublayers: the logical link control (LLC) and the media access control (MAC).

The IEEE 802.3, 802.4, and 802.5 working groups have formally drafted standards for the physical module and the MAC portion of the data-link module. The IEEE 802.2 working group set up the LLC portion of the data-link layer.

The IEEE 802.2 specification for the data-link module provides two classes for the delivery of packets: type 1, which is connectionless; and type 2, which is connection-oriented. Type 1 will be discussed first.

Type 1 service provides for *connectionless service*. Using this technique, data is simply transmitted onto the cable plant regardless of whether the receiving station accepted the packet. This service of the data-link layer depends on the networking software residing on the upper layers of the ISO model to provide this. There is no need for the data-link layer to first establish a connection between two communicating stations before data is transferred.

Networking software such as TCP/IP and XNS (each protocol is defined at the network and transport module of the ISO model; Chaps. 4 and 5 cover these layers) were defined to be independent of the data-link and physical layers of the ISO model. These networking protocols were developed in the early 1970s before Ethernet and Token Ring were developed. They were designed to allow remotely located hosts to be connected to dialup lines (the same line that you and I use to talk on the telephone). Since these hosts could establish multiple connections with other hosts, the networking software incorporated connec-

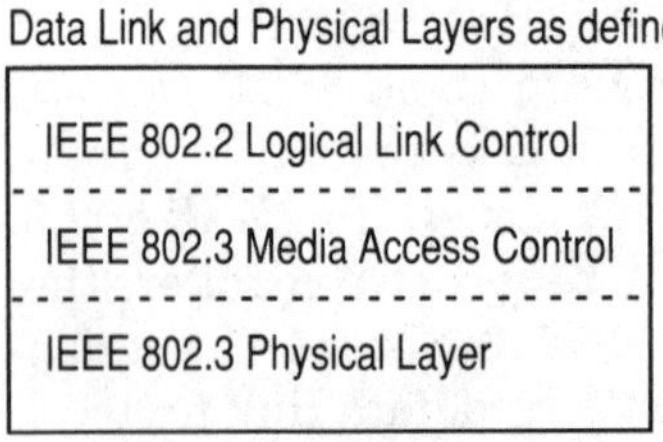

Data Link and Physical Layers as defined by the IEEE

| IEEE 802.2 Logical Link Control |
| IEEE 802.3 Media Access Control |
| IEEE 802.3 Physical Layer |

Figure 3.10   IEEE defined data-link and physical layers.

tion ID (identification) numbers to uniquely identify each session. Therefore, a session was initiated and given a session number, and then the two hosts would start to communicate.

The other algorithm invoked involved the telephone lines. These lines were very noisy, and therefore many different errors could occur when two hosts were transmitting and receiving to each other. To correct such errors, the networking protocols incorporated special algorithms to handle such errors.

Since the IEEE 802.2 specification was defined and published after most network software was already in use, this type 1 service allowed the above-mentioned software to run with the then newly defined IEEE 802.2 specification for LANs with very little modification to the networking software.

Type 2 operation is just the opposite of type 1. It is known as *connection-oriented service*. It applies the rules of the transport layer to the data-link layer.

A logical connection is established between two communicating stations before any user data is sent. The connection is maintained by using special packets that the sending and receiving stations understand and the connection is also terminated by this service. During this connection, sequence numbers are assigned to the packets to ensure that the data is received in the order that it was transmitted. Error control and flow control are provided with this service. It should be noted here that only unique source and destination addresses are used for this service. This service does not allow for broadcast or multicast addresses.

Stations on the network are identified by their class: class I and class II stations. Class I stations only support type 1 service, while class II stations support both type 1 and type 2 service.

Let's examine an IEEE 802.3 packet with the IEEE 802.2 information and explain the fields (see Fig. 3.11).

Notice that this frame is different from the Ethernet frame. Besides

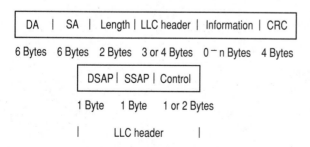

Figure 3.11   LLC data unit.

the obvious length field, the LLC header information (herein called the LLC data unit) is what provides the type 1 service or the type 2 service. First an explanation DSAP and SSAPs.

The SAP field basically provides the same functionality that the type field provided in the Ethernet packet. To distinguish between different data exchanges that involve the same station the term *service access point* (SAP) is used to identify a particular element in a network station that is involved in a single data exchange. A SAP involved in sending a particular LLC data unit is known as the SSAP and the SAP involved in receiving an LLC data unit is known as the DSAP.

The DSAP identifies the SAP for which the frame is intended. It is further expanded as detailed in Fig. 3.12.

The six DSAP address bits (D) and the user-defined address bit (U) form the address of the SAP for which the frame is intended. The U bit indicates whether the address is defined by the user (a binary zero) or is a group address (a binary 1) (see Fig. 3.13).

The six SSAP address bits and the user-defined bit identify the address of the SAP that originated the frame. The U bit indicates whether the address is defined by the user (a binary 0) or by the IEEE (a binary 1).

Following the DSAP and SSAP is the control field. The control field identifies the type LLC service. It will be 1 byte long for type 1 service and 2 bytes long in type 2 service.

There is a protocol that should also be described here. It is known as *subnetwork access protocol* (SNAP). What does SNAP allow? In its simplest terms SNAP allows an Ethernet frame to be encapsulated by

DSAP address field

D	D	D	D	D	D	U	I/G

D = DSAP address
U = user defined address bit
I/G = individual/group bit

Figure 3.12   DSAP address field.

SSAP field

S	S	S	S	S	S	U	C/R

S = SSAP address bits
U = user defined address bits
C/R = command response bit

Figure 3.13   SSAP address field.

an IEEE 802.2 logical protocol data unit (LPDU or IEEE 802.2 header). It uses the IEEE 802.3 type 1 service and a DSAP and DSAP of AA (hexadecimal). This will identify to the LLC layer that an Ethernet frame is to follow and treat the following packet accordingly. IBM has defined F0 as the SAP for the Netbios protocol, and 06 is the SAP for the TCP protocol.

This is a very simple approach that allowed the Ethernet drivers out there to reside within the IEEE 802.2 world, without having to completely rewrite their code.

We now know what all the components of an Ethernet LAN and exactly how the Ethernet operates. To build an Ethernet controller or any other Ethernet component is extremely complex, but to grasp the understanding of Ethernet and the components involved is not and should not be. As we continue to develop this network (with different protocols, bridges, and routers and some network management), it will become somewhat more difficult. Ethernet was the easy part!

Let's look at a figure to further explain the above verbiage. (Refer to Figure 3.14.)

Ethernet frame and addresses

Like the phone number in the telephone system, addressing in either a Token Ring or Ethernet network is the most basic way two stations will communicate with each other. All data, once the connection is established, will be transferred between the source and destination addresses of the two stations. The purpose of this section is to explain exactly what an address is, where it is located in an Ethernet or Token Ring packet (frame), and how the source and destination addresses are administered. This is for Ethernet addresses and not IEEE 802.3 addresses.

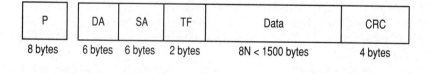

Figure 3.14   Ethernet frame.

Once you read through this chapter and understand an Ethernet address, imagine trying to remember these addresses for all stations on your network. The telephone system does force us to remember numbers in order to communicate with another person. If we cannot remember the exact phone number, the phone company has phone books that enable us to do a name-number translation.

Networks allow the same process of name-number translation although it is accomplished completely transparently to the user. This process is accomplished in the session layer (refer to Chap. 6).

To force a user to type in a 6-byte address to talk to another station on the network is not feasible. Most installed networks today do use a naming scheme so that we do not have to remember all the addresses on the network. But remember, this is only for human intervention. Stations on the network do not use names to communicate.

Like the telephone system, we simply have to remember who we are trying to call and the network software will dial the appropriate phone number. The connection is then set up between the two numbers, not the two names, talking to each other.

Ethernet addressing scheme

Ethernet addresses are 48 bits, expressed as 12 hexadecimal (hex) digits (0 to 9, plus A to F capitalized). These 12 hex digits consist of the first/left 6 digits (which should match the vendor of the Ethernet interface within the station) and the last/right 6 digits, which specify the interface serial number for that interface vendor.

Ethernet addresses might be written unhyphenated (i.e., 123456789ABC), or with one hyphen (i.e., 123456-789ABC). These addresses are physical station address, not multicast nor broadcast, so the second hex digit (reading from the left) will be even, not odd. These addresses are burned into a programmable read-only memory (PROM) to be read by the MAC layer software on initialization.

The 13th and 14th bytes of an Ethernet or IEEE 802.3 packet (after the preamble) consist of either the *type* or *length field*. The type field is managed by Xerox.

Understanding the addressing scheme of Ethernet and Token Ring is extremely important. Refer to Figures 3.15 and 3.16 to see the simplicity of this scheme. (Token Ring addressing is discussed in more detail in the next section.)

The first 3 bytes of each address, whether Ethernet or Token Ring, is the vendor ID. The IEEE assigns these numbers to each vendor possessing a Xerox Ethernet license. The globally assigned numbers are an attempt to allow Ethernet products from different vendors to reside on the same network without conflict. The first 3 bytes of each address

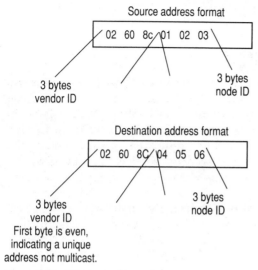

Source address format

Destination address format

First byte is even,
indicating a unique
address not multicast.

Figure 3.15   Ethernet address frames.

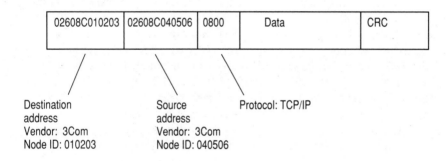

| 02608C010203 | 02608C040506 | 0800 | Data | CRC |

Destination
address
Vendor: 3Com
Node ID: 010203

Source
address
Vendor: 3Com
Node ID: 040506

Protocol: TCP/IP

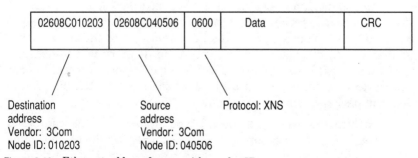

| 02608C010203 | 02608C040506 | 0600 | Data | CRC |

Destination
address
Vendor: 3Com
Node ID: 010203

Source
address
Vendor: 3Com
Node ID: 040506

Protocol: XNS

Figure 3.16   Ethernet address frames with vendor ID.

will always be unique to each vendor. The last 3 bytes can be duplicated from vendor to vendor.

For example, address 02608C is the address assigned to 3Com and
00DD00 is the address assigned to Tandem (formerly Ungermann-
Bass, Inc). Now the last 3 bytes indicate a physical station address, for
example, 010203. Now to totally confuse things, these last 3 bytes can
be duplicated from vendor to vendor. For example, 3Com may use the
address 010203, giving the total address of 02608C010203. Tandem
may use the same last 3 bytes, giving 00DD00010203. Even though
the last 3 bytes of this address can be duplicated by each vendor, the
first 3 bytes are always differentiated by vendor, thereby giving a
completely unique Ethernet address when used in a multivendor environment.

It should now be clear why it is extremely important for IEEE to
assign the Ethernet addresses and not for each vendor to assign their
own. There would be total chaos on the network and conflict between
machines on the network if it were left up to each vendor to assign
these addresses. (Appendix B covers the assigned vendor addresses.)

Token Ring is somewhat different. The address scheme is detailed
in the next section. The above rules still apply but something will look
different on the network when a protocol analyzer is placed on the network. A protocol analyzer is a machine that captures packets off of the
network and displays them on a screen for users to look at. You will
notice that all addresses begin with C (hex). The reason for this is
IBM. IBM recommends that all addresses on Token Ring should be in
the range of C00000XXXXXX–C00000XXXXXX, where XXXX is any
hexadecimal number in compliance with IEEE.

Certain rules are defined for the Ethernet or Token Ring addresses.
For Ethernet, the address may be in one of three forms: (1) unique station controller address, (2) multicast address, or (3) broadcast address.

1. A *unique station address* is much like a telephone number. There
is one number assigned per machine. When a packet is transmitted
onto the net, each station will receive the packet and look at the destination address. The adapter will do a comparison to the address that
was loaded into its memory at startup time. If there is a match, the
adapter then passes the packet on to the upper-layer software for that
software to determine the outcome. If there is no match on the address, the packet is simply discarded.

2. A *multicast address* is a special type of address. This address is
for a group of machines on the network that all have the same
multicast address. How does the adapter decide what is a multicast
address? This is very simple. If the first transmitted bit of the address
is a one, then it is multicast address. Another way to say this is: If the

Vendor ID (first 3 bytes of the packet) is an odd number, then the packet is a multicast address. For example, 3Com has been assigned an Ethernet address of 02608C. 3Com's multicast address is 03206C. Let's spread this out a little by looking at Figure 3.16. Represented in binary, the address would be 00000011 01100000 10001100 (03 60 8C). The first bit to be transmitted is the least significant bit of the first 8 bits. In binary, if the 1s bit is on (or set), then the resulting number will be an odd, not an even, number.

3. *Broadcast addresses* are a special form of multicast. When you hear the term *broadcast,* this means that the packet is destined for all stations on the network. All stations on the network will pick up this packet and notice that it is a broadcast packet and in turn will pass to the higher-layer software. For example, a destination Ethernet address of FFFFFFFFFFFF (6 bytes) is a broadcast address.

One reason why multicasting (item 2, above) has not been widely used is that hardware requirements to support multicasting are rather extensive. Typically an Ethernet controller chip can be in one of two states: promiscuous or nonpromiscuous mode. In promiscuous mode the Ethernet controller chip accepts all packets regardless of the address and forwards the entire packet to the software, which then decides what to do with the packet. Special multicast addresses are provided at the end of this chapter.

Broadcast packets (item 3, above) are discouraged on Ethernet. In some cases they are needed. What does the adapter do with the packet when it receives a packet with a broadcast Ethernet address? It automatically passes to the upper-layer software. You can see how this can slow the network down. If every packet were broadcast, the card would not filter packets out that were not destined for it and it would burden the upper-layer software with the unnecessary task of filtering. Well-known broadcast addresses are provided in Appendix D.

Summary

Ethernet addresses are 48 bits long and are commonly expressed as %0800020012AB or 08-00-02-00-12-AB. Referring to Figures 3.17 and 3.18, we see that an Ethernet packet (frame) has the general format shown in Figure 3.17.

Packets are transmitted bytewise in a serial fashion starting with the [destination addr] field and ending with the [CRC] field. All bytes

Destination address | Source address | Packet type | Data | CRC

Figure 3.17 Ethernet fields.

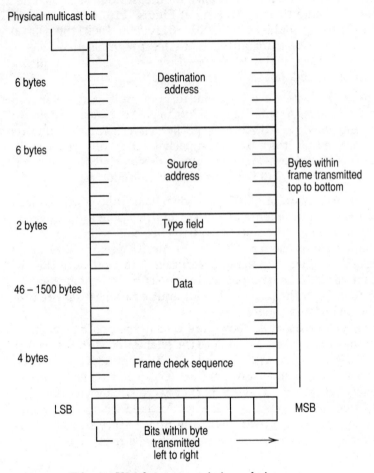

Figure 3.18 Ethernet V2.0 frame transmission ordering.

are transmitted least significant bit first. Given the order of transmission is LSB first:

The first bit transmitted is the 1s bit of the first byte in the destination address.

The second bit transmitted is the 2s bit of the first byte in the destination address.

The third bit transmitted is the 4s bit of the first byte in the destination address.

The fourth bit transmitted is the 8s bit of the first byte in the destination address.

The fifth bit transmitted is the 16s bit of the first byte in the destination address.

The sixth bit transmitted is the 32s bit of the first byte in the destination address.

The seventh bit transmitted is the 64s bit of the first byte in the destination address.

The eighth bit transmitted is the 128s bit of the first byte in the destination address.

The ninth bit transmitted is the 1s bit of the second byte in the destination address.

This process continues through the rest of the destination address, the source address, the packet type, the data, and on until the end of the CRC is transmitted.

That's it. Addressing is not a difficult concept, but is very unique and strictly controlled, which is good. Otherwise there would be chaos on the network.

In Appendix D you will notice that the 02608CXXXXXX address is assigned to 3Com and a type field of 0600 is assigned to the XNS protocol (see also Fig. 3.16). The destination and source address may vary from different vendors.

Network controller interfaces

Two types of controllers may be installed in a computer. The following figures are Ethernet controller cards for personal computers. The following discussion may be used for Token Ring interface controllers as well.

Ethernet controllers are rendered as both intelligent and nonintelligent. For personal computers especially, there are 8-, 16-, 32-bit controllers extended industry standard architecture (EISA), microchannel architecture (MCA; IBM PS/2 PC line), and Apple Macintosh adapters. Not every one needs a 32-bit controller.

The nonintelligent controller is exactly that. Referring to Figure 3.19, we see that it contains enough intelligence to receive and transmit data over the network. All software that is needed to run the network controller is contained in the computer memory (RAM).

The intelligent controller allows for the networking protocols to be downloaded onto the network controller card. Referring to Figure 3.20 the card in itself is a mini PC. It contains a CPU (central processing unit), a clock, and its own memory.

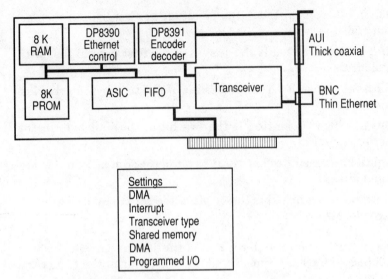

Figure 3.19 Nonintelligent Ethernet adapter (controller card). Uses 8K of RAM for packet buffering; ASIC chip contains the Ethernet algorithm; available with thin, thick, or twisted-pair connectors; contains on-board transceiver; usually consumes a half-expansion slot in the PC.

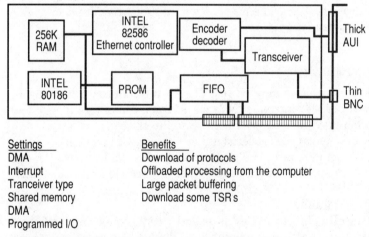

Figure 3.20 Intelligent Ethernet adapter (controller card).

For personal computers that operate in the DOS environment, this feature can represent a substantial savings in available memory to run your applications. All network software that needs to be loaded will take away from the available memory to run your applications. Careful thought should be taken when an intelligent controller is chosen.

Most intelligent network controllers run at an operating speed of 10 MHz. This operating speed is defined similar to that of your PC. Personal computers that operate over 16 MHz should not contain an intelligent controller. Any PC that has a CPU speed over 16 MHz will wait for the intelligent controller to process data and commands, effectively slowing down your rate of throughput on your PC.

The decision as to which controller to use is up to you. With the RAM (random-access memory)-saving applications that are available on the market today (the ability to load certain programs into another area of memory not used by DOS), most networking software has the capability to be utilized by these utilities, which allows for more memory for user applications. The intelligent card is not as popular as it once was. It is also a very expensive card (up to 2½ times the cost of nonintelligent cards). Nonintelligent cards are faster.

For most user personal computers an 8-bit card is sufficient. The 16- and 32-bit cards are usually used in a host or server (or network-intensive) type of computer.

Ethernet controllers for host mainframes or minis (not PCs) are supplied by the manufacturer of that computer, and the user seldom has a choice as to which type of card to choose. The manufacturer of the mini or mainframe will usually use an optimized network controller.

Technical Report: Token Ring

Token Ring (theory of operation deterministic, 4 and 16 Mbps) is probably the oldest ring technique, originally proposed in 1969. It has become the most popular ring access technique in the United States. This technique is the one ring access method selected for standardization by the IEEE 802 committee. IBM's product and those of a number of competitors are compatible with this standard.

Milestones

IBM first entered the Token Ring local area networking world with a series of four papers that it first presented to the IEEE 802 committee in March 1982 and at a conference in Florence, Italy, in April 1982.[1] The IEEE 802 presentation described a new architecture; the Florence presentation described some implementations of that architecture. In August of that same year, at an IBM users' group meeting, IBM presented a fifth paper outlining the wiring. IBM then took the IEEE 802

---

[1]Portions are reprinted with permission from *Inside the Token Ring* by J. Scott Haugdahl, Architecture Technology Corporation.

papers and presented them at an IEEE Computers Society semiannual conference, COMPCON in Fall 1982.

The next major development was a public demonstration of a Token Ring prototype at Telecom in 1983 in Geneva, Switzerland. This demonstration was a simplified version of today's Token Ring. An attached device gained access to the network by changing the status of a perpetually circulating 1-bit token from "free" to "busy"; the token is in the header of a message frame, and this frame is then filled with all or part of the message itself. The demonstration ring consisted of a wiring concentrator connected to several terminals: 3270 terminals, 8775 display terminals, a 3275 front-end processor, and 8100 distributed processors.

In May 1984, IBM announced the IBM Cabling System that was designed to connect all IBM data communications devices and accommodate the future Token Ring. In October 1985, IBM officially announced the Token Ring and a series of products, all for the IBM PC family. The products were developed by the IBM Telecommunications at Raleigh, North Carolina and were an outgrowth of the research performed by IBM Zurich (also known as the Zurich Ring). IBM felt that 4 Mbps was adequate for departmental and office-automation requirements, that the token passing protocol offers superior (over Ethernet) throughput under heavy loads, and that the protocol is better suited to supporting IBM's synchronous devices.

These product announcements included the MAU, support for telephone (type 3) wire, and the IBM PC Token Ring adapter, the asynchronous communications server, the Netbios emulation program, enhancements to the 3270 SNA emulation program, and APPC/PC. IBM stated that the IBM PC network program could operate as is but was later released as an upgrade (now called the PC LAN program), along with PC-DOS 3.2.

Much criticism and speculation was created over the announcements. Criticism stemmed from the ring supporting only 260 devices (10 more than the IEEE specification of 250) over a limited distance (no bridging or routing). The only physical attachment was for the PC. Later announcements in April to June 1986 specifying enhancements soon quieted the criticism.

IBM has remained distant from the IEEE 802.5 standard with its own proprietary Token Ring standards. When the IEEE 802.5 committee adopted their standard, it was IBM who helped shape their standard. With the IEEE 802.5 standard, the Token Ring access method became an open standard for all who wished to create products for it.

There are many elaborate definitions of Token Ring, many fields in the Token Ring frame, and many components in the physical layer itself. But what exactly does Token Ring accomplish?

Theory of operation

Operation of the Token Ring access method is completely different from that of the CSMA/CD algorithm for Ethernet. On a Token Ring network a certain 24 bit pattern is continuously transmitted on the ring. This particular bit pattern is called the *token*. Any station that has received this token and has data to transmit may then transmit onto the ring. Before any of this has taken place, there is a sequence of events that must be discussed. Let's start from the beginning.

When a station containing a Token Ring network interface card (controller) is powered on, the Token Ring card will initialize and prepare itself for insertion onto the ring.

You will often hear of the five-stage method for a Token Ring controller to insert itself on the ring. These processes are fully discussed below. (Do not try to fully understand the type of frames indicated below; they will be explained later.)

1. *Phase 0.* The lobe test is accomplished before the station has even attached itself to the ring. The *lobe* refers to the section of cable that attaches a station to a wiring concentrator (MAU). The lobe test performs a transmission of lobe test MAC frames onto the ring stations cable only. It does not transmit onto the ring whatsoever. This is to check out the cable and the cable attachment. If this test passes, the station then tests its receive logic by transmitting a frame called the *duplicate address test MAC frames*. These are simply test frames and are not used to actually test for a duplicate address. If this test passes, the station will then attach itself to the ring (open the relay in the MAU and listen for frames) and continue its test by initiating phase 1. Otherwise, it will return an error code and will not attach itself to the ring. Following this test, a device is physically connected to the ring and proceeds to phase 1.

2. *Phase 1.* The monitor check will start by initiating a timer. If, within this time, the station receives any of the special frame types ring purge MAC frame, active monitor present MAC frame, or a standby monitor present MAC frame, the station will assume that there is an active monitor present on the ring and will proceed to the next phase. If the station does not receive one of these frames before the timer expires, it will assume that (a) it is the first station on the

network, (b) no active monitor is present, or (c) inserting the station has broken the ring. The station will then initiate a token claim process. This is the process for initiating a ring and for the stations to contend to become the active monitor (discussed more in a moment) on the network.

3. *Phase 2.*   The third phase determines whether a duplicate physical address is already on the network. The network controller sends a packet out to the network to see if any other station on the network has the same physical address as its own. If a duplicate address is found, the station will notify the network manager software and deinsert (remove) itself from the ring.

4. *Phase 3.*   The fourth test, phase 3, "participation in neighbor notification," will allow the station to determine its "nearest available upstream neighbor" (NAUN) and to notify its downstream neighbor of its identity. The term *NAUN* is used to indicate a station's neighbor; i.e., the next immediate station that is active on the network. This is used for network management. When a station is powered off, it will deinsert itself from the network (the MAU will close the relay). Therefore, the station that was immediately below now has a new neighbor. They will be reported on the network and is very useful for network management.

5. *Phase 4.*   The last of these phases; phase 4, "request initialization," allows the station to identify itself to its LAN manager (IBM's LAN manager; this has nothing to do with Microsoft's working group network operating system—LAN manager). This identification includes individual addresses of the ring station's NAUN, product instance identification of the attached product, and the Token Ring controller's microcode revision level. If any of this information is incorrect or a threat to ring integrity, the LAN manager can request that this station be removed from the ring.

After all these phases, the Token Ring controller is now active on the ring. The station enters the "normal repeat" mode, and must wait for the token in order to transmit data onto the network.

Before we discuss how Token Ring repeats, transfers, and copies information from the network, we must study the Token Ring frame format. The IEEE 802.5 frame format is bit-specific, meaning that every bit in the packet (excluding the destination and source addresses) have significance. Let's start by a picture of the frame followed by short definition of the fields (Fig. 3.21).

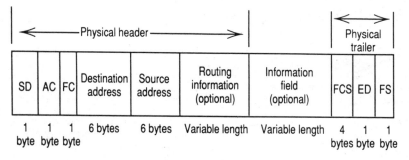

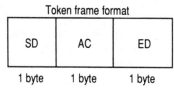

Token frame format

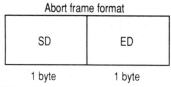

Abort frame format

Figure 3.21 Token Ring frame.

Token Ring frame definitions

Refer to Figures 3.21, 3.23 and Table 3.2. The Token Ring Frame contains the following.

Starting Delimiter (SD).   This first field of the Token Ring frame indicates the start of the frame. The starting delimiter is filled with the following pattern: JKOJKOOO. This field is static and will always be filled with that pattern. J and K are special nondata patterns that only the Token Ring controller will recognize.

Access Control (AC).   This field contains the 3 bits for priority settings, 3 bits reservation settings, 1 bit called the monitor bit, and 1 bit called the Token bit. The token bit is the bit that will indicate to the controller whether the frame is a Token frame or a data frame. If it is a Token frame then only the ED field would be next.

TABLE 3.2   Token Ring Frame Definitions

Bit	Description
	Access control
Priority (PPP)	Indicates the current priority of the token
Token (T)	Indicates whether the frame is a Token frame (1) or a data frame (0)
Monitor (M)	Used by the active monitor to prevent one frame from continuously circulating the ring. Also monitors priority bits
Reservation (R)	A field that is used to request that the next token that is issued be at a certain priority
	Frame control
Frame type (FF)	Indicates whether the current frame is a data frame or a MAC frame
	Ending delimiter
Intermediate frame (I)	Allows the receiver to identify whether the just received frame is the last (0) frame. A 1 in this field means more frames to follow
Error detected (E)	Set by any of the active stations on the network to indicate that an error has occurred in the frame
	Frame status
Address recognized (A)	A destination station recognizes the address
Frame copied (C)	The destination station has successfully copied the frame

Frame Control (FC).   This field indicates whether the frame contains data or is a nondata (maintenance) frame known as the MAC frame. If it is a MAC frame, the bits indicate the type of frame.

Destination Address (DA).   This field specifies the address of the network station that the frame is destined for. The field may contain any of the type of addresses discussed previously (unique, multicast, or broadcast). This field may contain either a 16 or 48 bit address. The 48 bit address is the most commonly found on networks. The 16 bit address is not assigned by the IEEE and is known as a locally administered address. If 16 bit addressing is implemented, then all stations on that particular network must use the 16 bit address technique. This applies to both the source and destination address.

Source Address (SA).   This field specifies the originator of the frame. It is always a unique address.

Information.   This field contains either user (LLC) data or control information (MAC frame information).

Framecheck Sequence (FCS).   This frame contains the CRC-32 error check that is performed on the FC, DA, SA, and information fields.

Ending Delimiter (ED).   This field contains special nondata bits and the I and E bits. The I and E bits are discussed in Table 3.2.

Frame Status (FS).   This frame contains the A and C bits. Since CRC error checking is not accomplished on this field, they are duplicated to insure the integrity of them.

Token Ring frame format

Now that we have defined the individual fields in the frame, you should have noticed that this frame is vastly different than the format of the Ethernet frame. Let's take a closer look into the token frame.

There are three basic types of frames that will traverse a Token Ring network: the token frame, the data frame, and a special management frame, the MAC frame. Let's explain the individual fields.

Refer to Figures 3.20 and 3.21 and Table 3.2. The starting delimiter (SD) field marks the beginning of a frame. It is represented by JK0JK000; J and K are nondata symbols and will be recognized by the Token Ring card as electrical phase violations. The card will read all 8 bits and note that this is a SD, indicating that a frame is approaching.

The next field is the access control (AC) field and has the following format PPPTMRRR. The first 3 bits of this field, PPP, are the priority bits. Every token has a priority associated with it containing values from 0 to 7. This will indicate the priority of the token or data frame.

The symbol T represents the token bit. If it is set to a 1, the frame is a token and if it is set to a 0, it is a data or MAC frame. If a station wishes to transmit and it reads this field as a token and its priority is higher or equal to the priority of the received frame, it will change the T bit to a 0 and append its data. Notice that it will check both the T bit and the 3 PPP bits. If the station's priority is lower, it will have to wait to transmit.

The next bit, the M bit, is the monitor bit. This bit is set to 0 by all stations except the active monitor. Once this frame is transmitted to the cable plant and passes by the active monitor, the active monitor will change this bit to a 1. The reason for this is to disallow a frame to be continuously repeated on the ring. How could this happen? A station may transmit a frame and then become disabled and be unable to remove the frame from the cable. Therefore, the active monitor will watch to see if this bit has previously been set. If so, the active monitor will abort the frame. (Remember that, with the exception of the active monitor, only the station that transmitted a frame may remove it from the ring.)

The next 3 bits, RRR, are reservation bits. These bits are initially set to 0 by any transmitting station. This field allows a station to reserve the next available token in its requested priority in the currently circulating data frame. So, when the currently circulating frame is returned to the originating station and a new token is generated, it will be at the requested value of rrr.

A priority listing for the rrr and ppp bits is presented in Table 3.3. Values are in binary.

The frame control (FC) field has the format FFZZZZZZ. This field indicates the type of transmission. Only two types of transmission are supported, those of frames containing MAC information and those containing data (also known as LLC data).

FF	Description
00	MAC Frame
01	Data (LLC data)
11	Reserved

What are the Z bits for? The ZZZ bits further break down this field: if the frame is a MAC frame, the Z bits indicate the type of MAC frame. The Z bits are designated as rrrYYY. This is further explained in the next section, on software components and MAC frames.

If the frame is a data frame (LLC frame), the Z bits are still split to rrr and YYY. The rrr bits are reserved for future use. The ZZZ bits indicate the priority of the data. These bits must be equal to or less than the priority in the access control PPP field.

The destination and source address fields are 48 bits (6 bytes) in length. Although the IEEE 802.5 committee does allow for 16-bit address fields, the present author has yet to run into it.

The source and destination fields indicate the originating station and the frame's final destination.

There are 2 bits of significance in the destination field. The first 2

TABLE 3.3   Priority Bits Definition

000	Normal user priority, MAC frames that need no token and response-type MAC frames
001	Normal user priority
010	Normal user priority
011	Normal user priority and MAC frames that need tokens
100	Bridge
101	Reserved by IBM for future use
110	Reserved by IBM for future use
111	Specialized station management

NOTE: Courtesy IBM Corp.

bits are designated as the individual or group (I/G) bit and the universally or locally (U/L) administered bit, respectively. The I/G bit is used to indicate whether a particular frame is destined for a group of stations (broadcast or multicast) or whether the destination is an individual station. The U/L bit indicates whether the address was locally or universally administered. *Universally administered* means that the address given was allotted by a central committee (i.e., the standards body of IEEE). See Figure 3.22. These fields are the same for IEEE 802.3.

In the source address, the I/G field will always be a unique address; so this field has a new meaning. *The U will indicate whether source routing is enabled or not.* It is called the Routing Information Indicator (RII). Source routing is fully discussed in Chap. 4.

The information field does exactly what its name implies: it holds information. This information may be of data or MAC frame information. There is no limit on the number of bytes in this field, like the 1500 byte limit in Ethernet, although the transmitting station may not transmit longer than it is allowed to hold the token (< 10 ms).

The framecheck sequence (FCS) is the field that contains the bit- error checking for the frame. This is also known as the 32-bit CRC, mentioned earlier.

The end delimiter (ED) has the format JK1JK1IE. This indicates the end of the frame. The J and K are nondata bits. This means that they are special bits that the Token Ring controller will recognize. The only bits that may be changed here are the I and E bits. This E bit is the error bit and may be changed by any station on the network. Every station checks each frame for errors. These errors include FCS error, illegal frame, or inappropriate nondata symbols. If one is found, this bit is set to a 1. Each station also keeps track of how many times they have set this bit.

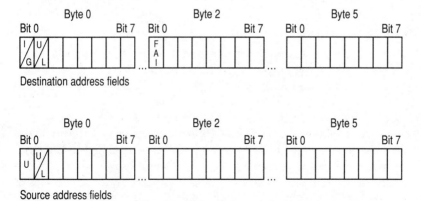

Figure 3.22 Token Ring (IEEE 802.x) Address Format (*Courtesy IBM Corp.*)

The I bit, the intermediate frame bit, indicates whether a frame is the last frame of a multiple-frame sequence or whether there are more frames to come. If I = 0, this indicates that it is the last or maybe the only frame to be transmitted. If it is set to a 1, then receiving station will know that there are more frames to follow.

The last field, the frame status (FS) field, has the format ACrrACrr. The r bits are reserved for future use and are automatically set to 0. The A bit represents the address-recognized bit. It is initialized to 0 by the transmitting station and will be set to a 1 by any station recognizing its address as the destination address or group address (including a broadcast address).

The C bit represents the frame-copied bit. Once again, this bit is initialized to 0 by the transmitting station. It will be set to a 1 by the station that copies (the destination station recognized the address as its own) the frame. The frame will be copied on the basis of three conditions:

1. The E bit is set to 0.

2. There is no FCS error.

3. The destination address was recognized.

The transmitting station may receive three types of AC frames back:

1. The station does not exist or is not active on the ring (A and C bits equal to 0).

2. The station exists but the frame was not copied (the A and C bit equal 0 and 1, respectively).

3. The frame was copied (the A and C bits both equal 1).

Never will the E, A, and C bits be set to a 1 at the same time. In order for the frame to be copied, the E bit must be set to a 0.

Software components and MAC frames

Since two types of frames may be transmitted on the network, MAC frames will be discussed separately. MAC frames are not data frames; they control certain management functions on the network. There are six total.

Table 3.4 lists the FC bits for MAC frames.

These active players in a Token Ring network cannot be detected without the use of a specialized protocol analyzer attached to the ring.

The most important component of any Token Ring network is the active monitor. One station on each ring will be assigned the duties of the active monitor, which provides token monitoring, among other

TABLE 3.4   MAC Frame FC Bits

Description	FFZZZZZZ
Claim token	00 0000011
Duplicate address test	00 000000
Active monitor present	00 000101
Standby monitor present	00 000110
Ring beaconing	00 000010
Ring purge	00 000100

NOTE: Courtesy IBM Corp.

things. This responsibility may be assigned to any active station on the ring. All other stations on the ring act as standby monitors. One standby monitor will become the active monitor in case the present active monitor fails.

The active monitor resolves certain error conditions that may occur on the ring, such as lost tokens, frames and priority tokens that circle the ring more than once, two active monitors present on the same physical ring, and clocking.

With the Ethernet specification, a preamble bit pattern was transmitted before each frame was sent to allow all receivers to synchronize their receivers to the incoming signal. Token Ring takes a different approach; the active monitor provides the ring's master clock, which ensures that all other stations on the ring are synchronized.

The active monitor introduces a 24-bit delay to the ring. This is accomplished by holding the token for 24 bit times in a buffer and then repeating the bits received. This is the only station that will buffer anything on a Token Ring network. All other stations on the network will repeat each bit as it is received. This will ensure that all stations will be able to transmit the full token before receiving it back. This is very important, for each station must be able to check the reservation bits to transmit a new token with the appropriate priority.

If you look at the Token Ring frame field formats (Fig. 3.23) you will notice a monitor bit in the access control (AC) field. This bit is used to detect whether a frame is continually circulating the ring. The possibility can arise for a station to transmit a frame and then be incapable of removing the frame from the ring. (Remember, the only station that may remove a frame from the ring, with the exception of the active monitor, is the station that originated the frame.) The active monitor will set this bit to a binary 1, and if it sees this frame again and the monitor bit set, it will purge the ring and transmit a new token.

Another function of the active monitor is to detect a lost frame and/ or token. The active monitor will set up a predetermined time that it knows is the longest time for a token to travel the full path of the ring.

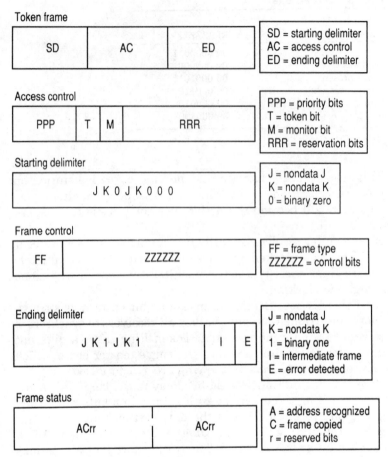

Figure 3.23 Token Ring field definitions.

(This timer is dynamic because the physical cable plant may change at any time.) The active monitor will start this timer countdown each time it transmits a starting delimiter. If this timer expires, the active monitor will assume that the token was lost. It will then purge the ring and initiate a new token.

How would the token become lost? In the simplest case, a token may become lost simply by a user shutting a PC down. In doing this, the MAU would lose its phantom voltage which is needed to keep the relay open for the token to travel the path from the MAU to the individual station. The token would be lost because of the relay closing in the MAU. This would cause the frame and/or token to become lost. The timer will then expire and the active monitor would purge the ring and initiate a new token.

Active monitor functions:

Lost tokens

Frames and priority token, that circulate the ring more than once

Other active monitors on the ring

"Short" ring (a ring with such a low bit delay that it cannot hold a token)

Clocking

In purging the ring, the active monitor broadcasts a certain type of frame, called the *ring purge MAC frame,* to all active stations on the network. If the active monitor can receive this frame, it will indicate to the active monitor that a frame can travel the ring safely.

Any station that believes it is the active monitor and receives a ring purge frame will automatically become a standby monitor on the ring. What are the functions of a standby monitor? The standby monitor performs two basic functions on the network: detects failures of the active monitor and detects any disruptions that may occur on the ring.

A standby monitor will wait for a predetermined amount of time for the active monitor present frame that will be sent out from the current active monitor on the ring. If any standby monitor on the ring does not receive this frame within the allotted time limit, it will assume that active monitor is not present on the ring and will try to become the active monitor by continuously transmitting a claim token MAC frame.

It will continue thus unless one of the following three conditions is met:

1. Another claim token MAC frame is received and the source address of that frame is higher than its own address.

2. A beacon MAC frame is received. A beacon MAC frame is transmitted in the case of a major ring failure such as cable break or a disabled or jabbering station.

3. A purge MAC frame is received. A purge MAC frame is sent by the active monitor after ring initialization or another station has won the token claim process. A new token will then be placed on the ring.

One final MAC frame is the duplicate address test (DAT) MAC frame. This frame is transmitted as part of a Token Ring card's initialization process, phase 3. The station sends this DAT frame with its own address in the destination address field. If the frame returns with the A (address recognized) bit set, the new station knows that its physical address is already being used on the network. The station will then notify the network manager and will deinsert itself from the network.

Now that we have a complete understanding of the Token Ring frame, it will be easier to understand exactly how Token Ring transmits, repeats, and copies data on the network. In undergoing each process mentioned above, certain bits are changed, as indicated in the following text. A Token Ring controller performs three basic functions: packet transmission, packet reception, and normal repeat mode.

Packet transmission.   Refer to Figure 3.21 and 3.24. When a controller does receive the token, the following algorithm is invoked: it will change one bit in the access control field (the T bit) from a 0 to a 1, which changes the whole status of the token. A Token Ring controller will assume that it has received the token when it receives a starting delimiter followed by an access control field with no code violations (J, K bits) in the priority bits and the bit that represents the token in the AC field is set to a 0. By changing this one bit, the token has be-

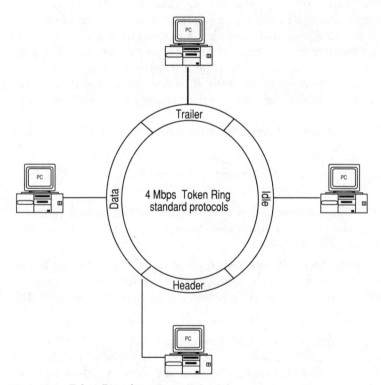

Figure 3.24   Token Ring data transmission.

come the header of a data or MAC frame, indicating to all other stations that this is now a data or MAC frame and not a token frame.

The controller will then check the token's priority bits. Two possibilities are presented:

1. The priority is equal to or less than the station's priority. If this is the case, the station will initiate the transmit data sequence.

2. The priority is higher than the station's priority. In this case, the station will set the reservation bits (rrr) and then the controller will wait for another token.

If the single-token method has been chosen (as opposed to the token early-release program, discussed toward the end of this chapter), the station must determine whether the frame transmitted was shorter than the ring length. (*Ring length* is the capability of a station to transmit a frame and be able to see that frame return before the end of its original transmission.) It is easy for a station to determine this and to take action accordingly.

How and why is a Token Ring length determined by a station? A Token Ring may never remain idle. There is always some sort of transmission on the cable, whether it is the token, a data or MAC frame, or simply idle characters (binary 0s) to fill the ring after transmission. With the single-token method, the station is not allowed to release the token without having started to receive its original transmission (the physical header) back. Why? It needs to check the reservation bits for any changes for the priority before release of the next token.

A station will indirectly determine the ring length according to whether it has received its original transmission back (the station does not really care about the actual cable length. If the station is finished transmitting the frame and has not yet received the frame back, there is a need to start transmitting idle characters after transmission of a frame. This is known as transmitting a frame that is shorter than the total ring length. You may say you can just add up the total amount of cable and that is the ring length. This is not true, for if a station is not powered on that particular station, it will not be active on the network. If it is not active on the network, then the token or data frame will not travel on that cable which attaches the inactive station to the MAU. This will shorten the traveling time of a frame and will shorten the ring length. It is safe to say that the ring length is a variable.

Returning to the transmission of the packet, if the controller enters the transmit mode, the station finds the SD and AC fields, and changes the T bit to a 1. The station will then wait for the ED field. Remember, the station does not read the token into a buffer. As the bits of each frame enter the station, each bit is repeated back onto the cable plant. If the station changes any bit in any field, that bit is automatically transmitted (repeated) back onto the cable.

If the controller does find the ED field, it will then transmit the rest of its frame. This includes, in the following order: the destination and source address fields, the optional routing information field (discussed in the next chapter), the information field (the data field), the framecheck sequence field, the ending delimiter, and finally the frame status field.

When the transmitted frame returns to the controller, the controller will compare the returned source address with its source address. If the two match, and regardless of whether the early token release option is selected and the token has not been released, or the early token release option is not selected, the station will transmit a token of the appropriate priority followed by idles. When all this is accomplished the controller will return to the normal repeat mode (discussed in a moment).

A very serious error can occur if the station does not receive the ED field immediately after the AC field and it has already changed the T bit in the AC field to a one; in such a case the controller knows that it has incorrectly interpreted the frame as a token frame and will immediately build an abort frame and transmit it. The station will then return and will then wait for the next token.

Packet reception.   When the packet reaches its destination station (as determined by the destination address), the destination station will copy the frame into its buffer and set the copy and address-recognized bits (or if an error is detected, the error-detected bit) while repeating the whole packet back on the ring. This is known as copying while repeating.

When a station does not have any data to transmit, it will act as a repeater on the network. This does not relieve the station from some responsibility. In normal repeat mode a station checks the data in the tokens and frames it has received and sets either the error-detected bit, the address-recognized bits, or the frame-copied, bits as appropriate. Remember that every station checks every packet for errors. If any station detects an error in any packet, it will set the error-detected bit as it repeats the frame. If the error bit was set and the packet has not yet traveled to the destination station, the frame will not be copied by the destination station.

Normal repeat mode. In normal repeat mode, a station will check only the data in the tokens and frames it receives and set the appropriate A, C, and E (address-recognized, frame-copied, and error-detected) bits as it repeats the token or frame. That's all that the normal repeat mode does.

Two key points should be remembered:

1. *Only when a station receives the token may it transmit data onto the ring.* This is known as *deterministic.* Two stations can never transmit onto the ring at the same time in the 4-Mbps non-early-release program Token Ring standard. When one station possesses the token, it may hold onto it for only a certain length of time. It must release the token. Otherwise other stations may assume that the token is lost and start error-recovery procedures prematurely.

2. *The destination station copies the frame into its receive buffer as it repeats the frame onto the network.* The destination, more or less, takes a snapshot of the packet as it is being repeated. The destination will change only the frame-copied and address-recognized bits. The rest of the packet is left intact for only the originating station to remove it from the cable.

Fault isolation and software error reporting

Lost or duplicate tokens do not present a problem for Token Ring. If the active monitor does not see the token for a specified period of time, it will issue a new token.

A duplicate token (non-early-release program) is a little more serious. One algorithm for this is: When a station sends a frame and the frame returns, check to make sure that the source address is its own. If not, the station will abort its current frame and will not issue a new token. Since it is presumed that both stations will perform the same activity, the token will eventually be lost.

Token early-release program

The last point to cover with Token Ring is the early-release program. To allow greater use of the bandwidth of the Token Ring architecture, there is a new algorithm involved, the early-release program. This algorithm is very simple. A station is allowed to transmit a token even without having received its original frame back. The station will release the token after transmitting the ending delimiter. If the header of the original frame has not been received, it releases the token with the reservation and priority bits set the same as when the controller received the original token enabling it to transmit.

Why implement the early-release program when it was stated before that even with the 24 bits of the token traveling the ring alone (which is the smallest frame that will ever travel the ring), it would take a tremendous amount of cable to introduce a sufficiently long delay for the whole token to be transmitted? The primary answer is the efficient use of the available bandwidth. There is no reason to allow stations to remain idle on the network when the possibility exists for more than one controller to transmit on the cable without interference. The early-release program is now an option on all Token Ring controller boards.

Advantages and disadvantages

Token Ring does offer some advantages over its counterpart, Ethernet. First, before the advent of unshielded twisted-pair (UTP) cable for Ethernet, Ethernet relied on a single-type cable technique. If this cable were ever broken, all stations attached to that cable would be disabled.

Token Ring, and now UTP for Ethernet, offer a star topology with each station possessing its own cable plant to the hub. If a single cable breaks there, only that one particular station is down.

There are no collisions on Token Ring. A station may not transmit until it receives the token frame. On Ethernet, a station may transmit whenever it perceives the cable (channel) to be clear. Other stations may perceive this and may transmit at the same time, thus causing a collision, a backoff algorithm to be invoked, and ultimately, transmission delays. Token Ring is deterministic. The token can be calculated as to when a station should see the arrival of the token.

Token Ring LANs are deterministic. The arrival time of the token at a station can be calculated. Every station must wait for the token. In general, LANs tend to be bursty: a lot of traffic, then no traffic. This is advantageous for Ethernet. Ethernet allows any station to transmit as long as the cable appears clear.

Under steady heavy loads, Token Ring tends to be more stable, whereas Ethernet generally falters. The degradation tends to be less severe as more users are added to the cable plant. You could argue this point in that if you design your Ethernet network correctly, you can easily prevent Ethernet from being overloaded.

IBM has its full support behind it. For some, this is a major advantage. Although recently, IBM has been surreptitiously supporting Ethernet. 3Com is currently supporting IBM with Ethernet cards and drivers.

Token Ring is very strong on built-in network management. The standard itself provides for network management capabilities.

4

The Network Layer and Extension of the Data-Link Layer

This chapter discusses an extension of the data-link layer and introduces the network layer.

Nontechnical Report: Internetworking

Internetworking and intranetworking products fall into four different categories: repeaters, routers, gateways, and bridges. One final category is *brouters,* which combines two of the previous categories (bridges and routers) into one device. Each handles different functions that directly correspond to the ISO layer at which the internetworking function is performed. To understand these functions it is necessary to be familiar with the role of each layer in the ISO model (refer to ISO layer model in Fig. 4.1).

Repeaters

Repeaters extend the geographic coverage of a local area network (LAN) by interconnecting multiple segments. For example, the IEEE standard specifies a maximum length of 500 m for a single segment, but with repeaters interconnecting five segments, an IEEE network can reach a maximum distance of up to 2500 m. Repeaters can also interconnect segments using different physical media such as thick coaxial, thin coaxial, twisted-pair, or fiber-optic cables. Repeaters are hardware devices that operate at the physical layer of the ISO model, repeating all electrical signals from one segment to the other. They have very little intelligence and do not provide any type of traf-

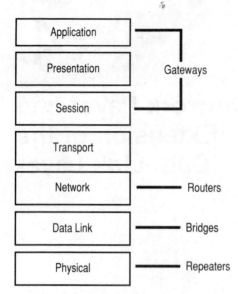

Figure 4.1 Internetworking and the ISO model.

fic isolation. Unlike bridges, repeaters do not act like an Ethernet station on the network.

Routers

Routers perform packet routing and forwarding functions. Operating at the network layer of the ISO model, they link networks that share the same network layer (i.e., the same network layer software). Most routers on the market today interconnect networks that use the same high-level protocols; these routers are respectively less mature and more complex and function in a single-protocol application. Routers are protocol-dependent. A router that is designated for use on an XNS network will route only XNS-based packets. They will not route TCP-based packets. Brouters will route multiple protocols within the same box.

Routers create a number of logical subnetworks, allowing large interconnected networks (known as internetworks) to be organized into different administrative domains. Routers, for example, may interconnect Ethernet segments either locally or remotely over point-to-point (leased telephone) lines. Another example is an application where routers interconnect Token Ring and Ethernet networks over a X.25 network.

Gateways

Gateways, the most complex of the internetwork products, interconnect networks that have totally different communications architectures. Since the network facilities and addressing schemes are incompatible, the gateway must provide complete conversion from one protocol stack to the other without altering the data that needs to be transmitted. Currently available gateways make such interconnections as TCP/IP to SNA or TCP/IP to X.25.

A TCP/IP-to-SNA gateway gives users on a multivendor TCP/IP LAN access to IBM hosts through the SNA protocols. Gateways between LANs and X.25 wide area networks connect LAN users to either X.25 hosts or a large database on an X.25 Public Data Network (PDN). They also connect users attached to a Packet Assemble-Disassemble (PAD) to hosts located throughout the X.25 network.

Bridges

Bridges interconnect local or remote networks at the media access control (MAC) sublayer of the data-link layer of the ISO model.

Bridges are transparent to high-level protocols such as XNS, TCP/IP, or OSI (this is known as *protocol-transparent*). Bridges isolate traffic to one or the other segments to which they connect. Their main purpose is to partition traffic on each interconnected segment. Bridges forward only traffic addressed to the other subnetworks, increasing the effective throughput of the entire network. Although all segments interconnected by a bridge form a single logical network, they are electrically isolated from one another.

Local bridges may connect similar networks such as Ethernet to Ethernet or Token Ring to Token Ring or dissimilar networks such as Ethernet to broadband and Ethernet to Token Ring.

Remote bridges use data communications link (a leased telephone line) such as T-1 line to join physically isolated networks.

Computing environment.   In environments with a variety of computer resources (PCs, workstations, mainframes), there are varying requirements for network bandwidth. For instance, clustered minicomputers, diskless workstations, or PCs sharing a file server place a great burden on a network because of numerous file transfers. When such traffic begins to seriously affect performance, the most efficient way to deal with the problem is to use a bridge to subdivide the network into two segments, thereby partitioning the traffic.

Before bridges came along, everything that could be placed on one cable plant was placed on there, regardless of the type of application. Therefore, graphics workstations were on the same cable plant with terminal servers (see Appendix G). Terminal servers do not generate that much network traffic when compared to a graphics workstation. Soon people found that the network was gradually getting slower (measured by response time, which is measured by the degree of user frustration). Some even went so far as to say that Ethernet had found its match. Ethernet can handle only so much traffic before it becomes saturated.

Before an uproar was started, a new networking concept arrived. Invent a device that will allow us to segment the cable plant based on network applications, yet give us total transparency. You could do this by running multiple cable plants with multiple hosts acting as routers, but something easier showed up before all that cable was pulled: *bridges.* Refer to Figs. 4.3 and 4.4.

Bridges are known by two other names: *MAC-layer bridges* and *Data-link bridges,* indicating operation at the data-link layer of the ISO model, specifically at the MAC layer of the data-link layer. For the most part, these other names have disappeared and their general term is now *bridges.*

Operation. An Ethernet bridge interconnects two or more Ethernet cable segments and watches all packets that traverse the cable (see Figs. 4.2 and 4.3). The bridge is set in promiscuous mode. With this capability a bridge has the authority to pick up and read any packets that are on the network.

Refer to Fig. 4.4. Specifically, a bridge watches both sides of the Ethernet for the source addresses of each packet on the cable. The bridge will look into its routing table to see if the address is located there. If not, the bridge will insert the address into its routing table. These addresses that it stores are the Ethernet addresses. This is known as *learning.*

A bridge also sees the destination address of each packet. Two circumstances exist here for which the bridge will make a decision. When the bridge receives a packet, it will look at the destination address. The bridge will first look in the routing table from the segment from which the packet was received. If the address of the destination is in the local routing table, the bridge will simply discard the packet. The bridge will then look at the remote (the second cable segment) routing table. If the bridge finds a match, the bridge will forward the packet. This is known as *filtering* and *forwarding.*

There is also one more decision that the bridge will have to make. What if the destination is not in either routing table? This situation may occur if the bridge is first powered on and has not had a chance to build its routing tables or if the destination node was just powered on and the bridge has not seen any packets from it yet. The architects of this standard also realized this, and therefore all bridges that encounter this condition will simply forward any packets that it does not

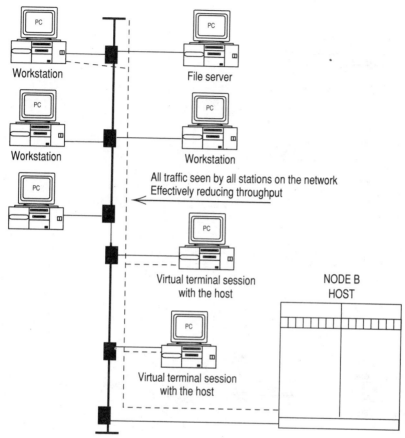

Figure 4.2 Ethernet segment without a bridge.

know about. This may seem inefficient, but considering that this condition should occur infrequently, it does not affect the throughput of the LAN.

In the design of the network, it may be possible to design two bridges that lead to the same Ethernet segments. This is known as a loop. It also causes unnecessary interruptions on a Ethernet segment. For example, if an originating station transmits a packet and two bridges that interconnect the same segments of Ethernet cable forward the packet, the destination station will receive duplicate packets. The destination's upper-layer software will be capable of discarding the packet, but it will have caused an unnecessary interruption in the network stations. (Refer to Fig. 4.8.)

An algorithm used for most Ethernet bridges that disable secondary loops is the spanning tree algorithm. With this algorithm, the bridges

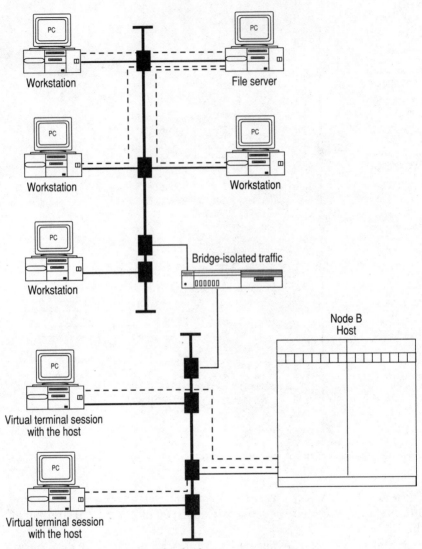

Figure 4.3 Ethernet segment with a bridge.

will pass certain control information between themselves trying to find redundant paths. When the bridges do find the redundant paths, they will disable (called blocking) them, allowing only a single path to remain to any station on the network. These control packets transfer to all the bridges about 2 to 15 s looking for changes in topology. In doing this, if an active path becomes disabled, the bridges will reconfigure themselves to enable disabled paths to become active,

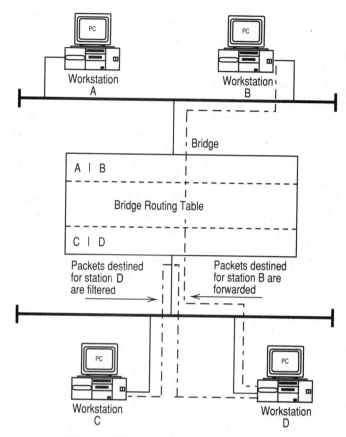

Figure 4.4   Ethernet Bridge filter and forwarding process.

thus allowing no interruption to any of the active stations on the network. This is known as the spanning tree algorithm (STA).

Token Ring bridges.   Bridges that support the Token Ring algorithm take a different approach for forwarding packets and allowing redundant paths. See Fig. 4.5.

A station that wishes to communicate with another first transmits an *all-stations* "dynamic route discovery packet," hoping to find the destination node on the local ring. If there is no response to this packet, the originating node will transmit either an "*all-routes* discovery packet" or a "*single-route* discovery packet." These are special broadcast packets.

A Token Ring bridge will copy this packet, and if it is an all-routes discovery packet, it will forward the packet onto the next ring. If it is a "single-route broadcast discovery packet," the bridge will first check to see if it is allowed to forward single-route broadcast packets. If it is allowed to forward, it will do so, and if it is not configured to forward the packet, it will simply repeat the packet to the same cable plant (not forwarding the packet).

As the packet crosses the bridges on its way to the destination station, it will collect routing information; inserted by each bridge that the packet traversed. This information includes what rings and bridges it traversed to get to the destination node.

Once the destination node receives this packet, it should respond, transmitting the packet via an all-routes broadcast. All Token Ring bridges will forward this packet back to the originator. If the originating station receives multiple response packets back, it will choose the path to forward its packets. It usually chooses the route, on the basis of the information that the packet collected, in the first packet it received back. Data will than be communicated between these two stations using that path.

Differences.   With Ethernet bridges and the spanning tree algorithm, all intelligence for routing is contained in the bridge. With this algorithm, a bridge may simply be inserted onto the network without redesigning any other components on the network. No changes to the MAC frame or any of the upper-layer protocols will be necessary on the network stations. This is known as transparent bridging.

Ethernet bridges, on powerup or a link state change, are the only components on the network that need to contain the intelligence to know that loops may be present on the network or that the network topology has changed. With special intelligence in the bridge, a special packet is sent out via a well-known multicast address so that the bridges can talk to each other to find loops and reconfigure the network accordingly. This special packet is sent out not only at boot time (when a bridge is first powered on) but every few seconds (usually settable by the network manager) so that whenever a bridge goes down, the network may automatically reconfigure itself, without affecting any of the users.

The network can contain multiple paths to the same destination, but no loops will be allowed. The network will automatically reconfigure itself when any bridge or bridge port fails completely transparently to all users. All intelligence is contained in the bridge, thereby eliminating any need to have the intelligence on the originating and destination stations, possibly consuming precious RAM.

The major drawback to this scheme is that redundant bridges remain in a standby state, never being used unless the network is forced to reconfigure itself. This could seem to be a waste of computing power and nonutilization of load sharing (except with remote bridges, those using telephone lines connecting to a remote network; redundancy is permitted here).

With this in mind, source routing takes an alternative approach by permitting redundant paths to exist; that is, all ports on a Token Ring bridge remain in the forwarding state. This is an advantage in that load sharing is produced, which could result in faster throughput. Also, IBM has allowed for up to 8 linear bridges to be in between two communicating nodes. Although this is inconceivable (because of upper-layer software synchronization, timing), it is eight bridges more than the spanning tree algorithm allows.

But what about the disadvantages in source routing? Source routing requires the originating node to have the intelligence for choosing the route that a packet will take. It also requires any node to respond to TEST or XID packets with a full complement of routing information so that two nodes may converse. This includes route discovery, route selection, and insertion of the routing information field in the MAC packet. This would produce changes in the packet frame format itself (see Fig. 4.5).

This might seem to be a minor consideration with minicomputers, mainframes, or any computing system that is multitasking or has no realistic requirement on memory. But since most PC networks operate on DOS with the infamous 640K application RAM barrier, this extra intelligence may require some of the computing power and the RAM as well.

The IEEE 802.1d committee adopted the spanning tree algorithm (STA) for use on all three IEEE 802 standards (802.3, 802.4, and 802.5). But with the IEEE 802.5 committee separately adopting of source routing, it has resulted in a controversy as to which routing algorithm to support. Since IBM is in full support of source routing and IEEE 802.5, source routing did gain a lot of support from those Token Ring vendors who claim to be IBM Token Ring–compatible. But the routing algorithm for bridges that has won the widest support is STA, with IBM slowly supporting this through their version called source route transparent.

Finally, a Token Ring LAN can connect to an Ethernet network as transparently as a Token Ring–Token Ring bridge or an Ethernet-to-Ethernet bridge. This is accomplished not only on the local level, but also on the remote level (those bridges connecting to geographically separated networks via leased telephone lines). The state of the art of these bridges is in its infancy.

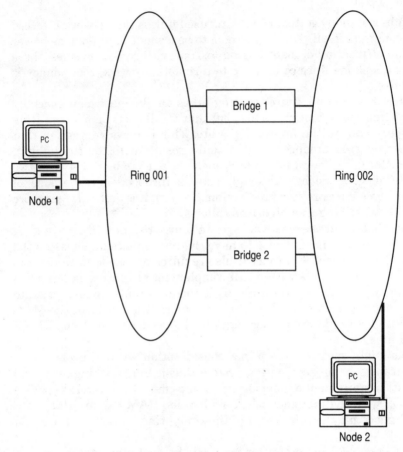

Figure 4.5 Token Ring filtering and forwarding process. Single-route broadcast route determination. Node 1 transmits a single-route broadcast to node 2. Bridge 1 forwards the frame to ring 2 and adds routing information data to the frame. Bridge 2 does not forward single-route broadcast frame. Node 2 responds to node 1 with an all-routes broadcast frame. Bridge 1 forwards the frame and adds routing information data; bridge 2 does the same. Node 1 selects a path from one of the two frames and sends a routed frame by flipping the direction bit. Node 2 responds by flipping the direction bit to reverse the path selected by node 1.

Source route transparent is the capability of a bridge to support both the spanning tree algorithm and source routing in the same bridge. Both algorithms are active at the same time.

Technical Report: Internetworking

Ethernet bridging

The concept of media access control (MAC) layer (bridges are known as MAC-layer bridges as they function at the MAC layer of the data-link layer of the ISO model) bridging offered powerful solutions for a number of internetworking problems. Unlike routers, a bridge operates at the data-link layer, a low level of the ISO model, so it can transparently pass traffic running different upper-layer protocols such as XNS, TCP/IP, and OSI protocols. This is known as being protocol-transparent. Bridges are thus a flexible and cost-effective choice for heterogeneous network protocol environments. While a bridge can interconnect networks running a wide variety of applications using such protocols as XNS, TCP/IP, or OSI, only devices running the same protocols can communicate with one another. For example, traffic from TCP/IP devices is understood only by other devices running TCP/IP. Bridges do not convert one protocol to another.

The theoretical speed of a bridge is based on a bridge having to look only at the destination and source address of each packet. The bridge will not look any further into the packet for information on which to base its decision regarding whether to forward the packet (unless manually circumvented). Special features are discussed later.

In addition to interconnecting networks running different protocols, bridges can connect networks using different media such as coaxial cable (baseband or broadband), fiber-optic cable, or twisted-pair cable. For instance, an interconnected network might consist of several coaxial cable networks or a mixture of coaxial, twisted-pair, and fiber-optic cable networks. The interconnected networks can also use different access methods, for example, CSMA/CD or Token Ring. One limitation of such an interceptor is the possible difference in maximum frame size supported by the various networks. It is essential that the upper-level protocols passing through the bridge do not violate the maximum packet size on any network segment.

In the Token Ring environment, there is no limitation on the size of the packet. In the Ethernet environment the packet is limited to 1518 bytes, including overhead. Therefore, if a Token Ring network transmits a packet that is 2048 bytes in size, the bridge will not be capable of fragmenting the packet and then transmitting it to the Ethernet port. Routers, on the other hand, do have this capability. (This is discussed in more detail later in the chapter.) Most network software upon initialization of a session between two stations will negotiate the largest frame (packet) size that can be received or transmitted.

Along with protocol transparency, another important benefit of a bridge is to provide simple traffic isolation between physical segments or cabling systems that make up the interconnected network. The bridge accomplishes this with a learning algorithm that alerts the bridge as to which packets should remain on the segment and which packets should be forwarded to another segment. These steps in traffic isolation process are known as learning, filtering, and forwarding. These are the basic operators of any bridge.

There are two main categories of bridges: local and remote. A local bridge interconnects two or more directly attached local networks, either Ethernet or Token Ring. A remote bridge connects multiple physically isolated networks by means of long-haul data communications links. Typically, these are point-to-point links with speeds ranging from 9600 baud to T-1 (leased telephone lines).

Basic principles

Learn algorithm. The basic operations for a bridge are learning, filtering, and forwarding. Any combination of these three operations may be turned on or off. For the learning algorithm to function, the bridge listens to all traffic on its attached segments. It then checks the source addresses of all packets received and the destination address. The bridge will then perform the following algorithm. The bridge will first check its routing table to see if the source address is registered. If it is not registered, the bridge will add the address to that table. If the bridge does find the address in its table, it will update the age function. (The age function is not available on all bridges. The age function determines how long ago the bridge last saw that particular source address.) If a predetermined time allotment has transpired, the bridge does have the capability to remove the address from the routing table, thus conserving the bridges RAM and the time for address lookup (see Fig. 4.6).

Filter and forward algorithm. Bridges also check the destination address of every packet received to determine whether it should be forwarded or filtered from the next segment. The bridge will first check its local table to see if the destination address is on the port that the packet was received from. If the destination address is on the local table, the packet is simply discarded (filtered). If the address is not there, it will check the address table for the port of the next segment. If the address is found on the table of the next segment, the bridge will forward the packet on that particular port. If the destination address is not found on the other port again, the bridge will forward the packet, assuming that the address is remote and has simply not seen it yet. A bridge's tables are built on the source address only. The destination address is looked at only to see if the packet should be forwarded.

Filtering and forwarding are relatively simple in the case of a local bridge connecting only two networks but become increasingly complex for local or remote bridges interconnecting multiple networks.

The filtering and forwarding processes (see Fig. 4.7) help illustrate

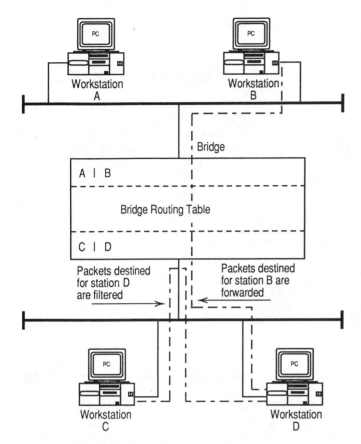

Figure 4.6 Ethernet bridge with routing table.

the filtering and forwarding processes. The first time station A sends a packet on the network, for example, to station B, the bridge forwards the packet to network 1, since it does not yet know where station B resides. When station B responds, the bridge then learns that it is on network 2. The next time station A sends a packet to station B, the bridge will filter it so that it is not forwarded to network 1. Similarly, a transaction between stations A and C alerts the bridge to station C's location. In Figure 4.7, the bridge forwards to network 2 only those packets destined for stations (any equipment physically attached to the network) on that network.

As does any other station on the local segment, the bridge regenerates each packet it receives. Therefore, the number of stations on the segment or the distance the packet travels before reaching the bridge has no effect on the quality of packets being forwarded to another seg-

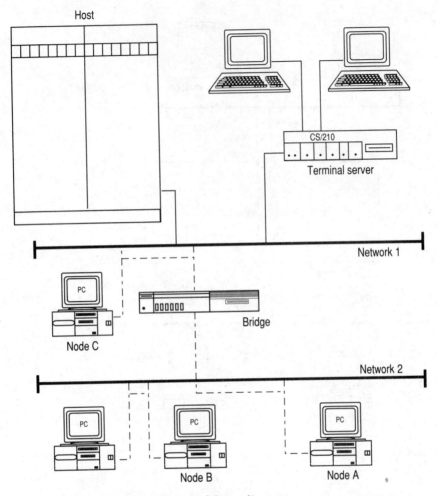

Figure 4.7 Ethernet bridge filtering and forwarding process.

ment. Any delay related to distance, however, must meet the requirements of the high-level protocols involved. This extends the 2500 m limit of Ethernet as mentioned in the next paragraph.

The number of bridges that a packet is allowed to traverse is usually limited to a linear 8, meaning that the source and destination stations be separated by no more than eight bridges. The reason for this is *not* based on a limitation of the bridge itself. The main reason is that if a bridge does introduce a delay in the forwarding of the packet and if the total delay is long enough, the upper-layer protocols of the originating station may time out and retransmit the packet again. If the packet were simply delayed and not lost as a result of a collision, for instance, and the final destination station responded to the original packet, that destination station would receive duplicate packets, causing undetermined problems on the network. If the network was also designed correctly, there should be no need for a packet to span through eight or more bridges without being separated by a router.

The forwarding and learning processes assume that the topology of the overall network is a tree or that there is only one path between any two stations located on LANs separated by bridges. If active loops (parallel paths) exist, problems may occur, such as packets being duplicated or traveling endlessly throughout the interconnected network. The loops in bridged networks shown in Fig. 4.8 illustrates this

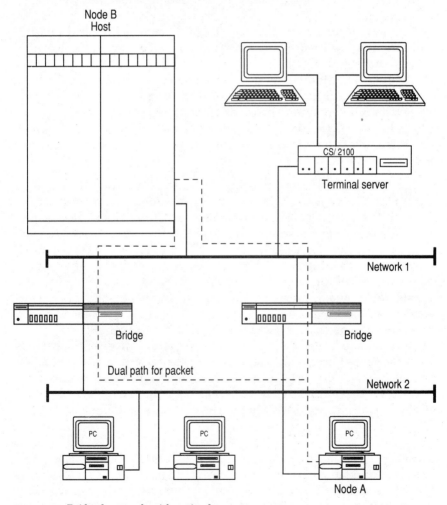

Figure 4.8 Bridged network with active loops.

potential difficulty. For example, a packet sent from station A to station B is automatically sent twice since there are two bridges interconnecting networks 1 and 2. Both of these bridges will forward the packet. This is not a fatal error, for the destination station will know that it has already received the packet and will simply discard it. The problem is that the destination station had to consume time processing this duplicate packet.

In order to deal with this problem, some bridges implement intelligent algorithms to detect loops and shut down alternate paths. The STA (an IEEE 802.1d committee recommendation) is one example. If the active path fails, one of the inactive paths takes over automatically. (The STA is fully discussed in the section immediately following this section.)

The three basic processes for a bridge (learning, filtering, and forwarding) may be used in any combination. For example, the learning process may be turned off, disabling the bridge to learn any new address on its own. Individual addresses may be entered manually. The bridge would still forward and filter according to the addresses that were manually entered (this is called *static routing*).

The bridge may also have forwarding turned off. This would disable the bridge from forwarding any packets. This is sometimes used for security or for network management.

Remote bridges. For remote bridges, parallel lines from the same local bridge to a remote bridge do not constitute a loop, so bridges can balance the internetwork traffic among multiple lines. This allows planners to design networks with some level of redundancy. (See the star topology flowchart in Fig. 4.11, in the section on topology, below.)

When remote bridges with parallel lines participate in the spanning tree protocol, all remote links connected to the same remote bridge are considered as one network interface. The STA puts all the links in forwarding or blocking state. This ensures that the network topology can maximize the use of the bandwidth provided by parallel links.

Some remote bridges will divide the physical address of the packets to be forwarded up among the remote links. According to the address, the bridge will forward the packet on one assigned path and will always take that path (except on a topology change). This allows all paths to stay in the forwarding state and allows simple load balancing.

Topology. The most common topology for bridges are cascaded networks or backbone networks for local applications and star topologies for remote applications. A choice among these depends on the number of computing devices networked and how much partitioning they require. In a case where the performance of a network is no longer satisfactory because of traffic bottlenecks, bridges can divide the network into segments, forming a cascaded network (see cascaded network in Fig. 4.9). The bridges control and monitor intersegment traffic, restoring the efficiency of each segment. For example, a bridge might isolate a group of PCs or workstations sharing the same file server. Whatever the case, a cascaded network should probably include no more than five or six segments. Otherwise, the delays introduced by successive bridges may become excessive for the higher-layer protocols, as well as intolerable to users.

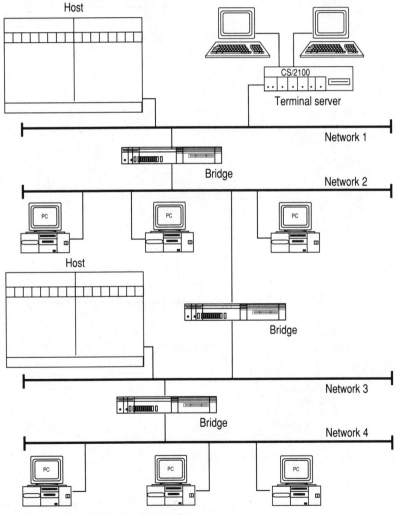

Figure 4.9 Cascaded bridged network.

A high-speed backbone is a reasonable alternative in cases where many segments need to be linked. One prime advantage is that such configuration allows systematic network growth. In contrast, many cascaded networks are the result of pressure from unplanned growth. Another benefit of backbone configuration is improved performance, since intersegment traffic passes over only one intervening segment between the source and destination segments (unlike a cascaded network, where traffic must traverse all intervening networks).

A backbone topology, (Fig. 4.10) is extremely efficient in an office

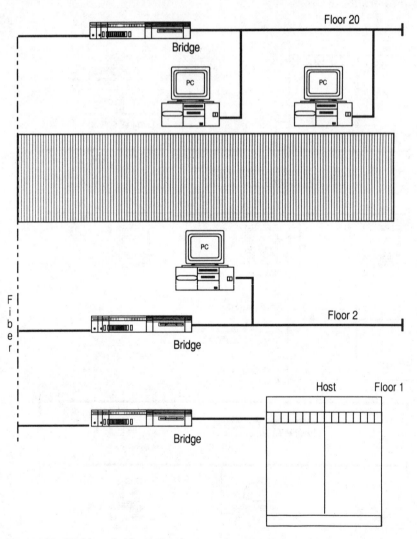

Figure 4.10   Backbone bridge network.

tower with many floors, as illustrated in the backbone configuration office tower in Figure 4.10. In this case, an Ethernet backbone—usually thick coaxial or fiber-optic cable—runs the full height of the building. Ethernet ribs extend from the backbone onto each floor. Bridges partition the traffic among the floors, maximizing the performance of each segment.

The *star topology* is the most common choice for remote bridge applications. It allows remote sites to be interconnected with a minimum number of intervening segments and without loops. For instance, a large corporation with several divisions and remote sales offices can solve its connectivity problems with bridges in a star configuration. Divisions with high network bandwidth requirements are connected to their headquarters through high-speed T-1 links and 56-kbps backup link, whereas small remote offices are interconnected with lower-speed lines (see Fig. 4.11).

Spanning tree algorithm. For Ethernet and IEEE 802.3 networks, all bridges follow the spanning tree algorithm. This algorithm is used to close loops in the network caused by the addition of two or more bridges connecting the same two physical networks together.[1]

Before the IEEE 802.1d standard, network designers had two choices: avoid designing loops in the network or keep redundant bridges that created these loops powered off until needed. (Some bridge vendors designed their bridges with proprietary loop algorithms embedded; so, for example, you would power up one bridge first and then the other. The latter bridge would find a loop and bring its ports down until no loop was found.)

Loops in a network create many problems. Any node may receive one packet twice, or packets may loop through the network endlessly. In the TCP/IP routers, loops are allowed, for one of the fields in the IP (Internetwork Protocol) header of a TCP packet is a time-to-live (TTL) field which each of the routers decrement as the packet passes each router. The router that decrements this field to a 0 will send a control message to the destination exclaiming that the host was not found. Therefore, a packet should not traverse a network endlessly.

Looking at the loops in a bridged network in Fig. 4.8, we see that if node A wanted to converse with node B, bridges A and B would both pick up the packet and check their respective routing tables. Each would see that node B is not on the same side as node A and would forward the packet onto the other side. Remembering that only one physical node may transmit at a time on Ethernet and that bridges must follow this, two packets would arrive at different times to node

---

[1]Portions of the following paragraphs were reprinted from the *Internetwork Bridge Operation Guide* with permission from 3Com Corp.

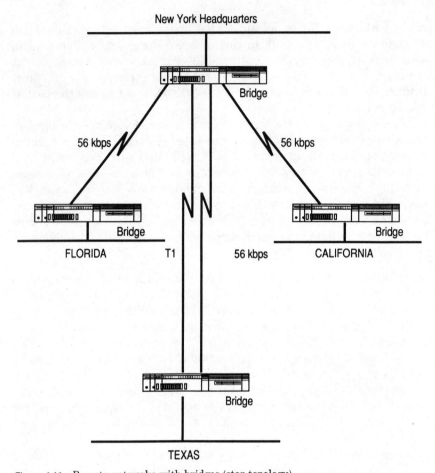

Figure 4.11   Remote networks with bridges (star topology).

B, each as a good packet, just duplicated. This is not a fatal error, except that it resulted in a duplicate packet being received and processed by node b. Node B's upper-layer protocols would realize that it already received the packet and would simply discard it. This requires additional processing time by node B when it could have been doing something else.

The STA eliminates this problem. The bridges are able to exchange certain control information to each other, selecting certain bridges to "block" or turn off their ports, enabling the network to form a tree topology (see Fig. 4.12).

Terminology and definition.   Before we define the algorithm, some terms need to be introduced. The following terms are used by STA.

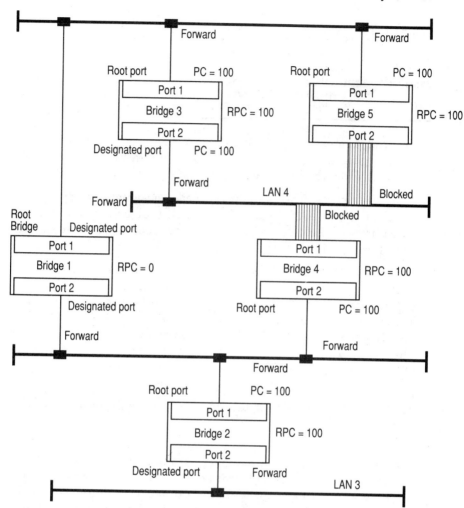

Figure 4.12 The spanning tree algorithm. RCP = Root Path Cost; PC = Path Cost.

Bridge identifier. This is determined by a combination of a bridge's Ethernet or hardware (data-link) address and bridge priority. A lower bridge identifier results in a higher priority for the bridge and increases its probability of being selected by STA as the root bridge.

Designated bridge. This is the bridge attached to each LAN segment in the network with the lowest path cost to the root bridge. In the case where all bridges have the same root path cost, the bridge with the lowest bridge identifier becomes the designated bridge. The designated bridge conveys network topology information to all

TABLE 4.1 Path Cost

Type	Speed	Path cost
FDDI	100 Mbps	10
Ethernet	10 Mbps	100
T1	1.544 Mbps	651
DDS	56 kbps	18867

the other bridges that are connected to the same physical LAN via the designated port. The root bridge is the designated bridge for each LAN for which it is attached.

Designated port. This is the port on each designated bridge that is attached to the LAN segment for which that bridge is the designated bridge. The designated port conveys topology information received from the root bridge to the other bridges on the network.

Path cost. The path cost is a number that is inversely proportional to the speed of the port interface. For example, a bridge may be assigned a path cost of 100 with the port interface speed of 10 Mbps. These values are usually settable by the network administrator. Table 4.1 gives an example of the recommended standard. For other interfaces, divide 1,000 Mbps (million bits per second) by the speed of the interface to obtain the cost.

Port identifier. This is the identification for each port of the bridge. This identifier contains a settable priority field and a fixed port number.

Port states. The following two steady states are possible on each port on the bridge: *blocking* and *forwarding*. All root ports and designated ports are in a forwarding state; all other ports are in a blocking state. Blocking of some ports ensures that no multiple paths exist between any two LANs. Both the port from which a packet is received and the port to which it is destined must be in the forwarding state for a packet to be forwarded.

Root bridge. This is the bridge in the network with the lowest bridge identifier. The root bridge transmits topology frames to both attached networks.

Root port. This is the port on each bridge that has the lowest path cost to the root bridge. Topology information from the direction of the root bridge arrives at the root port. Except for the root bridge, each bridge has a root port.

For the STA to function properly, the following list of requirements is assumed:

1. Each bridge can recognize a unique destination address.

2. Each bridge has a unique identifier (bridge ID), which contains priority field and a data-link address.

3. Each port of a bridge has a unique identifier (port ID), which contains a priority field and a port number.

4. Each port is associated with a path cost, which is determined by the speed of its network interface: the faster the speed, the lower the cost.

On the basis of the bridge ID, the port ID, and the path costs, the STA configures the network to become loop-free by the following algorithm:

1. Select a bridge that acts as the root of the spanning tree network. It should be the one that has the lowest bridge ID (6-byte physical address) among all the bridges on the extended network.

2. Select a root port on each bridge (except the root bridge) that incurs the lowest path cost when the bridge forwards a packet to the root bridge.

3. Select a designated bridge on each LAN that incurs the lowest path cost when forwarding a packet from that LAN to the root bridge. The port by which the designated bridge is attached to the LAN is called the *designated port*.

4. Enable all the root ports and designated ports so that they can forward packets; block all other ports.

Let's look at some diagrams to further explain all these terms. Using Figs. 4.12 and 4.13, the following dictates an example of the STA in action.

1. When the bridges are powered on, each bridge assumes that it is the root bridge and then transmits a *configuration bridge protocol data unit* (CBPDU), which is a group of packets through all of its ports. A CBPDU contains information such as the ID of the bridge that the transmitting bridge "thinks" is the root bridge, the transmitting bridge's root path cost and the path cost associated with the source port. Refer to Fig. 4.13.

PROT ID	PROT VER ID	BPDU Type	Flags	Root ID	Root path cost	Bridge ID	Port ID	MSG age	MAX age	Hello time	FWD DEL

Figure 4.13 Bridge Hello packet fields (CBPDU frame).

2. When a bridge receives a CBPDU that contains superior information, it stores the information at that port. The information is considered "superior" if it is more up to date and reflects more accurately the current conditions of the network than the information held by the receiving port. If this CBPDU is received at the bridge's root port, the bridge also forwards it to all of its attached LANs for which it is the designated bridge. If a bridge receives a CBPDU that contains information inferior to that currently stored at that port, it discards the CBPDU. If the bridge is a designated bridge for the LAN from which the CBPDU is received, it sends to that LAN a CBPDU containing the information stored at that port. As a result, inferior information is discarded and superior information is propagated on the extended network.

Assume that each port in Fig. 4.12 is equipped with an Ethernet interface which has a path cost of 100. Further assume that the priority fields in bridge 1's and bridge 3's IDs are the same. Having the lowest bridge ID (because the data-link address is the smallest), bridge 1 becomes the root bridge, and its CBPDU is superior to the CBPDUs from other bridges. After exchanging a few CBPDUs and discarding the inferior ones, all the bridges contain the same information indicating that bridge 1 is the root bridge. Because a root bridge is automatically the designated bridge for all the LANs to which it is attached, bridge 1 is also the designated bridge for LAN 1 and LAN 2.

3. Each bridge (except the root bridge) has to select a root port, the port which incurs the least cost when the bridge forwards a packet to the root. The cost depends partly on the port's cost (determined by the speed of its network interface) and partly on the root path cost of the designated bridge for the LAN to which this port is attached. For example, while port 1 and port 2 of bridge 3 have the same network interface and hence the same path cost, bridge 3 incurs less cost if it forwards a packet from port 1 than from port 2. The algorithm then decides that port 1 should be the root port for bridge 3.

4. If a LAN is attached to a single bridge, that bridge is the LAN's designated bridge. For example, in Fig. 4.12, bridge 2 is the designated bridge for LAN 3 because LAN 3 is attached to bridge 2 only. For a LAN attached to more than one bridge, a designated bridge must be selected. For example, in Fig. 4.12, because LAN 4 is attached to bridges 3, 4, and 5, the algorithm must compare the root path costs of these bridges. In this case, their root path costs are the same. Having the lowest bridge ID, bridge 3 becomes the designated bridge for LAN 4. Because bridge 3 is attached to LAN 4 via port 2, port 2 is the designated port for LAN 4. Bridge 1, which is the root bridge, is automatically the designated bridge for all its attached LANs (i.e., LAN 1 and LAN 2). Because bridge 2 is the only bridge attached to LAN 3, it becomes LAN 3's designated bridge.

5. Only root ports and designated ports are put in forwarding state; other ports such as port 1 of bridge 4 are put in blocking state. When a port is in forwarding state, it performs the learning, filtering, and forwarding functions. When it is in blocking state, it performs none of these functions. Because some of the ports are put in blocking state, the bridges can now forward packets properly and none of the packets will circulate on the extended network indefinitely.

The information that a bridge exchanges with other bridges in order to configure a loop free network is accomplished using the Hello Bridge Protocol Data Unit (BPDU), see Fig. 4.13. This is a special packet that will contain all the information that other bridges will use to maintain a configuration, and it is the only packet that a bridge will transmit for management functions. The information that is within the packet is only of use for another bridge. The packet must be transmitted on the network with respect to maintaining low overhead. How do the bridges exchange this spanning tree configuration information between themselves with respect to low overhead? The bridges transmit packets to each other via a special multicast address (default is 0180c2000000) pertaining only to bridges (this address is listed in Appendix C), to discover and establish a minimum cost spanning tree topology.

What this produces is a tree topology, with a minimum number of hops. These STA packets are continuously transmitted (via the special multicast address) at a predetermined amount of time settable by the network administrator, usually every 4 to 15 s. If another loop is found, the algorithm is started all over again. The packets are very small and generate very little overhead traffic on the LAN.

Remote bridges. When remote bridges with parallel lines participate in the spanning tree protocol, all the remote links connected to the *same* remote bridge are considered as one network interface. The algorithm puts all of them in forwarding or blocking state. This ensures that the network topology can maximize the use of the bandwidth provided by parallel network links. Multiple remote bridges with interfaces to the same LAN destination are not considered one interface and will participate in the STA procedure.

Reconfiguration. The STA reconfigures the network topology when bridges are added or removed, the root bridge fails, or the network manager changes the parameters determining the topology.

Whenever a bridge detects a topology change, and if it is a designated bridge for a LAN, it sends out a *topology change notification* BPDU through its root port. This information is eventually relayed to the root bridge. The root bridge then sets the *topology change flag* in its CBPDU so that the information is broadcast to all the bridges. It transmits this CBPDU for a fixed period of time to ensure that all bridges are informed that there is a topology change.

If a port is changed from blocking state to forwarding state as a result of the topology change, the algorithm ensures that it propagates the topology information to all the ports before that port starts forwarding data. This prevents temporary data loops.

Normally, a bridge removes from its routing table the addresses from which it receives no packets within a fixed period of time. After reconfiguration, the bridge removes these addresses faster to ensure that each active port still forwards packets to the right network after a topology change.

Security, protection, and special features. A special feature available only to bridges is their ability to filter packets based on a particular pattern. As mentioned previously, bridges dynamically learn the addresses on each segment and filter those packets that are on the same cable segment. Bridges can also be manually configured to watch for a particular pattern in any packet, and if it finds that pattern, it will filter the packet. This can be accomplished while it is filtering on addresses.

The network manager can do this by specifying a particular pattern anywhere within an Ethernet frame (see Fig. 4.16 later in this chapter in section on routers). This pattern can correspond to a protocol type, a protocol header, a source address, or any data pattern. For example, a bridge can *filter* all XNS traffic or can prevent network stations on a segment from accessing a computer located on another segment.

Let's say you have two Ethernet segments separated by a bridge. On one segment you want only XNS packet types and on the other, TCP/IP packet types. But if the packet type is local area transport (LAT; a packet type used by DEC for terminal traffic) you still want the bridge to forward those packets. This is where filters can assist you. The Ethernet type field is used to identify the type of packet, whether XNS, TCP, or LAT. For XNS, the type field would be filled in with a 0600h, and TCP would be 0800h. The network manager would set special filters with these type fields, and the bridges would automatically filter them. Not all bridges have this capability. To find out which vendor implements this technology, use the vendor address listing in Appendix C and contact the bridge vendor.

The 3Com Corporation has been making bridges for over 6 years and was one of the first vendors to introduce the special filtering concept. The capabilities of their bridges go far beyond the simplex explanation given in this book. 3Com's address and phone number is listed in Appendix C.

Performance. Another important area requiring careful study is performance. A bridge receives all the packets transmitted on each attached network. This means that the bridge must be able to receive and check packets at a rate corresponding to the maximum anticipated usage for each network segment. If the bridge cannot accommodate this traffic load, it has the ability to drop packets, causing the originating station to retransmit them. This results in performance degradation and possibly session disconnections.

The maximum possible usage of a network is often much less than its theoretical limit. A 10-Mbps Ethernet network can theoretically carry small-size (64-byte) packets at a rate of 14,880 packets per second. Because of the access method used by Ethernet, 100 percent utilization of the available bandwidth can be achieved only by a single station or synchronized transmitting stations. Otherwise, too many collisions would occur and overall network throughput would be adversely affected. Even very large Ethernet networks rarely exceed 50 percent utilization for a long period of time. In practice, a local bridge that can handle an aggregate filtering rate of 19,000 packets per second is appropriate for virtually all traffic conditions.

Another parameter that requires closer examination is the forwarding rate. Bridges partition the load on the different segments so that the amount of intersegment traffic is relatively limited. For instance, users and their file server (host or any other attachment) should be on the same network segment. Graphics workstations should be on their own segment, and hosts should possibly have their own segment. Aggregate forwarding rates of about 5000-9000 packets per second are sufficient for all applications and are within the range of existing local bridges.

From the previous discussion, you should be able to see how bridges not only simplify the network but also allow better management of the network. Bridges are completely self-sufficient and with the exception of special filters, can simply be taken out of the box and placed on the network. Even loops are not a problem.

Bridges are available for Token Ring and Ethernet and even a combination of Token Ring to Ethernet LANs. At the time of this writing, the state of the art of this type of interconnection is in its infancy. Before Ethernet and Token Ring are connected through a bridge, a number of considerations are necessary. These issues will be covered at the end of this chapter.

Token Ring bridging

Source routing. Much to the STA enthusiasts' dismay, IBM has not abandoned this approach but has adopted a new algorithm called *source route transparent* (SRT), which will incorporate both the STA and the source route algorithms. IBM has not been able to convince all standards committee working groups of the merits of the source routing. To fully understand why it is being changed and to understand the new approach taken by IBM, a discussion is in order.

Source routing takes a different approach to route a packet through a bridge or series of bridges. Using this approach, the originating station, not the bridge, contains the intelligence of how to route the packet. (This is different from STA, where the bridges contain the intelligence to determine which bridge ports are able to forward and which bridge ports are in blocking mode.) Bridges utilizing the source routing algorithm will never have a bridge port that is in blocking state for forwarding data. All ports on all bridges are in forwarding state, and the originating node wishing to transmit a packet determines which bridge route to use. Bridges that support source routing do not build routing tables that contain Token Ring addresses for each ring they connect. Stations determine the route through a search, as detailed below.

Theory of operation. This whole procedure is accomplished by the originating station sending a special frame onto the network. This frame is called a TEST or XID (eXchange IDentification) LPDU [logical (link control) data protocol unit, also known as a packet] onto its local network. In this frame, the Token Ring station is attempting to find the destination station on the local LAN. In other terms it is called a *dynamic route discovery packet*. The destination's address is in the destination field. The DSAP & SSAP fields are set to null. This packet is on LLC type 1 packet. A packet that has source routing fields will also set the I/G bit to a 1 in the source address field of the packet. See Fig. 3.2 and 3.9.

If the originating station does not receive a response to this packet, the originating station will assume that the destination station does not reside on the local LAN. The originating station has other options to discover the destination station. The two most common techniques are described below.

All-routes broadcast route determination. The originating station sends the same dynamic route discovery packet out to all rings. This packet will then traverse through all rings via the bridges, collecting routing information while crossing the bridges. When the packet is forwarded through the bridges, each bridge will insert routing information into the packet. If more than one route to the destination station exists, then more than one packet will reach the destination. When the destination node receives each packet, it will in turn respond with a TEST or XID response LPDU (packet), returning all the acquired routing information to the originating station. This response packet will follow the original path in reverse.

If more than one route to the destination station was found (multiple bridges forwarded the packet), all response LPDUs (packets) will be returned to the originating station. These LPDUs are returned with the destination address set to the originating station and not to broadcast. It is up to the originating station to then choose the path to reach the destination station. The originating station chooses a preferred route by the first nonbroadcast packet it receives. The originating station then uses this route for all subsequent communicating packets. This is source routing.

Single-route broadcast determination. An alternative to the all-routes broadcast for route determination is the single-route broadcast for route determination. A node, in trying to determine the route to a destination, will issue a dynamic route discovery frame to the ring so that only one frame will appear on each ring.

On receiving the frame, the destination will issue a response XID or TEST frame and will send this response frame via an all-routes broadcast. The originating station will receive multiple copies of the response packet and will then choose the preferred route (according to which packet it receives first). This is a different algorithm in that only one bridge was allowed to forward the dynamic route discovery request packet. The response packet was still broadcast, via an all-routes broadcast, to all bridges, and all bridges forwarded the response packet.

The main difference is that the single-route broadcast provides for spanning tree configuration for the network. What's this??? You thought that spanning tree and source routing were two different routing techniques used for bridging and that they were completely different? All of that is true. IBM has chosen to incorporate the STA to determine which bridge is allowed to forward a single route broadcast message. They did not choose one algorithm over the other. Let's look a little closer at the single-route broadcast for route determination.

Single-route broadcast for route determination ensures that only one copy of a limited broadcast frame traverses each network segment. Bridges in the spanning tree are configured for forwarding single-route broadcast frames. These bridges can be configured for this either manually or automatically. If they are configured for automatic configuration, the bridges incorporate the STA as described previously. Refer to Fig. 4.14.

The single-route determination is the preferred method for route determination. A good example of why it is preferred is for frames that are transmitted for group or functional address. A functional address is a special address usually used to identify the management servers

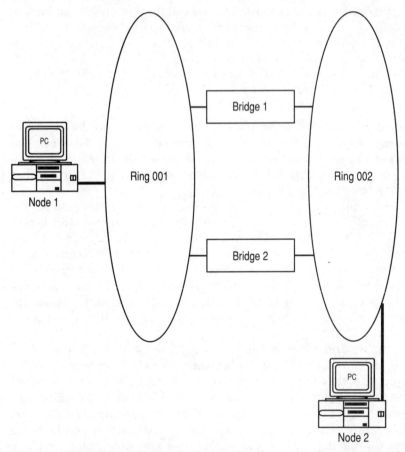

Figure 4.14 Token Ring bridging. Single-route broadcast route determination. Node 1 transmits a single-route broadcast to node 2. Bridge 1 forwards the frame to ring 2 and adds routing information data to the frame. Bridge 2 does not forward single-route broadcast frame. Node 2 responds to node 1 with an all-routes broadcast frame. Bridge 1 forwards the frame and adds routing information data; bridge 2 does the same. Node 1 selects a path from one of the two frames and sends a routed frame by flipping the direction bit. Node 2 responds by flipping the direction bit to reverse the path selected by node 1.

on the ring. Some addresses are used to identify a bridge or Netbios. If a ring network is configured for all-routes broadcast only, these packets would be duplicated for as many bridges that are on the network. This would mean that all nodes that receive these special packets would be interrupted many times, possibly slowing the network down. In a single-route broadcast network, these nodes would receive only one copy of frame and be interrupted only that one time. These particular stations would not copy the response frame, for the response frame had a unique destination address. They would simply repeat the packet.

A new algorithm incorporates both the STA and source route algorithms, giving you the best of both. With this, Token Ring networks use the bandwidth of the network much more efficiently. This algorithm gives the bridge the capability to distinguish between each type of algorithm for the packets it receives.

With source route, the bridges need to contain very little intelligence. What does the bridge do with the all-routes broadcast or single-route broadcast that it receives? The bridge does a number of things, including inserting the ring number of the ring that the bridge received the frame from, its own bridge number, and the ring number of the ring onto which it forwarded the frame. In a multiple-bridge environment, the first bridge that the packet is received on also inserts a maximum packet size indicator, defining the largest packet that it can forward. Subsequent bridges examine this field and compare it to a value indicating the largest packet size that it can forward. If this number is smaller, that bridge will insert its own value in this field.

This algorithm also contains the intelligence to prevent a frame from continuously circulating the ring. A source routing bridge will only forward a packet that has not already traversed the next ring. When a bridge receives this packet, it will examine the routing information in the received packet. If the ring number of the next ring is already present in the routing information field, the bridge will not forward the frame.

Before defining Token Bridge operation, some terms need to be introduced.

Token Ring bridge operation

Bridge number	A unique number assigned to each bridge to be used as its identifier.
Hop Count Limit	Specifies the number of rings an all-routes broadcast frame may traverse before it will be discarded by a bridge.
Largest Frame Size	The size of the largest frame that can be

	accepted by either of the two rings that the bridge interconnects or by the bridge itself.
Ring number	A unique number assigned to each ring on a Token Ring network to be used as its identifier (the bridge is characterized by the numbers of the two rings it connects).
Single-route broadcast indicator	Specifies whether the bridge is configured to forward single-route broadcast frames.

Each node that transmits a frame onto the ring will transmit a destination address, source address, and possibly routing information. The routing information consists of an ordered list of ring and bridge identifiers through which a transmitted frame is to travel to reach its destination (specified by the destination address). Bridges will add their information to the frame only when they forward an all-routes or single-route broadcast frame. Bridges will also make frame forwarding decisions according to whether their information is in the routing information field of each nonbroadcast frame. When a bridge forwards the broadcast frame to the next ring, it will add the ring number of the ring from which it received the frame, its own bridge number, and the ring number of the ring to which the frame was forwarded. The bridge will also add the largest frame size that it can forward. Subsequent bridges will then add the bridge number and ring number of the ring that they forward the ring to. These subsequent bridges will also check the maximum frame size field and change it accordingly. If that bridge or its connected ring can forward a larger packet than indicated by the received packet, it will not change it. The bridges have no way of fragmenting and reassembling the packets. This is a capability reserved for routers.

If a bridge receives a frame and forwarding that frame would exceed the hop count, the bridge will not forward the frame. A maximum of 8 bridges may be configured.

When the frame reaches its destination, all subsequent response packets will use this path until the end of the session or until a bridge link fails, eliminating the need to use broadcast packets and efficiently conserving bandwidth. Only then will the node have to transmit another all-routes broadcast or single-route broadcast to determine the path to take to converse with a destination station.

Routing information frame formats. As shown in Fig. 4.15, specifically the routing control field, the first field that the bridge will try to in-

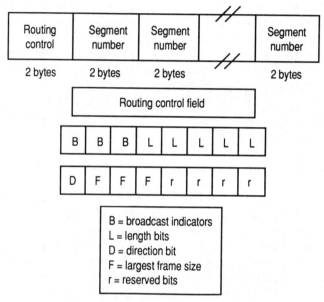

Figure 4.15   Token ring routing information field.

terpret is B, the broadcast indicators. The broadcast indicators specify to the bridge whether the frame is a nonbroadcast frame (forwarding the packet based on a unique path), an all-routes broadcast (meaning that all bridges will forward this packet, resulting in duplicate packets), or a single-route broadcast. Single-route broadcast is a broadcast packet that is routed on a specified path. Refer to Figure 3.20 to see where the routing information field is located in a Token Ring frame for those Token Ring stations that support source routing.

The bits are interpreted as follows:

0xx   Nonbroadcast
10x   All-routes broadcast
11x   Single-route broadcast

Please note that an all-routes or single route broadcast is different from an all-stations broadcast. An all-stations broadcast indicates to the bridge that all stations on the local ring that it received the frame from should copy the frame. A Token Ring bridge will not forward an all-stations broadcast unless accompanied with an all route or single-route broadcast field.

The x in the field means that the bit may be a binary 0 or a binary 1. It does not affect the meaning of the packet if it is set either way.

The next bits to interpret are the length bits (LLLLL). These 5 bits will indicate the length, in bytes, of the routing information field. This will enable any station to know where the routing information header fields stop. This is important in that the routing information field is dynamic, meaning that it can change size depending on how many bridges are on the rings. It is also used to enable a bridge to know where to append its routing information.

Each bridge checks this field. If the length is an odd number of bytes or if it is less than 2 bytes or greater than 18 bytes, a bridge will not forward the frame. Each bridge appends 2 bytes to this field with the exception of the first bridge which appends 4 bytes. A simple formula for determining how many bridges have been crossed can be calculated using this field: $[(length - 2)/2] - 1$.

The next bit is the direction bit. This bit will enable the bridge to correctly read the routing information field. If the direction bit is set to a 0, the bridge reads the routing information field entries from left to right. If it is a 1, the bridge will read the routing information field from right to left. By implementing this bit, the routing information field remains in the same byte order no matter which way the frame is traveling. For individual nodes communicating with one another, the originating node sets this bit to a binary 0 while the responder sets this bit to a binary 1. This bit is extremely powerful. When stations communicate over a bridge, they will have to use the routing fields of the frame. By flipping the one bit, it will indicate to a bridge which way the packet is traveling. This alleviates the stations from reinserting, in reverse order, the routing fields when responding to a packet. This direction bit is used for nonbroadcast frames (used after a station has selected a route or in response to a dynamic route discovery packet).

The next field of importance is the largest frame bits (B). These bits specify the largest frame (this excludes headers) that can be transmitted between two communicating nodes on a given path.

The field is very important when heterogeneous networks (i.e., mixed IEEE 802.3 and IEEE 802.5 networks in the same site) are used. This field can be broken down as follows.

000   Indicates the largest frame size of 516 bytes; this is the smallest maximum frame size that a MAC must support under the standard ISO

8802/2 (IEEE 802.2) LLC and connectionless-mode network service (ISO 8473)

001   Indicates that up to 1500 bytes may be in the information field; this is the maximum data size supported in ISO 8802/3 (IEEE 802.3 and Ethernet)

010   As many as 2052 bytes are allowed in the information field; this is the typical size used on PC LANs for it allows for a screenful of data (80 × 24 screen) to be transmitted at one time

011   As many as 4472 bytes may be in the information field; this size is the largest data size supported in the Fiber Data Distributed Interface (FDDI) ANSI X3T9.5 specification. It is also the largest frame size possible for ISO 8802/5 networks

101   The information field may contain a maximum of 11,407 bytes

110   The information field may contain a maximum of 17,800 bytes; this is the largest information size that the medium access control supports for ISO 8802.5 standard stations

111   Used in all-routes broadcast frames

The reserved bits are reserved for future use. They are initialized to binary zeros.

Then, finally, we get to the real meat of the routing information field, the route designator fields. This field is split into two parts: the first 12 bits (left to right) are designated as the ring number and the last 4 bits are the individual bridge number.

The ring number portion indicates the individual ring number or the two rings that the bridge interconnects. Bridges attached to different rings will have different values for the ring number portion of this field. Bridges attached to the same ring will naturally have the same ring number.

The individual bridge number identifies a bridge. Bridges attached to the same ring can have the same number for the individual bridge portion of this field. Parallel bridges (those connecting the same two rings) must be identified with different numbers.

Because the end of any route will be a ring (a bridge could not be an endpoint on a ring), the individual bridge portion of the last route designator in the routing information field will not be defined and will be set to all binary zeros.

Remember that IEEE 802.5 Token Ring does not specify a maximum frame size. However, it does specify how long any node may hold the token; this is 10 ms (10 ms = 0.010 s).

Bandwidth considerations. A node utilizing source routing, not source route transparent, requires the discovery of the destination via a dynamic route discovery packet. Depending on the size of the network, this overhead generates traffic on the network. But how much?

The following approach should be used as a general rule of thumb, and it will give you some idea of the traffic generated. The number of frame copies transmitted for route discovery is in the order of A^B, where A is the average number of bridges on each LAN and B is the number of LANs in the network. Therefore, if the network has 12 LANs with an average of two bridges per LAN, the network traffic generated for this overhead would be 2^{12} of 4096 frames for each route discovery. This is the number of frames, not bytes! With many nodes on the network, this can add up to a tremendous amount of network overhead. Quite a price to pay to do load sharing.

The new algorithm for single-route broadcast for route determination has reduced much of the traffic overhead involved with source routing. The formula in the preceding paragraph assumes an all-routes broadcast for route determination.

Routers

Routers are devices that interconnect multiple networks, primarily, running the same high-level protocols. They operate at the network layer of the ISO model. With more software intelligence than bridges, routers are well suited for complex environments or large internetworks. In particular, they support active redundant paths (loops) and allow logical separation of network segments (so that each segment can have its own network number, analogous to the first three digits on a telephone). Routers also better solve the problems associated with interconnected network segments using different media such as Token Ring and Ethernet. For instance, the packet size is controlled by the network layer and is identical on both sides. The problem of address resolution is also addressed in a better way in that routers, unlike bridges, do not pass MAC-layer addresses from end to end, but rather each router knows the MAC-layer address of the next router in the path. This approach avoids the delicate problem of converting Ethernet and Token Ring layer addresses from one format to the other before transmitting a packet.

Routers offer the capability to handle different-size packets. For Ethernet, the largest packet size is 1518, and there is no maximum length requirement for Token Ring. Routers have the capability to fragment the packet into multiple packets and then reassemble them at the remote end. Bridges do not have this capability.

Routers look a little further into the packet for information on routing (see Fig. 4.16). They also must choose the best route to take, for active loops are allowed in a routed network. The speed of a router is

Ethernet Frame

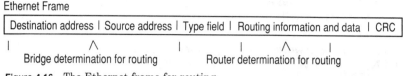

Figure 4.16   The Ethernet frame for routing.

about two-thirds that of a bridge at best. But speed is not what routers are primarily used for.

Theory of operation.   Routers work with network numbers, which are similar to geographic area code numbers. For local calls one simply dials the seven-digit number. The switching offices of the telephone system will automatically route the call to its destination because it is a local call.

For long-distance calls (i.e., a call to a number in another area code, e.g., from New York to Virginia), you must dial a 1 and then the area code for that state in order to complete the call. The telephone switching offices in New York will look at the area code and notice that it is assigned to Virginia. It will route the call to Virginia, where the local switching offices there will route the call to its final destination. This is similar to the routing functions in a wide area network–LAN connection.

Packets that are bound for nonlocal networks (i.e., stations that usually are geographically separated) are sent to a router by the software that resides in the network layer of the ISO model. Depending on your type of network operating software (TCP/IP, XNS, etc.) there are many different ways of traversing the routers. The following example closely resembles the Internet Datagram Protocol (IDP) of the XNS (Xerox Network Systems) environment. Other routing functions are similar. The following is provided as an example.

For networks that allow the use of routers, they must employ what is known as a *network number*. This network number is not the same physical address that identifies a station on the network. For XNS, this is usually a 32-bit number that represents an individual logical network. The combination of the network number with the physical address of the station on the network will identify any station on a wide area network. The same is true for a telephone number. The combination of the area code and phone number can address any individual phone in the United States. How do these two numbers interoperate? Network stations will be grouped using one network ID. A separate and distinct network ID would be used for stations on the other side of the router.

First, it requires specialized software in a network station on the

LAN. Not all stations on a LAN require this software to be resident. If the network station will not employ routers to transmit its data, the network layer (router) software need not be there. This is true for most workgroup network operating systems operating on a single logical LAN.

If the station does have this network layer software resident, it can be used in the following manner. When the network layer software of the network operating system receives a packet from its upper-layer software that is bound for a station that is across a router, the normal process is to look at the network address of the destination packet and compare it to its local network address. (Remember, this is not the 6-byte physical address of the station; this is the "area code" in which it resides.) If the network number is different, the network layer software will know that the packet is bound for a remote network. (The destination is across a router.) It will then attempt to find a router that can process this packet via the shortest number of hops. (A hop is defined as a router that a packet will traverse.)

The network layer software that resides in a station on a network will hold a table of routers that it knows about. These entries contain the router's physical address, which network numbers the router is associated with, and the number called the hop count. The hop count is a number that indicates to the originating station how many routers (hops) the packet must traverse before reaching its final destination. If the router is in the table, the network layer software will build a packet and send the packet addressed directly to that router. If the network layer software on the network station does not have an entry for that particular network, it will transmit a special type of packet to the LAN requesting routing information from the routers for that network.

All routers will pick up this packet, and while processing it will notice that it is a routing update request; then each router on the network will transmit its routing information back to the original requester. In this response is information of how to get to the remote station via a hop count. The hop count is the number of routers that a packet will have to traverse before reaching the final destination. Some network stations have the capability to listen to the network for the responses of the router table update. These stations will then update their router tables.

The requesting station will then use this information to address its packet to be handled by a router or series of routers to enable the packet to reach its final destination. Once formatted, it will submit a packet to the network with the destination address set not to its final destination but to a particular router.

That router will pick up and process the packet. In this, the router looks in the fields of the packet that contain the routing information, particularly the destination network number. If the network number is direct (i.e., directly on the other side of the router), it will simply forward the packet to the other side. If not, it will transmit the packet to the next router to enable that packet to reach its final destination station.

This is different from bridging in that the physical address headers (destination and source address) will change (the Ethernet or Token Ring 6-byte address). When two stations are communicating on a local LAN (i.e., the two stations are not separated by a router), the data-link packet headers (destination and source address) will contain the Ethernet or Token Ring physical destination and source addresses.

If any packet is destined to traverse across a router, the originating station will submit the packet with the destination address set to the router's physical address. It is up to the router to make sure that the packet traverses across the router(s) and reaches the final destination station.

When the packet reaches its final destination network, the destination address will be that of the final destination. The source address will be that of the router. The destination station will then submit a packet back to the router and the router or routers will send the packet back to the original requesting station.

In looking at the Ethernet frame (Fig. 4.16), the network layer software will append its information beginning with the end of the type field. The routers will read the information that is located in this field of bytes to determine how to route the packet.

With routing, requesting stations will send their packets to the routers and the routers will route the packet to the destination for them. Source and destination stations are not talking directly to each other. They talk via the routers. All this is accomplished by the network layer software appending its routing information into the packet. Inside the packet will be the physical addressing information of the original source and destination hosts. On ethernet frames, the network layer software will append its information into the data field. It will not be mistaken for data for the destination will know that the routing information is placed there.

Since routers impose no topology constraints, they provide sophisticated routing or flow control as well as traffic isolation. How routers perform these functions depends largely on the network protocol they use and the particular implementation thereof (i.e., XNS, TCP/IP). Unlike bridges, routers *do* require full participation of sending and receiving stations in addressing packets.

Routers give network managers the ability to define boundaries for administrative control. Using a hierarchical addressing scheme, a network manager can divide a large internetwork into small administrative domains. An example is a university campus with a backbone network linking different departments. With routers, each department's network can remain logically separate and under the administrative control of the department.

Because routers selectively forward packets, loops are allowed in the internetwork topology. In addition, most routers implement a time-to-live program for packets. This process, which consists of destroying packets that have traveled too long or through too many routers, prevents defective packets from congesting the network. The router may notify the originating station that the packet was destroyed.

Static versus dynamic routing. There are two ways that bridges and routers may be allowed to route packets: statically or dynamically. Learing may be turned off on a bridge for security reasons.

In the static configuration, all routing tables on all routers must be updated manually; a network administrator is required to update the routing tables. As new bridges and/or routers are added to the network, the network administrator is required to update all the routing tables in each bridge or router to allow it to participate in the network.

If a router breaks and is removed from the network, it is considerably time-consuming and frustrating for the network administrator to manually update all the routing tables on all the routers placed on the network. Then, when the router becomes operational and is placed back on the network, the routing tables again must be updated to allow other routers to know that this router is once again operational.

In dynamically configured routers and bridges, the routing tables are configured "on the fly." Routers will periodically send routing tables to one another to identify the routes available to one another. Therefore, whenever a new router is added to the network, all other routers will automatically find this router and update their tables as to the new routers' available paths. At that point in time, if the routers find a new and better route, packets will then traverse the new route. Dynamic routing is by far the most advantageous. The network administrator is usually not involved in this process, with the possible exception of assigning some parameters to the associated routers' and bridges' paths.

Networking environment. In multiprotocol environments, bridges provide, at this time, a more flexible and mature solution. They are transparent to high-level communications protocols and accommodate many different applications. For instance, bridges would be a good solution in a case where users want to interconnect networks supporting a mix of protocols such as DECnet, XNS, and TCP/IP.

Over the past few years, an increasing number of computer and networking vendors have introduced products using the TCP/IP protocol suite, making it somewhat of a de facto standard. Therefore, multivendor, single-protocol environments have become increasingly common. In these cases, routers are a possible solution. Network complexity will probably determine whether a bridge or a router is used. In small configurations, bridges are a sensible choice. As complexity increases, so does the need for traffic isolation and control capabilities of routers. A combination of bridges and routers, however, can solve particularly complex internetworking problems.

Network administration.   Bridges and routers offer equal capabilities in the areas of network statistics and monitoring. Both can provide automatic audit trial and, along with a network management station, sophisticated analysis of such information. How an organization wishes to administer its internetwork will most likely determine what internetworking product it uses. On one hand, if the network manager wishes to administer the entire internetwork from a central location, a bridge makes good sense. A bridged internetwork acts as a single logical network. For example, the network manager must take into account all stations of a bridged internetwork when adding or removing a station.

On the other hand, an organization may want or need decentralized network management, thus making a router the better choice. A network interconnected by routers allows each segment to be logically independent. Interconnected networks that have many distant sites or that are relatively large may require several network managers.

For ease of installation and maintenance, bridges offer definite advantages over routers. Bridges require little intervention from the network manager. They can make extremely basic routing decisions themselves. Routers, however, are more sophisticated devices.

Vendor interoperability.   The last point to be considered on bridges or routers is interoperability among vendors. Can bridges or routers, whether local or remote, interoperate with other vendors? The answer is "Sometimes." Let's consider each one separately.

For bridges, strict compliance with the IEEE 802.1d standard should allow bridges from different vendors to interoperate. The key point is the STA algorithm. The STA packet that is transmitted between bridges has a special multicast address mentioned earlier. If the bridge is set up to accept that multicast address, it should allow any bridge from any vendor to operate with other bridges. Usually customers will buy their bridges from one vendor and continue to do business with that vendor. The nice thing about standards is that they allow multiple vendors who follow the standard to operate together, that is, to interoperate. Extreme care should be taken when a vendor claims to follow the IEEE 802.1d standard, which allows a vendor to operate with another vendor's bridges. The best case to present is remote bridges, or those bridges that operate over telephone lines.

Remote bridges have another interface to encounter: the telephone line interface. Usually vendors that have bridges or routers that operate remotely use a protocol known as *High-Level Data-Link Control* (HDLC) to communicate between the bridges. The Ethernet or Token Ring packet is encapsulated by an HDLC frame and transmitted serially over the telephone link.

The problem that arises here is that most vendors' HDLC link between the bridges (over the telephone line link) is proprietary; in other words, each vendor implements the protocol differently. This does not allow compatibility among the different vendor's remote links.

A protocol known as an *emerging standard,* called point-to-point protocol (ppp), was designed to resolve this problem. This protocol will work with remote bridges as well as remote routers using any protocol. It will standardize the protocol used between the bridges (the protocol used to allow bridges to communicate over the telephone link, HDLC).

Very few vendors are supporting this protocol at present. But as most standards are today, this protocol should become a standard very soon. If it does, and if it allows multiple vendors to interoperate with their bridges and routers, it will soon become popular and the user community will mandate it.

So, the final word is that different vendors' products sometimes will interoperate. Routers, as long as they are local (i.e., not using a telephone link to communicate with another router), should interoperate. Local bridges, if they are in strict compliance with the IEEE 802.1d standard, should also interoperate. If they don't, you have the option of turning the STA algorithm off in any bridge, which should ensure that bridges will interoperate. But without STA (allowing multiple paths to the same destination station), bridges allow only a subset of their full functionality.

Conclusion

Routers. Routers offer much in comparison to a bridge:

1. Routers are self-configuring in that they know of all other routers and the best route to take on each interconnected segment. Routers

exchange routing tables with other routers and broadcast information packets to the stations on their local segment.

2. Routers automatically allow for redundancy (loops are allowed) without the use of STA or source routing.

3. Routers offer some intelligence in that they will respond to an originating station when the destination is unreachable or if there is a better route (that is, send the packets to another router) to take.

4. Routers allow for different-size packets on the network. If one segment of the network allows for only 1518 bytes and the other segment allows for 512, routers will fragment the packet and then reassemble it at the other end.

5. Routers allow for load balancing. If one channel becomes congested, the router will select another path.

6. Routers segment the network into logical subnets by assigning an ID number to each segment. This allows for better network management.

7. Routers do not forward broadcast packets. This can eliminate what is known as "broadcast storms." Broadcast packets are special packets (use a special address) that all stations will automatically pass to their upper layer software.

Bridges. Bridges have several advantages over routers.

1. Bridges are faster than routers and create less overhead on the network. Bridges make a simple decision as to forward or filter according to the destination address.

2. Bridges are less expensive than routers, although that cost is becoming negligible (within $500.00 only).

3. Ethernet bridges allow for loops but will turn off one of the redundant paths until there is a topology change. Token Ring bridges allow multiple paths that will make ports on the bridge active.

4. Bridges, like routers, are available in local and remote versions.

5. Bridges are less complicated devices.

6. Bridges are "invisible" to other stations on the network; bridges talk only to other bridges. Network stations do not need specialized software to operate with a bridge.

7. Bridges increase the available bandwidth (throughput) of a LAN by physically segmenting network stations to their respective LANs.

So now, you ask, since routers and bridges have their distinct advantages and disadvantages, which one should you choose? This question or issue is becoming less of a decision. There is a new product emerging called a *brouter*. What is a brouter?

Brouters. A brouter is a special device that allows for routing and bridging in the same box. For example, if you have the protocol suite known as TCP/IP running on some stations on the network and a small working-group system running the XNS protocol suite and some DEC equipment running the local area transport (LAT) protocol suite for terminal servers, a brouter can be configured to route the TCP/IP and the XNS traffic, and it will bridge all other traffic (bridge the LAT traffic). It will accomplish this through all the same ports that it interconnects.

It is like stuffing multiple routers into one bridge box. The cost difference is small. 3Com offers a brouter (NB200x) that offers TCP/IP, XNS, OSI, IPX, and DECNET routing capabilities with bridging, and as of October 1990 the cost difference between their bridge and router was $500.00. Not much of a price to pay, when not long ago, you would have had to buy one router and one bridge costing twice as much and also having to tap twice onto the cable plant.

Use brouters whenever possible. Both large and small networks will benefit.

The following figures (Figs. 4.17, 4.18, 4.19) show the packet processing flow for bridging, routing (XNS protocols), and a brouter. Please note that source explicit forwarding (SEF) is the ability of a bridge to use static source address entries in a routing table to allow forwarding of a packet based on the source address. If the source address of the packet to be forwarded is not in the table, then the packet will not be forwarded. This is not available on all bridges and this parameter may be set to on or off on 3Com bridges. It is used as a security feature.

In Fig. 4.19, Firewall is a protection feature built into the brouter that ensures that a uniquely addressed packet of a protocol type that is supported by the routing function of a brouter is not forwarded by the bridging function of the brouter. In other words, any packet employing a routing function should address packets directly to the brouter. Refer to the routing section earlier in this chapter.

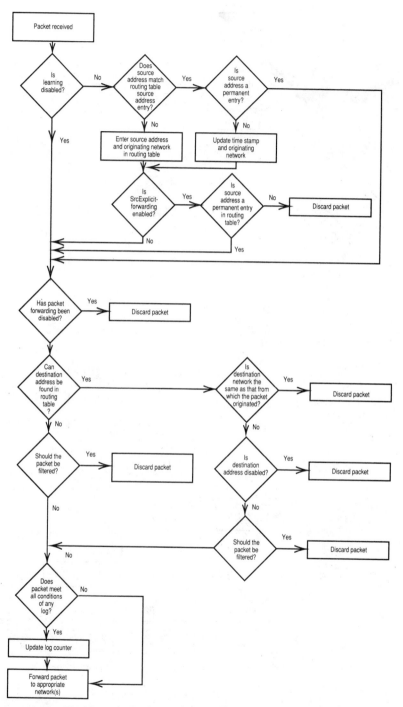

Figure 4.17 Flowchart for bridge packet handling. (Courtesy of 3Com Corp.)

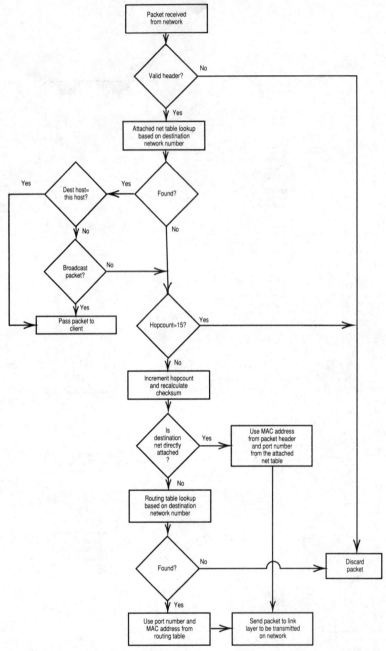

Figure 4.18 Flowchart for XNS router's packet handling. (Courtesy of 3Com Corp.)

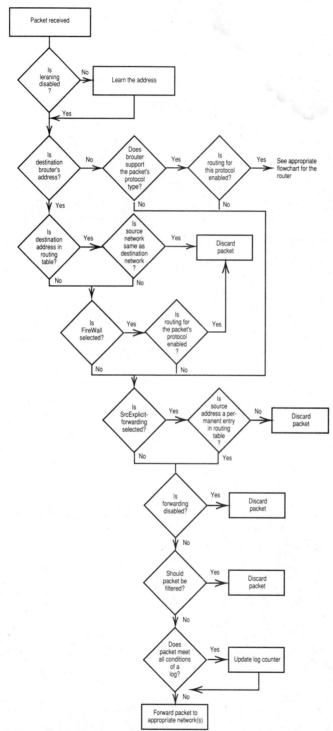

Figure 4.19 Flowchart for Brouter's packet handling. (Courtesy of 3Com Corp.)

5

The Transport Layer

Since the transport layer is basically transparent to a user, the basic concepts will be described below. Although it is important when making a network decision whether to choose TCP/IP, XNS, or IPX, the layer will be transparent. The transport layer does not correspond to a single piece of user software or hardware like the other layers do.

Since XNS was written specifically for Ethernet, we will look at that particular protocol. The following information is based on the Sequence Packet Protocol (SPP) of the XNS protocol suite. It is used as an example only. Different protocol suites such as TCP of TCP/IP are similar with respect to the functions they provide.

The transport layer of the ISO model is tasked with providing reliable data transfer for a session between two stations, that is, guarantee the delivery of data between two stations. The transport layer accomplishes this as follows. For XNS, the transport layer provides connection control, source connection ID, destination connection ID, sequence numbers, acknowledge numbers, and allocation numbers.

Connection control.   Used to request a send acknowledgment, request attention, and indicate an end-of-message from the receiver.

Source connection ID.   An integer number assigned to a connection to identify a particular session. One connection ID is specified by each end of the connection at the time of its creation, and the IDs are checked on all later transmissions.

Destination connection ID.   Same as source connection ID.

Sequence number.   Proves that packets arrive in the correct order. The packets sent on the connection are counted. The first packet is assigned a beginning number, and the count proceeds sequentially from there. The destination host will use the sequence number to determine the order of the packets, acknowledge them so that no duplicates are sent, and specify flow control information.

Acknowledge number.   Specifies the sequence number up to and including which packets will be accepted from the other end.

Since multiple sessions may be connected either to or from a station, the transport layer software must have a way of distinguishing which connection the reliable data service will be supported. The connection ID provided by the transport layer is used to signify which connection the transport layer is providing the reliable data service for.

The transport layer is used by the session layer to provide the session layer with a connection ID number. This is done when the session layer is requested by its upper-layer software (usually a network application) to provide connection to a remote resource.

Once the session layer has requested a new client ID from the transport layer, the transport layer will provide it with one. The ID number that is sent to the session layer is kept in a memory resident table within the transport layer software.

If a connection between two or more network stations has been established and the session layer has been provided with a connection ID, the session layer may send data to the transport layer. The transport layer appends a source and destination connection ID and a sequence number to the data and will submit the data to be processed by the network layer (if there is one). The data will then be submitted to be processed by the data-link layer (Ethernet or Token Ring) and sent over the network to the remote station.

The transport layers at each source and destination station communicate with each other. Refer to figure 5.1. In other words, the transport layer on the source of the connection communicates only with the transport layer on the destination of the connection. The transport layer appends distinguishable header information into the packet that will be read by the destination station. This header information does not contain user data but control information that the destination transport layer will take the appropriate action on.

Setup

To set up a reliable session, the tasks to be performed between the two transport layers are as follows. The transport layer software on the source station will attempt to open a connection to a remote station. The transport layer software in each station trying to connect will attempt a connection providing each with a connection ID number. Since a network station may accept multiple connections from multiple stations, the transport layer software will use this ID to uniquely identify which particular session is to receive or transmit the data.

Once these connection calls are accomplished, the transport layer software on one of the stations will send a beginning sequence number to the remote station. The remote station will usually acknowledge this packet by sending an acknowledgment packet back to the originating station. Embedded in this packet is the number of the next sequence number that the remote station expects. On some transport layer software implementations, the remote station will start its own sequence number to be acknowledged by its remote station.

A reliable session is now established and identified and data transfer between the two stations may begin. As data packets are sent and received, sequence numbers are continually checked by each respective station, usually by a station submitting an acknowledgment packet with the next sequence number that it expects. This will continue until an error occurs.

An error may occur, for example, when the destination station submits an acknowledgment packet and the packet does not reach the recipient. In this case the originating station of the packet will timeout while waiting for an acknowledgment for the packet. The originating station will then resubmit the packet with the same sequence number. When the packet does arrive at its destination station, the receiver of the packet will check it and notice that the sequence number has already been acknowledged. The receiving station will discard the information in the packet, but it will usually submit an acknowledgment back to the source station. The source station will then notice that it is an acknowledgment, and data flow will resume.

Sequence numbers and acknowledgments are the transport layer's way of ensuring the integrity of the data (ensuring that the data was received in good condition at the transport layer of the remote station). An analogy would be as follows. Suppose you are telling a story to someone and you wanted to make sure that the person comprehends the story. You would probably look for signs such as a response to at least a part of your story, a nodding or shaking of the head, etc. These are signs that the person is listening and understanding what you are saying. Usually, if any part of your story is not understandable, the person will stop you and ask you to repeat part of it. This is similar to the way in which the transport layer software between a local and a remote station ensures the integrity of the data. This dialog will continue until the source or destination station submits a connection close request.

You should now see how—with the combination of the source connection ID, destination connection ID, and sequence-acknowledgment data flow—the transport layer software reliably transfers data between two stations. All this information is placed in the packet, and the packet is then handed down to be processed by the next-lower layer of software.

This is not all that transport layer software accomplishes, but for the purposes of this book, it is as far into the transport layer as we should venture. The transport layer software will be discussed further in connection with the session layer software in Chap. 6.

Socket Numbers

A socket number is assigned to a service. What service is this? This could be file service, name service, terminal service, or any other service that is provided on the remote connection. The socket number is used to identify to the destination station the service to which the packet is requesting.

For example, when the network software on a source host is tasked with setting up a connection with a terminal emulation process that runs on a remote host, it will first make up a number known as the *source socket.*

The terminal emulation process that runs on the remote host is assigned a unique identifier known as a "well-known port number." That terminal service on the remote host is assigned this port number (an integer number that calling programs may use to request a specified service of the host). This number will never change and will be used by all stations on the network requesting terminal service from this particular host.

The local station will notify the remote host of the service requested by providing the remote host with this number. The service in this case could be assigned a port address of 23 for terminal emulation service. The network software would then attempt to set up a connection for service number (port number 23). If the remote host can accommodate this, the remote host will spawn the request off as a separate process to be run. To identify the process with this connection, the host will respond to the requesting station with the port number for the program that it spawned off, so that the requesting application may identify the remote service. The two port numbers are then used in pairs to identify to each station (local and remote) the service endpoints of this connection. The combination of a network number, a network physical address, and this identifiable port number is known as the *socket for the connection.*

Client-Server Computing

Client-server computing is currently a hot topic for debate. Ask anyone this question, and you will be guaranteed a different answer every time. A number of articles have been written about this, discussing anything from its origins to its present-day meaning.

On any LAN, there will always be two entities: The client (the source station, the station that makes requests) and the server (the destination station, the station that responds to those requests) (see Fig. 5.1). This concept originated in the design of operating systems and was implemented with the experimental Ethernet in 1973. In the 1980s, the concept was enhanced again with the introduction of the personal computer and file servers.

This concept is hotter than ever now, in the 1990s. This time the term *client-server computing* is used not only by engineers to explain networks on an engineering level but by marketing personnel, who have coined the phrase to sell their products.

Before LANs, terminals were directly connected to the minicomputer or mainframe and all commands were processed directly between the terminal and its host processor. Since the computer hardware was moved from a "centralized" location, the computer room, out to where the users were located, a design was needed to allow centralized computing on a decentralized scale. How do you allow the commands—which were once centralized and that integrated the user with the mainframe—out to the desktop? Enter client-server computing.

The functions of client-server computing are the same today as they were in 1973. The client will make a request and the server will respond to the request. A server may also be a client in the respect that it can make requests to other servers. The only difference in function of network client-server computing between 1973 and today is that it has matured over the last 17 or so years.

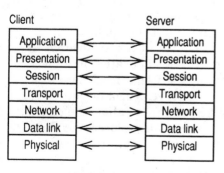

Figure 5.1 ISO model layer communications. Each layer communicates with its associated layer at the client or server by means of the layer headers that are appended to the packet.

First-generation network client-server model

When LANs first arrived in the commercial community most hosts were directly connected with a terminal. Very few personal computers were used in the business community at that time. Few hosts had the capacity for direct connection to a LAN. So a device was invented to act as an intermediate between the host and the terminal. It is known as a *terminal server*. (For a complete description of terminal servers, refer to Appendix G.)

The client (a terminal server with a terminal attached to it) would make a request of the server (usually another terminal server with a host attached to it). The request would usually be one of three functions: a request for a connection, a request to transfer data, or a request to tear down the connection. A request would be initiated from the client to the terminal server to establish a connection. Once the connection was established, data would flow on the session that was set up. When the user was ready to quit, the session would be disconnected. This was a simple client-server relationship. The client side made the request, and the server side responded to the request.

Second-generation network client-server model

The 1980s brought on the personal computer and the client-server relationship expanded. The original requests were still there, but the needs and the functions of personal computers were much more complicated than those of the terminal servers, and the client-server concept expanded.

The applications that originally ran on a personal computer were now stored on a server PC station, called a file server, located somewhere on the network. This file server would service user requests (file and print) from remote PCs.

A user would still initiate a connection, but this time it was from their local PC to the file server PC on the network. Looking at this connection, one might think that an extra disk drive had been added to the client station. The user would then request the application program from the server. The server would download the application to the client PC, and the client PC would run the application local, just as if the application had been located on the user's local hard-disk drive. The user could also save data to this server's disk drive.

The file servers would also contain the software to allow the direct attachment of a printer. Using print queues, multiple users could redirect their local printer ports to the file server and print their data on the file server's printer.

The file server could accept multiple connections from any stations that were on the network. The same application software program could be executed from these remote stations. The result would be one copy of software on the server PC and many users requiring access to it. This is how most PC LAN operating systems work today. The printer queues could accept multiple connections to it, allowing companies to buy one printer and allowing multiple users access to it all through application of the client-server relationship.

Third-generation client-server model

Today, with database engines becoming as powerful as those that are run on some minicomputers, the client-server model has expanded again. The original concepts are still in place, but new functions have been added.

The client-server concept has expanded to allow an application program not to be downloaded to the client PC but to be distributed between the client and the server. This means that part of the application would run on the server and the other half, on the client PC. The client-server concept has even changed names: back-end/front-end computing.

The best example of this is an application known as the *SQLserver* from Microsoft. The SQLserver is run on the file server and is known as the *back end*. A client starts an application program on a PC such as DBASE IV from Ashton-Tate. The application program will then initiate SQL commands that would be transmitted on the network requesting data records from the server. In this case, the whole database file is not downloaded to the client PC. The client PC simply makes a request for whatever record or records is currently needed. This concept of distributed computing allows multiple client stations on the network to request the same records from the same file on the server. SQLserver will ensure that only one user at a time modifies any part of a file.

This is the impending future function of client-server computing. All three models and methods are still in existence today. All three can work on the same LAN. Front-end applications are becoming available from spreadsheet database and even word processing companies.

The beginning of any client-server relationship is based on the session layer, which is the next topic for discussion in Chap. 6.

6

The Session Layer

The rest of the book contains information on how a communication session is established and maintained between two communicating stations. This information will focus on PC LANs or, as they are more commonly known, *workgroup systems*. The information in the previous chapters can pertain to any device that can attach to a LAN, including PC LANs. Netbios is a good, simple example of a session layer protocol. However, it is used primarily on PC LANs, and the following information focuses on this application.

The Netbios interface has been selected to explain this application. As we have studied previously, there may be many different protocols running on your network. All these protocols (XNS, TCP/IP, IPX, etc.) have their own session layer, but all session layer implementations create, maintain, and then disconnect a session in similar ways, and all three of these protocols can use Netbios as a session layer.

The last concept that should be understood is the session layer also ac-

client and its host server. When a workstation wants to make a connection between itself and another network station, a series of handshaking protocols must take place before the connection is established.

This series of events to establish a session is analogous to someone making a phone call. First, you pick up the phone receiver and ensure that it is operating when you hear the dial tone. You know the name of the person you want to call, but to make the call you must also know that person's unique phone number. Once you have obtained that number, you can place the call.

A series of events may follow. The person whose number you have dialed may not be there and the phone rings until you are tired of waiting and you hang up. Or perhaps the person who answers the phone is not the person you wish to talk to. The line could also be busy, or the person might not be able to talk to you at this time.

If the person whom you are calling answers and is available to talk to you, the conversation may begin and continue until one party decides to terminate it. You then say the appropriate good-byes and hang up the receiver. With the phone systems of today, you may even put one call on hold while you place or receive another call.

This is exactly how a session is established, maintained, and then disconnected during communication between a client workstation and its host server.

Referring back to our analogy, let's combine it with the way a client station attempts to make connection to a server station. When making any original connection, you should acquire the name of the server station you wish to connect to by whatever means you can (the Netbios naming scheme is explained in detail in a moment). Once you have the name of the server, you make the connection request to the server (dial the phone number). From here the same series of events may follow. The server may not be up and running (may not be there), may answer but might not allow you to access the information that resides on its hard disk (someone is there, but this is not the person you wanted to talk to), or may be busy with too many sessions or doing something else at the time you called (the person cannot talk to you at this time).

If the server does answer, your client personal computer and the server will then exchange a few packets (frames) to ensure that both are talking the same dialect (exchange information on version of software, largest packet size, and so forth), and the connection is then established and will be maintained for as long as you desire (or as long as the network administrator desires).

In English, this all seems okay and easily understandable. Let's take a closer look at the Netbios protocol and see, in network terms, exactly what is happening.

Theory of operation

Netbios is a client-server application program interface (API) that provides multiple services.

First, let's explain what an API is. Spelled out, Netbios an *application program interface,* is an *interface* to the network for *application programs.* It provides an application with an interface to request network functions to be performed.

What advantage does this have? Since Netbios is an API, it allows communication programmers to write their application programs without knowing the underlying network. All the programmers need to know is the Netbios interface. Any Netbios-based application program should be able to run on any network station that supports Netbios. This means that the same Netbios-based application program that runs on a Microsoft Lan Manager network will run on a Novell Netware network as well as a Banyan Vines network, without having to do a major code rewrite of the application program.

Electronic mail application programs such as cc:mail and Network Courier are known as Netbios-based applications. Most SNA (system network architecture, by IBM) emulation programs for LANs; as such, Attachmate's SNA products are based on Netbios. They are application programs that operate over the network by making calls to an API such as the Netbios software that resides on a PC. These programs are specially written to operate over the network using Netbios. The largest application for Netbios is called the redirector by Microsoft. This program is explained in detail later.

municating stations. For example, a TCP/IP (fourth and third layers of the ISO model) with a program based on Netbios (fifth layer of the ISO model) would be able to communicate with only another TCP/IP Netbios-based station. See Fig. 6.1a and 6.1b for a better understanding of this setup.

The connection between the client and the server shown in Fig. 6.1b will not work. Even though Netbios is loaded on both stations, the lower-layer protocols cannot communicate.

One final note on interoperability. There is one standard that currently exists for multivendor Netbios interoperability. This is known as *RFC-compliant Netbios* (RFC standard numbers 1001, 1002). If any vendor claims full compliance to this standard, it should allow Netbios-based programs to be distributed among multivendor LAN platforms running TCP/IP. This is not a guarantee of interoperability, merely a statement that RFC compliance should work. I have worked with 3Com Corporation's version of the protocol suite and observed that it has allowed application programs to communicate between two vendor LAN operating systems. Another example of why public-domain or open standards provide the best alternatives for the customers: multivendor interoperability!

Without this standard, if an application program is run on vendor A's system, there is no guarantee that vendor A's workstation can establish a connection to and then send data to vendor B's system, even

Client station   Server station

Mail client software	Mail server software
Netbios	Netbios
TCP	TCP
IP	IP
Ethernet	Ethernet
Wire	Wire
|- -|	

(a)

Client station   Server station

Mail client software	Mail server software
Netbios	Netbios
TCP	SPP
IP	IDP
Ethernet	Ethernet
Wire	Wire
|- -|	

(b)

Figure 6.1   Station communications with the same protocol (a) and with different protocols (b).

though the two stations are running Netbios. The lower-layer protocols, unless publicly standardized (e.g., RFC 1001, 1002) will interfere and will not allow the two stations to communicate. What is important here is the application. A Netbios-based application is usually portable to most systems. Always check with the vendor first!

This ease of use and portability allowed for an onslaught of Netbios-based (networked) programs. These programs include E-Mail (electronic mail) systems, and even most of the 3270 gateways programs use Netbios.

Milestones

The Network Basic Input/Output System (Netbios) was originally developed by a company named Sytek, for IBM's broadband IBM PC network. IBM reiterated the importance of Netbios by offering a Netbios emulator when they announced their second-generation networking scheme of Token Ring, allowing applications originally developed for their first networking product PC network to be ported and run on the new LAN architecture of Token Ring. A third Netbios milestone occurred when IBM announced the PC LAN Support Program (which includes a Netbios driver), in conjunction with Personal System/2.

Netbios would not have become a de facto standard had it not been for the backing of IBM. IBM provided the *IBM PC Network Technical Reference Manual* with a full technical listing of the Netbios interface. Included with this book were source code assembly-language programs that provided application programmers a jump on writing a Netbios application.

a. CALL

b. LISTEN

       c. SEND
       d. SEND NO-ACK
       e. CHAIN SEND
       f. CHAIN SEND
       g. CHAIN SEND NO-ACK
       h. RECEIVE
       i. RECEIVE ANY
       j. HANGUP
       k. SESSION STATUS

4. General commands
       a. RESET
       b. CANCEL
       c. ADAPTER STATUS
       d. UNLINK

Name support.   Each station in a Netbios-based LAN is unique and is identified by its name. Any station may possess more than one name, the maximum settable by each vendor's implementation. Multiple Netbios-based applications may be used on the same PC (one at a time on DOS or many simultaneously on OS/2). With unique naming, there may not be two of the same names of the network.

Each network name can be up to 15 characters in length. The name may consist of alphanumeric characters (case-sensitive). There are restrictions, though; an asterisk or a binary zero cannot be the first character of a name, and the letters IBM are reserved by IBM for the first three characters. Microsoft has further defined the naming scheme to 16 characters; the last (16th) character is a termination character. The 16th character is reserved (allowing only 15 character names). IBM reserves 00h-1Fh as the 16th character.

For the Microsoft Lan Manager file server operating system, the 16th character represents which part of client-server software the message is coming from.

00h	Redirector
03h	Receiver
05h	Messenger
20h	Server

The redirector (explained in the next section) indicates that the Netbios name has the Microsoft redirector installed and can communicate through the LAN. The receiver indicates that the Netbios name can receive alerts, sends, and so forth; the messenger indicates that the Netbios name can send messages. The last termination is the server, and indicates that this Netbios name is a SMB (server-message-block) protocol server (discussed in a moment).

When Netbios is first initialized it will issue a RESET packet. It will then try to register its name. Any station on the network must register its name on the network to ensure that no other PC is using the name. Netbios does this by initiating an ADD NAME and ADD GROUP NAME. ADD NAME initializes an individual (unique) name, while ADD GROUP NAME will add a single name that is used by multiple stations on the network.

The PC will issue this packet onto the network. If no other PC on the network is using this name (this will be known, for any other PC with the same name that sees this packet will issue its own NAME CLAIM packet in response), the name is considered registered. Netbios will write this name into its name table with an associated 1-byte number. This number is used by Netbios to identify a name in its name table. This number is an unsigned 1-byte number allowing a possible 256 numbers to be assigned. Since 0 and 255 are reserved, the maximum of 254 numbers (names) may be assigned. This does not mean that there may only be 254 names on a Netbios network. It means each name table may hold up to 254 names. As many as 10 million different names may be used on any Netbios network, with the stipulation that all are unique. This number should not be confused with the LSN (local session number), to be explained later.

There is no central naming administration with Netbios. That is, there is not a central controller for maintaining a database of Netbios names on the network. The Netbios specification does not specify this. Some vendors have implemented proprietary schemes for this, but they are proprietary! Each PC will keep its own name table to identify other names on the network.

one (1). For example, if your network station address is 02608c010203, your first entry in the name table would be 00000000000000-000002608c010203 (15 bytes). This is accomplished transparently to the user when the network controller boots on Netbios initialization time.

Once this name is registered, it can be deregistered by issuing a DE-LETE NAME function. You can delete any name except for the first name (the permanent node name). A hard reboot or soft reboot of the PC or LAN software will also clear these names.

Datagram function.   Once the name process has taken place, Netbios has become active on the network. To send messages to other Netbios-based applications, the functions of sending a datagram or creating a session come into play.

Datagrams are short (512 bytes for Netbios) unacknowledged (messages not requiring the recipient of the packet to respond with an acknowledgment to the message) packets. This is also known as "best-effort delivery."

An analogy to sending a datagram packet would be as follows. You write a letter to a friend. You address it with your friend's address and your return address and put the letter in the mail. From that point on you have no idea whether the letter was actually delivered to your friend's address. All you can do is hope that the postal system delivered the letter.

Datagrams can be sent with either a broadcast address (remember Chap. 3 on addressing) datagrams or unique (single-station) address.

Datagrams are usually used to send simple messages that do not necessarily require the destination station to respond to receipt of that packet. Error messages and simple broadcast messages on the network use this method of transmission. The purpose behind this is less overhead. Since the recipient did not have to generate a return message, there will be one less packet on the network for that particular message. Multiply this by the hundreds of nodes that tend to be on networks today and the tens of thousands of overhead packets that were deleted. Network management stations are also users of datagrams.

Datagrams are seldom used for established sessions between a client and a server. Datagrams are usually good for sending messages and network management functions.

Session communications.   An alternative to the datagram for information transfer is the session. A session or multiple sessions can be established between any two names on a network. A session is sometimes referred to as *virtual circuit* (a circuit connected through software, not hardware). The names involved in a session are usually on separate nodes but can be on the same station, or they can even be the same name on the same station. The same two names can also be used to establish multiple sessions.

Once a session is established on a station, it is assigned a unique number to differentiate it from all other sessions on that station. This is the local session number (LSN). Data can be reliably transferred between two stations (i.e., the data is guaranteed to arrive at the destination in the same order that it was sent from the source) only after this session has been established. The LSN is unique for every session that a workstation has. This LSN will correlate to the connection IDs in the transport layer.

A commonly used term, a *virtual circuit,* is introduced here. We now understand the access methods of Ethernet and Token Ring and how the session layer works with those methods to enable us to establish a session with another computer. The connection that is eventually established between two stations is also known as a virtual circuit. It is a circuit that is virtually there. It is not physically there, but we know that a link is established between the two communication stations. This is commonly called a virtual circuit.

The link that we just established could have been established by running individual cables between the two communicating stations. Network hardware and software create the same links as the hardwired cable used to do, except that we establish these links via software and networking hardware. *Sessions established between two communicating stations on a network is accomplished via software and is known as a virtual circuit.*

Internetwork communications.   Netbios in its native form is not used on an internetwork, that is, one that is used with routers. Netbios is a

tered Netbios names must still be unique across all the LANs that the bridges interconnect. Bridges operate at the data-link layer and base their packet-forwarding decisions on this. Bridges know nothing about the Netbios naming scheme and will pass any packet based on the destination address. Care should be taken when implementing a Netbios-based LAN with bridges.

A session setup is shown in Fig. 6.2.

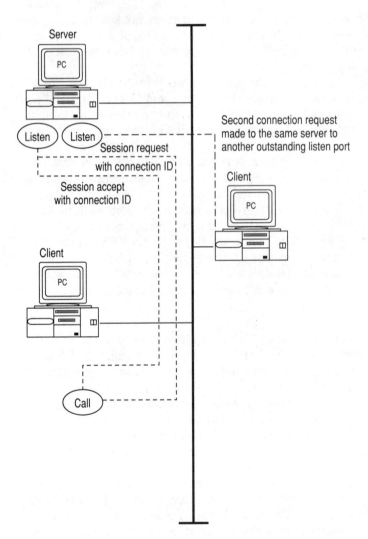

Figure 6.2 Netbios session setup. Connection is set up by a call made by the client with a client connection ID. The connection request is accepted if there is an outstanding LISTEN port available. A server connection ID is sent with the response. Data is sent on the connection IDs. Session is closed by a HANGUP request.

Technical Report: Netbios

Netbios session operations and definitions

The basic operation for establishing a connection and exchanging data between two names on the network is as follows:

1. CLAIM and ADD names to the respective application's local name table at that station.

2. Establish a session between the two names (using the number associated for the names) using the CALL and LISTEN commands.

3. Transfer data using the SEND and RECEIVE commands (using the LSN).

4. End the session using the HANGUP or RESET commands.

The other name for Netbios is called INT5Ch (or interrupt 5C hex). What is this? Whenever an application wishes to communicate with the Netbios software, it needs to know how to call it. Netbios (at least in the PC DOS community) is called via a software interrupt known as *Interrupt 5C*. An application wishing to communicate with Netbios will build what is known as a *network control block* (NCB) (see Table 6.1). These NCBs are how an application communicates with Netbios and how Netbios will communicate with an application. The NCB table is 64 bytes long and contains the information listed in Table 6.1.

TABLE 6.1   Network Control Block

COMMAND (1 byte)	RETCODE (1 byte)

NUM   Number returned by Netbios; represents a local NAME. NUM may range from 2 to 254; 0 and 255 are never used, and a 1 represents the permanent node name.

BUFFER@   Double-word pointer to the data buffer to be used. The @ symbol is used to represent the word address in memory.

LENGTH   Number of bytes of data to be sent or received.

CALLNAME   A name of the station (remote) you want to communicate with.

NAME   A name on the local station.

RTO   Receive timeout. Each increment equals 500 ms (milliseconds or 0.5 s).

STO   Send timeout. Each increment equals 500 ms.

POST@   Double-word pointer to the applications routine to be executed when a NO-WAIT command has completed processing. The @ symbol is used to represent the word address.

LANA NUM   Local adapter number used to route the NCB to correct adapter in the workstation.

CMD CPLT   Command complete—indicates status of the NCB.

RESERVE   Reserved field used by Netbios to store temporary variables.

Functions

To communicate with the Netbios interface, an application would fill out a NCB with the appropriate information and submit the NCB to be processed by Netbios by giving the location (address in memory) of the NCB to Netbios and calling interrupt 5C. Some Netbios interfaces allow a Netbios call to INT2Ah (i.e., Software Interrupt 2A hex). Calling this interrupt allows an application to isolate itself from any future Netbios enhancements.

Netbios would find the NCB and would interpret each field to understand the task it is to accomplish. Netbios uses the NCB and only interprets the fields and takes action on them; the NCB is not transmitted over the network. Netbios will build its own packet header containing its information and submit the packet to its next-lower layer of software. It's that simple.

Building this table is similar to filling out a questionnaire. For example, if you wanted to establish your Netbios name on the network, you would fill in the fields described in the following paragraphs.

NAME CLAIM function. Refer to Table 6.1. The COMMAND field would be filled with a 30h or B0h (h signifies that the number is in the hexadecimal numbering system). The NAME field would contain a valid Netbios name. The second number shown here (B0) is to tell Netbios that it is a no-wait command. The application program will not wait for Netbios to complete the function. This is known as asynchronous commands. Netbios will interrupt the calling application when the command is complete. It will interrupt the program by an address specified in post@. You would then submit this block of data to Netbios by calling INT 5Ch.

According to the information contained in the NCB, Netbios

would take the following actions. Netbios would first look at the CALLNAME to see if it is an asterisk (*) or the entry is a NULL (00). If so, Netbios would inform the calling program that the CALLNAME is illegal. Netbios would then look in its local name table to see if the name is already in its table. If the name is in conflict with the name that is in its local name table (a unique name), it will inform the calling program; otherwise, it will inform the calling program of the name's number and that it is a duplicate name.

Netbios will check to see if the name table is full; if it is not full, it will submit the name in broadcast mode to the network and wait for some type of error response. (Usually Netbios will transmit the CLAIM NAME packet on the network several times, depending on the vendor.) At this point, all active stations on the network will receive this packet and search their own name tables to see if the name exists. If they find an entry, these remote stations will transmit a CLAIM NAME indicating the name is already taken response packet on the network. Netbios on the station that tried to register the name in error will then issue a delete name for its own use.

Netbios will return with information in the RETCODE field indicating the result of the call. If the call was successful (indicated by the RETCODE field), the NUM field would contain the number associated with that particular name. This number will be used for all subsequent calls with that particular name involved. You would not use the Netbios name from that point on; the number that Netbios assigned to that name would be used.

We now would like to establish a session with a remote station on the network. We would fill out another NCB with the following information.

Call function. Refer to Tab¹
or 90h. The CALLNAMᴿ
with which you wish
anywhere on the r
are sending thᵣ
group name. T.
local name tabl

The RTO fiel(
0.5-s increments)
mand issued durinᵧ
cate no timeout. Onᴄ
the field may not chanᵧ
The STO field designateᴄ
0.5s increments) before successful completion of any SEND command issued during this session. A zero entry in this field would indicate no

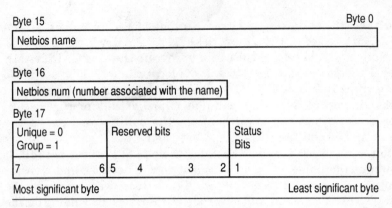

Figure 6.3   Name table fields.

SEND timeout. Once a session is established between two stations, this field may not change.

On completion of this command, the RETCODE field would indicate a successful and unsuccessful completion of the command.

Before any call is accepted by a remote station, the remote must have previously issued a listen request as explained below.

LISTEN function.   The LISTEN function is used on a station that is willing to accept a connection from a remote station that issued a CALL function. It is not issued across the network. Before any connection is accepted (a free listen port awaiting a connection), a LISTEN command must be outstanding.

A LISTEN command is issued according to the following procedure: Netbios accomplishes some error checking. First, to see if the local resource is available, search for the name in the local name table; then see if the local session table is full. If any of the above errors is true, Netbios will inform the calling program. The calling program, which is vendor-dependent, will inform the end user with some type of descriptive text message.

Otherwise, Netbios will wait for a connection request from a remote station or wait for NAME CLAIM packet to detect for name conflicts. If Netbios receives a request for a specific LISTEN, Netbios will check for the source for the session request packet. If the source of the SESSION REQUEST packet is the same as the remote, Netbios will indicate that a LISTEN SPECIFIC call has been satisfied.

The other type of LISTEN (the most common) that Netbios receives is a LISTEN ANY. This function allows a station to accept a connection from any station on the network. The station is not looking for a call from one particular station on the network. Once Netbios receives this packet, it updates its tables with a SESSION REQUEST COM-

PLETED indicator. Netbios will also respond to the requesting station with a connection ID that will distinguish it from all other sessions on that station.

Netbios will respond to the requesting station with a SESSION AC-CEPT packet and wait for the first packet on that session. When the first packet arrives, it will set the SESSION ESTABLISHED indicator in the session table and return the source of the SESSION REQUEST packet, the local session number (LSN), and a COMMAND COM-PLETED status to the calling program.

Once the session has been established, Netbios will transmit data via the SEND and RECEIVE functions. The following is an example of two stations communicating with the Netbios SEND and RECEIVE functions.

SEND DATA. Netbios sends data to another station via the LSN. When Netbios is requested to send data, a NCB is complete and Netbios is called to read the NCB. Netbios will first do some error checking. Netbios will check its session table to see whether the LSN is valid. If the LSN is not valid, it will return an error to the calling program. If the LSN is valid, Netbios will check to see if the session is closed or aborted; if it is, Netbios will return the appropriate error message to the calling program.

If Netbios determines the session to be active, Netbios will send the data packet(s) to the destination station and wait the appropriate timeout for an acknowledgment to the packet. If the acknowledgment is received within the timeout period, Netbios will return an appropri-ate status message to the calling program. Otherwise, Netbios will abort the session.

RECEIVE DATA. When Netbios is required to receive data, the follow-ing algorithm is used. Netbios will first do some error checking. This error checking is the same as that for the SEND DATA command: check for invalid LSN and check for session aborted or closed status. If any of the error checking produces an error status, an appropriate er-ror message would be responded to the calling application program.

If the session is active, Netbios will wait for data packet(s) from a remote station. If the session data is received within the timeout pe-riod, specified by the RTO field, Netbios will transmit an ACK packet to the appropriate remote station and submit the data to the calling application program's buffer space in the station. If the session timed out, Netbios will inform the calling program of this.

Netbios will also submit the actual length of the data received to the calling program. Netbios will check to see if there is enough free buffer space to place the data. If there is not, Netbios will set the appropriate error message status and submit it to the calling program; otherwise, it will inform the calling program of a successful RE-CEIVE. Netbios can receive from one particular station or receive from any station.

HANGUP.   Finally, we need to close the session between the two communicating stations. This is accomplished via the HANGUP command as follows.

Netbios will perform some local error checking as to illegal session number, session already closed and not reported, or session already aborted and not reported. If any of these conditions exists, Netbios will inform the calling application appropriately.

Netbios will check if there are any outstanding RECEIVE commands waiting for this session. If so, Netbios will immediately abort all outstanding RECEIVE commands. If there are any outstanding SEND commands, Netbios will wait for the completion of all pending SEND commands or timeouts on any SEND commands before initiating the HANGUP command. If the SEND command timed out, Netbios immediately aborts the session.

Netbios will inform the remote station that it wishes to HANGUP the session by transmitting a close packet to the remote station and wait for a close packet from this remote station or a timeout. If a CLOSE packet is received before a timeout, Netbios closes the session; if it is received during a timeout, Netbios simply aborts the session. Netbios will then inform the calling program of its status.

Whenever Netbios returns information to the appropriate calling program, it is usually reported to the end user via a text message. This text message is seldom of the same format as when Netbios returned the message to your application program. This informational text message is vendor-specific and can report anything.

ADAPTER and SESSION STATUS functions.   The last functions are the ADAPTER and SESSION STATUS functions. Any calling program may request the status of any session. Status information may be obtained from remote stations as well as a local station. Netbios will return with the following information on the session(s):

Netbios will return the following information upon request of a session status call. It will return the adapter name number, the number of sessions associated with this name, the number of RECEIVE DATAGRAMS, and the number of RECEIVE ANY commands that are outstanding (meaning the number of times that the name may receive data).

It will also report local session number assigned to this session, the current state of the session (any commands that are currently pending, i.e., waiting to complete), the local name and the remote name associated with this session, the total number of RECEIVE and SEND commands for this session.

Acquiring the session status for one session or all sessions is possible. (See Table 6.3).

The ADAPTER STATUS report will contain the information listed in Table 6.2. In the table, except where noted, each square represents 1 byte.

Name table data. The first 16 bytes (bytes 0 to 15) in each name table entry are used for the name itself. The 17th byte (byte 16) is the number assigned to the name. This is the number returned in the NUM field of a NCB after successful completion of an ADD NAME or an ADD GROUP name.

The assigned number represents the name. The last byte (byte 17) provides information on the name itself. This field is as shown in Fig. 6.3.

TABLE 6.2   Adapter Status Table

Byte number and description	
Unit ID (6 bytes long)	For Ethernet and Token Ring, it is the address of the controller board itself; the unique physical address
06 Reserved	
08 Software version number	
0A Length of reporting period (in minutes)	Since last power-on reset
0C Reserved	
0F Number of collisions detected	
12 Number of transmissions aborted	
14 Number of packets transmitted	
18 Number of packets received	
1C Number of Retransmissions	
1E Reserved	
28 Number of free NCBs	
2A Total number of free NCBs	Since last power-on reset
2C Total maximum of NCBs prior reset	
2E Reserved	
32 Number of sessions pending	
34 Configured maximum sessions	
36 Total maximum sessions prior reset	
38 Maximum session data packet size	
3A Number of names in name table	
3C Name table (18 bytes per entry)	

Status bits are as follows:

000   Attempting to register its name

100   This name is registered

101   The name has been deregistered

110   This name is a duplicate

111   The name is a duplicate, deregistering pending

Table 6.3 lists SESSION STATUS functions and commands. The session state contains the following codes:

01h   LISTEN command pending

02h   CALL command pending

03h   Session established

04h   HANGUP command pending

05h   HANGUP command complete

06h   Session aborted or not reported

The previous information is used when an application is directly written for Netbios—for example, a mail program. The mail program client side runs on one station, while the mail server runs on another station. But what about those applications that are not aware of the Netbios interface, such as Microsoft Word, WordPerfect, or Lotus? These applications were written to run directly on a PC and are unaware that they are being run on a network.

A common approach to define the data that is transmitted or received between the two stations is a piece of software known as the *redirector* (see Figs. 6.4 and 6.6) using a protocol known as server message block (SMB) protocol. We will study this protocol next.

The information contained in the rest of the book will pertain to PC LANs. The information is specific for the 3Com/Microsoft LAN Man-

TABLE 6.3   Session Status Table

Byte	Description	Byte	Description
00	Adapter name NCB_NUM (1 byte)	01	Number of sessions (1 byte)
02	Number of RECEIVE datagrams (1 byte)	03	Number of RECEIVE ANY commands (1 byte)
04	Local session number NCB_LSN (1 byte)	05	Session state (1 byte)
06	Local name NCB_NAME (16 bytes)		
16	Remote name NCB_CALLNAME (16 bytes)		
26	Number of RECEIVE commands (1 byte)	27	Number of SEND commands (1 byte)

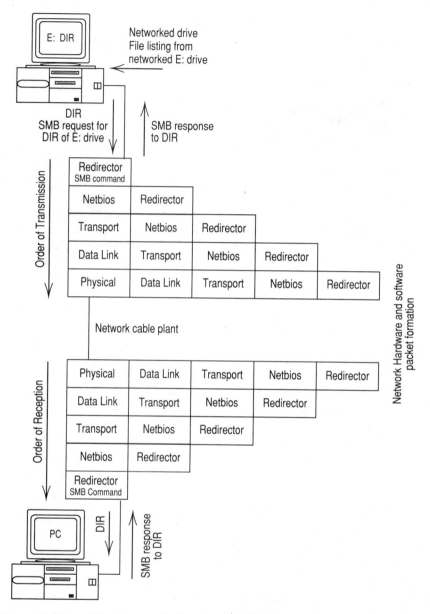

Figure 6.14 Network hardware and software packet formation. As data is transmitted down from the application, each layer will append its header information on the packet to be interpreted by the same layers at the remote station. This figure is shown for a workgroup LAN operating system without network layer software. If network layer software were installed it would append its header information between the data-link and transport header information.

ager. This representation is not exact but is sufficiently close to provide you with a feel for the internal workings of LAN operating software.

Server message block protocol

As mentioned above, SMB protocol can be used to define data transmitted and received between two stations, utilizing a redirector program. The redirector is a software program that is loaded into the computer that provides basically three main functions: (1) request file-print service connection on the network, (2) intercept operating system calls, and (3) request an end to the connection to a file-print server on the network.

The redirector is a software module that gets loaded when the LAN operating system is invoked. The redirector will allow us to create a virtual link, pass certain commands across this link, and then allow us to disconnect the link. By now, you might say that Netbios supposedly provided us with those functions. Netbios does! Just as Netbios-based application program informs Netbios of the actions to take, it is the redirector that informs Netbios of the action to be taken. The redirector resides on top of Netbios and is an application for Netbios.

It is like a car and its driver. A car provides the means for transportation wherever the driver wants to go. But it is the driver that informs the car, through a series of actions, of what the car is supposed to do. Netbios is like this; Netbios is used as a vehicle to provide a communications path between two stations on the network.

Let's consider an example. Let's say you are sitting at your PC and it has accomplished its boot procedure. During this boot procedure, the DOS operating system and the LAN software were loaded. No connections were made to any stations on the network yet.

Connection setup.   You now want to make a connection to a file server out on the network. You will type in a command that tells the network software that a connection to a particular station on the network is needed. Once you type in this connection request command, the network software—in this case, the redirector—will intercept this call. The redirector will decipher that the call is a connection request and will then form a command message [network control block (NCB)] and pass this to Netbios. Netbios will decipher the command and notice that a connection is being requested. Netbios will then pass a "new client" call to the transport layer software asking for a client ID. The transport layer software will pass the client ID back to the Netbios software. Netbios will then issue a packet back to the transport layer to be sent out to the network, requesting this connection. The transport layer will assign a socket ID number to the packet and give the packet to the data-link layer (either Token Ring or Ethernet); this packet will then be sent to the network (see general flowchart in Fig. 6.5).

If the file server responds within a timeout period, it will respond with an acknowledgment to the originating station with the following information with a server-assigned socket number. Netbios then assigns a session number. Netbios will have an entry in its table with the session ID and the client ID. The session is then set up. The connection to the file server is accomplished (see Table 6.4).

The redirector will then initiate a negotiate protocol so that the workstation and the server may inform each other of their characteristics (maximum packet size, buffer space, etc.). Once the workstation receives a response from the server to this negotiation protocol, the workstation redirector will pass a file-service request to the server. If

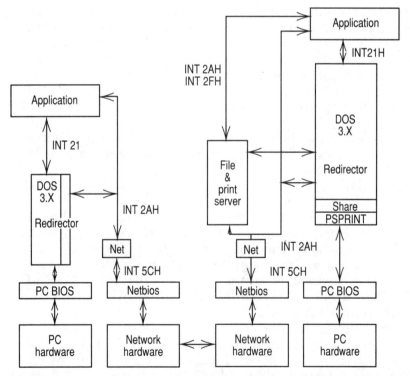

Figure 6.5 Netbios flowchart. Sharing information in a Netbios-based LAN requires three pieces of software: (1) PC DOS 3.X, (2) Netbios itself, and (3) the redirector. (Courtesy: *Inside Netbios*, J. Scott Haugdahl, Architecture Technology Corp.).

TABLE 6.4 Tables kept on the Workstation Redirector

Redirector Table		
Session ID	Drive linked	Sharename
15	d:	\\server1\apps
Netbios Table		
Session ID	Client ID	
15	10	
Transport Layer Table		
Client ID	Socket number pair	
10	110 150	

the server can accommodate this request, a virtual circuit is established and the redirector places an entry in its table with the session ID and driver ID and the file-service name that was requested (see Table 6.4).

Once the connection has been established between a client and its server, the second function that the redirector provides is to intercept all operating system Interrupt 21 calls to check and see if the information in the call is for the redirector. The redirector checks to see whether the call is requesting some type of service that includes any type of network function. If the information in the call is not for the network, the redirector will pass the call to the DOS for local processing.

System calls are nothing more than typing DIR A:, which is a command that a user will type into a personal computer running the DOS operating system requesting listing of the files on the floppy-disk drive A:. The PC will respond by printing to the screen of the PC a listing of all the files located there.

Starting with DOS 3.1, all system calls should be made through a software interrupt, Interrupt 21. When the DOS operating system or even an application program calls the interrupt, DOS will look at the function call that was passed by Interrupt 21 to see what action needs to be performed. Some common Interrupt 21 calls include MAKE DIRECTORY (MD), REMOVE DIRECTORY (RD), WRITE TO A FILE, and READ FROM A FILE.

Referring to Fig. 6.6, when the user types DIR A:, a series of Interrupt 21 calls are made. The first check that the redirector will accomplish is to check for the drive ID. The drive ID signifies the drive letter of disk drive. All disk drives are identified by assigning an alphabetic letter and a colon to them. Floppy-disk drives are assigned to the letters A: and B: and hard-disk drives are assigned C:, D:, and E:. With the LAN operating system installed on the PC, disk drives may be assigned from D to the letter Z:.

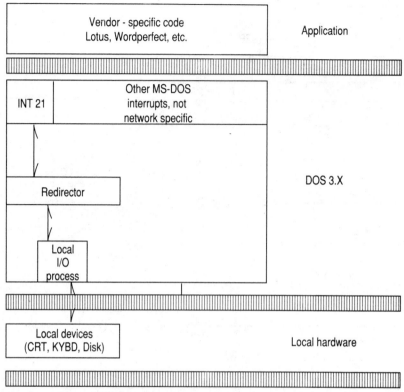

Figure 6.6   Normal PC data flow.

The redirector trapped the Interrupt 21 call and looked at the drive ID (A:, C:, D:, etc.). The redirector compares this ID with its table of devices that are "redirected" to the LAN. If the drive ID is not located in its table, the redirector will pass the call to DOS and wait for the next Interrupt 21. As simple as that. Once again, please notice that this type of call is an example of the Microsoft LAN Manager. It is similar only in function to other types of LAN operating systems such as those used by Novell and Banyan (see Fig. 6.7).

An example of the content of the redirector table is given in Table 6.4.

A sharename is a file server mapping to a directory on the disk drive. A file server shares its subdirectories with other network stations on the network. When linking to the file server instead of having the users type the whole subdirectory of the serve, the server will map a simple name known as a *sharename* to its actual subdirectory. For the Microsoft redirector, the server shares its files on the basis of the following naming scheme:

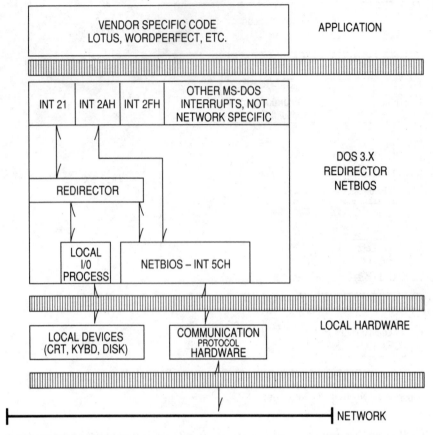

Figure 6.7 Networked PC data flow.

```
\\ < servername > \ < sharename >
```

Where the servername is the Netbios name of the server on the network and the sharename is the mapped directory on the server you wish to use. For example, \\servername\word.

This is easier to type in and remember, and maintains the file servers naming structure.

How are all these tables and the information in the tables used? As illustrated in Fig. 6.5, when the user types in a command such as DIR D:\, a series of Interrupt 21 calls are made. The redirector will intercept these calls and first looks at the drive ID. The redirector will look in its table to see if this drive is there. The redirector will discover the drive is located on the network. It will then take this call and form a SMB packet which is related to the DOS Interrupt 21h DIR function call. It will then take the session number from its table based on the drive ID.

Netbios is then called and the redirector gives the session ID and the SMB command to Netbios. Netbios acquires the Ethernet or Token Ring address and client ID from its table according to the session number. Netbios will then pass the information to the transport layer software. The transport layer software will then look in its table according to the client ID passed to it from Netbios. The transport layer appends its information to the packet and sends the packet to the data-link layer (Ethernet or Token Ring). The data-link layer will pass the packet to the network.

This process is reversed at the remote end. The data-link layer of the indicated server (noted by the physical address of the packet) will pick up this packet and will strip off its associated headers and pass the packet to the transport layer of the server. The transport layer will identify the process, strip off its associated headers, and pass the packet on to Netbios. Netbios will identify the process, strip off its headers, and pass the SMB information to the redirector on the server. The redirector on the server decodes the SMB packet and notices that it is a DIR function. The server, if allowed, will gather the directory information and form a SMB response packet and send it back to the workstation. This type of communication process is continued until the redirection is disconnected (session is hung up).

Overview. Moving on up through the ISO model, we now know how sessions are created and maintained, but after the session is established, how do we tell the receiving station what to do with our commands? This is where the SMB protocol comes into play (see also Fig. 6.8 for a review of client-server basics with respect to SMB protocol). The SMB protocols were developed by Microsoft, Intel, and IBM. This, loosely speaking, is a way of distributing the operating system across the LAN between your PC and the server. This is not the only method of defining data submitted between a server and its client, but is becoming extremely popular. The SMB protocol is an "open" protocol, meaning that the protocol is within the public domain and is not proprietary to any one company. It is used with the 3Com Lan Manager; Xenixnet from Santa Cruz Operations and a host of other vendors are currently supporting this protocol for message translations. The following information pertains to Microsoft's Lan Manager, a working-group PC LAN network operating system.

For example, let's look at Fig. 6.5. We have established a connection between PC A and server 1. Now we need to tell the server that we would like to see a directory of the sharename to which we have established a connection. An SMB command will be issued and passed to the redirector. The redirector will pass this to the network as explained before. The redirector at the server will receive this SMB com-

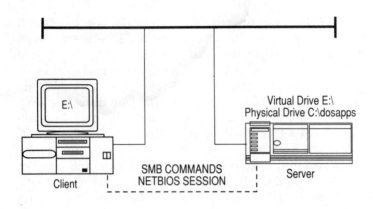

Check address table _____ Respond to the connect request

Send data _____ Receive data

Receive data _____ Send data

Send data _____ Receive data

Receive data _____ Send data

Send data _____ Receive data

Issue a hangup _____ Close connection response

Figure 6.8 Client-server basics.

mand and perform the DIR. The output from the command will be passed back to the client PC that requested it.

The redirector and server function of LAN Manager implement SMB. SMB operates at the application level, and thus it is required for LAN Manager operation. SMB is designed to be machine- and operating system–independent.

SMB is an open protocol as published by IBM, and many vendors have chosen to implement it in their PC LANs. Vendors such as Novell have implemented their own redirector (the shell) and server protocols for reasons of efficiency and added functionality.

Table 6.5 lists examples of some of the SMB messages that the redirector uses to communicate with other SMB stations on the network. Notice that these commands resemble the same command that you may use on your local PC (without a network installed).

TABLE 6.5   SMB Function Fields

Value	Meaning
00h	Create directory
01h	Delete directory
02h	Open file
03h	Create file
04h	Close file
05h	Commit all files
06h	Delete file
07h	Rename file
08h	Get file attribute
09h	Set file attribute
0Ah	Read byte block
0Bh	Write byte block
0Ch	Lock byte block
0Dh	Unlock byte block
0Eh	Create unique file
0Fh	Create new file
10h	Check directory
11h	End of process
12h	LSEEK
70h	Start connection
71h	End connection
72h	Verify dialect
80h	Get disk attributes
81h	Search multiple files (DIR)
C0h	Create spool file
C1h	Spool byte block
C2h	Close spool file
C3h	Return print queue
D0h	Send message
D1h	Send broadcast
D2h	Forward user name
D3h	Cancel forward
D4h	Get machine name
D5h	Start multiblock message
D6h	End multiblock message
D7h	Multiblock message text

Establishing a session. Another explanation of the establishment of a session using Figures 6.6 and 6.7 is explained here. When a user attempts to connect to the resources of a server, the redirector (the code that resides in a user's workstation) attempts to establish a session with the server. If there is room in the local adapter's address table, then a session starts, in which the redirector and server agree on a protocol and begin communicating.

Over the server side, the redirector requests that a connection be set up to the share resource such as a subdirectory. The server will make sure that the requested resource exists and, if so, will check the optional securities to make sure that the user or requesting resource may obtain the right to access the remote resource. The server then responds with a maximum server transmission block size and a connection handle called the *network path ID* (similar to the handle returned by PC DOS when opening a file) for all future requests to the resources. When the connection terminates, the redirector requests of the server to end the connection and free the handle.

Normal PC operation is as follows. For example, if you are sitting at your PC and the DOS prompt is staring at you, you might ask yourself: "Exactly how does this machine know whether I am about to communicate over the LAN, or will I just interface to the local hardware that I have on my PC?"

The answer is very simple. Refer to Fig. 6.6. If should be obvious by now that there is software loaded somewhere in your PC that will "watch" what you are about to type and intercept it to see if it is anything that will involve the network. This piece of software is known in Microsoft Lan Manager as the redirector and as the *requester* in Novell.

The operation of the redirector is very simple. It will intercept any Interrupt 21 calls to see if the request made by this interrupt is for anything that is local on your PC or whether the redirector needs to redirect the information across the network.

What is an Interrupt 21 call? Most "well-behaved" application programs that place calls to the DOS are made through this interrupt. This includes calls for opening a file, closing a file, writing to a file, and writing to the screen. An interrupt is an application's way of telling the computer that it needs outside assistance to complete a particular task.

The redirector watches for these calls and simply looks to see if the request is being made of a local device or a device that the user has redirected to a remote location.

Interfacing to the PC

The central processing unit (CPU) of a computer communicates with its peripheral devices in the following basic ways:

Interrupts
I/O base address
Direct memory access (DMA)
Shared memory window address
Bus mastering

Before any LAN adapter is installed in the personal computer, you must first check the system for its current configuration. With any personal computer you will find many expansion boards depending on the personal computer. For example, when the first personal computers were rolled out in 1981, all serial and parallel communications, video, and even some of the main memory were external to the motherboard. These were external boards that were placed in the expansion slots of the personal computer.

The PCs of today will usually have all the memory, serial and parallel communications, and the video card placed on the main (mother) board of the computer.

Nevertheless, you must still concern yourself with four important features that every expansion board must comply with. These are fully explained in the following paragraphs.

I/O Port Addresses

Ports enable the CPU to correspond to the rest of its peripheral devices. A port is something like a telephone line that the computer can call up on. Any part of the computer's circuitry that the microprocessor needs to talk to is given a port number, and the CPU uses that number like a telephone number to call up the particular port. For example, one port number is used to talk to the keyboard; another is used for the programmable timer. Controlling the disk drives and transferring data back and forth is also done through the ports. The display screen is also controlled by using ports, but the data that appears on the display is controlled through memory.

The CPU has 65,536 (2 bytes) port numbers available for it to use. Not all of them are connected. The designers of any CPU decide which port numbers to use for various purposes, and the circuit elements of the computer are wired up to respond to these port numbers. The computer's bus is used to indicate which port that CPU wants to talk to. All peripheral devices see this port number on the bus, but only one will respond.

Interrupts

The interrupt feature allows the computer to suspend whatever it is doing and switch to something else, in response to something that causes the interruption, such as pressing a key on the keyboard.

The ability to be interrupted solves many problems in getting the CPU's attention. The CPU has the inherent (built-in) ability to be interrupted, combined with a convenient way of putting the work that has been interrupted on hold while the interrupt is being processed.

Every part of the computer which might need to request the CPU's attention is given its own special interrupt number to use. The keyboard has its own interrupt, so that every time we press a key on the keyboard, the CPU knows about it. The PC's internal clock also has its own interrupt to let the computer's time-keeping program know each time the clock has ticked—18.3 times a second. Disk drives also have interrupts signaling when a read is completed, etc.

These are all IBM-defined hardware interrupts. There are also software interrupts for use of the ROM basic input/output system and others, but discussion of these elements is not within the scope of this book.

Direct Memory Access

Some devices have the ability to directly access memory without having to pass directly through the CPU. This process, known as direct memory access, is a special controller to facilitate this action.

Although the CPU is capable of transferring the data between the LAN adapter and its own memory, this DNA chip was specially designed to perform this task and in most cases will perform it in half the time that the CPU could. This function is not always enabled and on some LAN adapters may actually be disabled.

Shared Memory Window Access

This is an addressable piece of memory that both the LAN adapter and the PC will share (both can address). The address is usually above 640K (A0000–E0000). Information transferred from and received to the PC will be in this piece of memory. The address space may also be used by those LAN adapter cards that support diskless boot. This is the capability for the PC to boot its network operating software from the file server and not from its local disk drives.

B

LAN Vendor Listings

The following lists contain the names and addresses of Ethernet (including hubs), Token Ring [including media access units (MAUs)], bridge, and router vendors.[1] To use this guide, simply find the name of the vendor that you have an interest in. Then call the number associated with the company. When the company answers, ask to speak to a sales representative. Once connected to that person, ask for a literature packet on the products that they manufacture. A company background is always helpful to instill confidence in the stability of the company. *Note:* C, H—Vendor sells both the adapter card and the hub. Otherwise, the vendor sells only the specific adapter card.

Ethernet Card and Hub Listing

Abacus Network Devices (C, H)
1101 Pine Street
St. Paul, MN 55346
(612) 982-5900

Accton Technology (C, H)
2109 O'Toole Ave. Suite S
San Jose, CA 95131
(408) 432-3042

Acer America
401 Charcot Ave.
San Jose, CA 95131
(800) 538-1542

Adaptec
691 South Milpitas Blvd.
Milpitas, CA 95035
(408) 432-8600

Allen-Bradley (C, H)
555 Briarwood Circle
Ann Arbor, MI 48108
(800) 288-4362

Allied Telesis
627 National Ave.
Mountain View, CA 94043
(415) 964-0944

---

[1]This list is provided courtesy of *Lan Magazine*.

Alloy Computer Products (C, H)
165 Forest St.
Marlborough, MA 01752
(800) 544-7551

Americable (C, H)
7450 Flying Cloud Dr.
Eden Prairie, MN 55344
(800) 234-2580

American Concord Techage (C, H)
10543 Progress Way
Cypress, CA 90630
(714) 761-4477

American Research
1101 Monterey Pass Rd.
Monterey Park, CA 91754
(800) 423-3877

Anthem Technologies
2157 O'Toole Ave., Suite E
San Jose, CA 95131
(408) 943-6630

Apple Computer
20525 Mariani Ave.
Cupertino, CA 95014
(408) 996-1010

Aquila Communications (C, H)
846 Del Rey Ave.
Sunnyvale, CA 94086
(408) 732-0700

Arche Technologies (C, H)
48881 Kato Rd.
Fremont, CA 94539
(800) 422-4674

Artisoft
575 East River Rd.
Tucson, AZ 85704
(602) 293-6363

Asnate Technologies
1050 East Duane Ave., Suite G
Sunnyvale, CA 94086
(408) 736-3360

AST Research
16215 Alton Pkwy.
Irvine, CA 92718
(714) 727-4141

AT&T Computer Systems (C, H)
1 Speedwell Ave.
Morristown, NJ 07960
(714) 727-4141

Axon Systems
9465 Wilshire Blvd.
Beverly Hills, CA 90212
(213) 271-5448

Bethel Computer
1723 21st. St.
Santa Monica, CA 90404
(213) 828-1415

BICC Data Networks (C, H)
1800 West Park Dr.
Westborough, MA 01581
(800) 4-ISOLAN

Cabletron Systems (C, H)
35 Industrial Way
Rochester, NH 03867
(603) 332-9400

Cayman Systems
26 Landsdowns St.
Cambridge, MA 02139
(617) 494-1999

C&C Technology (C, H)
Bldg. 9, Unit 60
245 West Roosevelt Rd.
West Chicago, IL 60195
(708) 231-0015

Chipcom (C, H)
Southborough Office Park
118 Turnpike Rd.
Southborough, MA 01772
(800) 228-9930

CMC
125 Cremona Dr.
Santa Barbara, CA 93117
(805) 968-4262
(800) CMC-8023

CNet Technology (C, H)
62 Bonaventura Dr.
Sunnyvale, CA 95134
(408) 954-8000

Codenoll Technology (C, H)
1086 North Broadway
Yonkers, NY 10701
(914) 965-6300

Cogent Data Technology
175 West St., P.O. Box 926
Friday Harbor, WA 98250
(206) 378-2929

Compaq Computer
P.O. Box 692000
Houston, TX 77269
(713) 370-0670

Compatible Systems
P.O. Box 17220
Boulder, CO 80308
(800) 356-0283

Compex (C, H)
4065 East La Palma, Unit C
Anaheim, CA 92807
(714) 630-6302

Computer Products
2900 Gateway Dr.
Pompano Beach, FL 33069
(305) 974-5500

Corvus Systems
160 Great Oaks Blvd.
San Jose, CA 95119
(800) 4-CORVUS

CSS Laboratories
1641 McGaw Ave.
Irvine, CA 92714
(714) 852-8161

Cubix
2800 Lockheed Way
Carson City, NV 89706
(800) 829-0550

Dataco
Smedeholm 12-14
Herley, Denmark DK-2730
(45 44) 53-01-00

Data General
4400 Computer Dr.
Westboro, MA 01580
(508) 366-8911
(800) DATAGEN

David Systems (C, H)
701 East Evelyn Ave.
Sunnyvale, CA 94086
(408) 720-6867

DCA (C, H)
1000 Alderman Dr.
Alpharetta, GA 30201
(404) 442-4553

DFI
2544 Port St.
West Sacramento, CA 95691
(916) 373-1234

Digital Equipment (C, H)
146 Main St.
Maynard, MA 01754
(508) 493-5111

D-Link Systems
5 Musick
Irvine, CA 92718
(714) 455-1688

Dove Computer
1200 North 23rd St.
Wilmington, NC 28405
(919) 763-7918
(800) 622-7627

DSC Communications
2940 North First St.
San Jose, CA 95134
(800) BUY-NEXOS

DTK Computer
15711 East Valley Rd.
City of Industry, CA 91744
(818) 333-5429

Earth Computer Technologies
10525 Lawson River Ave.
Fountain Valley, CA 92728
(714) 964-5784

Edimax Computer (C, H)
3020 Scott Blvd.
Santa Clara, CA 95054
(408) 496-1105

Everex Systems
48431 Milmont Dr.
Fremont, CA 94538
(415) 498-1111

Farallon Computing (C, H)
2000 Powell St., Suite 600
Emeryville, CA 94608
(415) 596-9100

Fibercom
3353 Orange Ave. NE
Roanoke, VA 24012
(800) 423-1183

Four Dimension Computer (C, H)
Fifth Floor, Suite 335
Section 3, Roosevelt Rd.
Taipel, Taiwan 10763
(886 2) 363-0855

Frontier Technologies
3510 North Oakland Ave.
Milwaukee, WI 53211
(414) 964-8689

Fugitsu Microelectronics
50 Rio Robies
San Jose, CA 95134
(800) 865-8680

Fujitsu Technologies
50 Rio Robies
San Jose, CA 95134
(800) 866-8680

Gateway Communications (C, H)
2941 Alton Ave.
Irvine, CA 92714
(800) 367-6555

Harris Adacom
16001 Dallas Pkwy.
Dallas, TX 75248
(214) 386-2000

Hewlett-Packard (C, H)
3000 Hannover St.
Palo Alto, CA 94304
Call local HP Sales Office

Hirshmann (C, H)
Industrial Row, P.O. Box 229
Riverdale, NJ 07457
(201) 835-5002

Hughes Lan Systems
1225 Charleston Rd.
Mountain View, CA 94043

ICE
17945 Skypark Circle, Suite G
Irvine, CA 92714
(800) 486-7800

ICL (C, H)
9801 Muirlands Blvd.
Irvine, CA 92718
(714) 458-7282

IMC Networks (C, H)
1342 Bell Ave., Unit 3-E
Tustin, CA 92680
(714) 259-1020

IQ Technologies
22032 23rd Dr. SE
Bothell, WA 98021
(206) 485-8949

Inmac (C, H)
2951 Zanker Ave.
San Jose, CA 95134
(408) 435-1575

Integrated Technologies
128 East 56th St.
New York, NY 10022
(212) 486-7036

Interphase
13800 Seniac
Dallas, TX 75234
(214) 919-9200

JC Information Systems (C, H)
161 Wjotmey Pl.
Fremont, CA 94539
(415)659-8449

Kodiak Technology
2340 Harris Way
San Jose, CA 95131
(408) 954-8070

Lancer Research
557 West Covina Blvd.
San Dimas, CA 91773
(800) 966-8866

Lanking Computer (C, H)
931 Fanwood Ave.
Westfield, NJ 07090
(201) 654-1462

Lanmaster
1401 North 14th St.
Temple, TX 76501
(800) 441-6189

Lans Plus
1648 Geneva Circle
Longmont, CO 80503
(303) 651-7463

Lantana Technology (C, H)
4393 Viewridge Ave., Suite A
San Diego, CA 92123
(619) 565-0798

Longshine (C, H)
2013 North Capitol Ave.
San Jose, CA 95132
(408) 942-1746

MBA Technique
239-4 Kin-Hwa St.
Taipei, Taiwan
(886 2) 341-1260

Multi-Tech Systems (C, H)
2205 Woodale Dr.
Mounds View, MN 55112
(800) 328-9717

Network Interface (C, H)
15109 West 95th St.
Lenexa, KA 66215
(800) 343-2853

Networth (C, H)
8101 Ridgepoint Dr., Suite 107
Irving, TX 75063
(800) 544-5255

Nuvotech (C, H)
2105 Bridgeway, Suite 204
Sausalito, CA 94965
(415) 331-7815

Optical Data Systems
1101 East Arapaho Rd.
Richardson, TX 75081
(214) 234-6400

Plexcom (C, H)
65 Moreland Rd.
Simi Valley, CA 93065
(805) 522-3333

Prime Computer
Prime Park
Natick, MA 01701
(508) 655-8000

Pro-Log
2555 Farden Rd.
Monterey, CA 93940
(800) 538-9570

PureData (C, H)
1740 South i-35
Carrollton, TX 75006
(214) 242-2040

Quam (C, H)
2817 Anthony Ln. South
Minneapolis, MN 91311
(621) 788-1099

Racal-Interlan (C, H)
155 Swanson Rd.
Boxborough, MA 01719
(800) LAN-TALK

RAD Data Communications (C, H)
151 West Passaic St.
Rochelle Park, NJ 07662
(800) 969-4RAD

Retix (C, H)
2844 30th St.
Santa Monica, CA 90405
(213) 399-2200

Samsung
3725 North First St.
San Jose, CA 95134
(408) 434-5482

SBE
2400 Bossp Lane
Concord, CA 94520
(415) 680-7722

Ship Star Associates
36 Woodhill Drive
Newark, DE 19711
(302) 738-7782

Standard Microsystems (C, H)
35 Marcus Blvd.
Hauppauge, NY 11788
(516) 273-3100

Sun Microsystems
2550 Garcia Ave.
Mountain View, CA 94043
(800) 334-7866

Sureman Computer
20270 Carrey Rd.
Walnut Creek, CA 91789
(714) 594-5880

SynOptics (H)
501 East Middlefield Rd.
Mountain View, CA 94043
(800) PRO-8023

TCL (C, H)
41829 Albrae St.
Fremont, CA 94538
(415) 657-3800

Televideo Systems
550 East Brokaw Rd.
San Jose, CA 95161
(800) 835-3228

The NTI Group (C, H)
3265 Kifer Rd.
Santa Clara, CA 95051
(408) 739-2180

Thirdware Computer Products
4747 Northwest 72nd Ave.
Miami, FL 33166
(305) 592-7522

3Com (C, H)
3165 Kifer Road
Santa Clara, CA 95052
(408) 562-6400

Tiara Computer Systems
1091 Shoreline Blvd.
Mountain View, CA 94943
(800) NETIARA

Top Microsystems (C, H)
2005 De La Cruz Blvd., Suite 118
Santa Clara, CA 95050
(800) 827-8721

Tri-Data System
3750 Kifer Rd.
Sunnyvale, CA 94086
(408) 746-2900

Ungermann-Bass, Inc. (C, H)
3900 Freedom Circle
Santa Clara, CA 95054
(800) 999-3236

Unicom Electric (C, H)
11980 Telegraph Rd.
Santa Fe Springs, CA 90670
(800) 346-6668

Vaes Technology
Beemdenstraat 38
NL-6004 CT Weert, Netherlands
(31 4950) 77777

Wang Laboratories
1 Industrial Ave.
Lowell, MA 01851
(800) 225-0654

Western Digital (C, H)
2445 McCabe Way
Irvine, CA 92714
(714) 863-0120

Xinetron (C, H)
2330-B Walsh Ave.
Santa Clara, CA 95051
(800) 345-4415

Xircom
22231 Mulholland Hwy., Suite 114
Woodland Hills, CA 91634

Yamatech Connectivity Solutions
(C, H)
1 Transborder Dr., P.O. Box 800
Champlain, NY 12919
(514) 737-5434

Zenith Electronics (C, H)
1000 Milwaukee Ave., Room 512
Glenview, IL 60025
(708) 391-8919

Zytec Systems
5323 Spring Valley Rd.
Dallas, TX 75240
(214) 991-9966

Note: C, H—Vendor sells both Token Ring card and hub (MAU); otherwise vendor sells only the card.

Token Ring Vendors

Abacus Network Devices (C, H)
1101 Pine Street
St. Paul, MN 55346
(612) 982-5900

Accton Technology (C, H)
2109 O'Toole Ave., Suite S
San Jose, CA 95131
(408) 432-3042

Americable (C, H)
7450 Flying Cloud Dr.
Eden Prairie, MN 55344
(800) 234-2580

Andrew Network Products (C, H)
2771 Plaza del Amo
Torrance, CA 90503
(800) 733-0331

Apple Computer
20525 Mariani Ave.
Cupertino, CA 95014
(408) 996-1010

Asante Technologies
1050 Easy Duane Ave., Suite G
Sunnyvale, CA 94086
(408) 736-3360

Avatar
65 South St.
Hopkinton, ME 01748
(800) 289-2526

Barr Systems
4131 NW 28th Lane
Gainesville, FL 32606
(800) BARRSYS

Cabletron Systems (C, H)
35 Industrial Way
Rochester, NH 03867
(603) 332-9400

Cablexpress (C, H)
500 East Brighton Ave.
Syracuse, NY 13210
(315) 476-3000

Cnet Technology (C, H)
62 Bonaventura Drive
Sunnyvale, CA 95134
(408) 954-8000

Compaq Computer
P.O. Box 692000
Houston, TX 77269
(713) 370-0670

Compex
4065 East La Palma, Unit C
Anaheim, CA 92807
(714) 630-6302

Corvus Systems
160 Great Oaks Blvd.
San Jose, CA 95119
(800) 4-CORVUS

D-Link Systems
5 Musick
Irvine, CA 92718
(714) 455-1688

Dukane Network Integration
2900 Dukane Dr.
St. Charles, IL 60174
(708) 584-2300

Everex Systems (C, H)
48431 Milmont Dr.
Fremont, CA 94538
(415) 498-1111

Fibermux
9310 Topanga Canyon Blvd.
Chatsworth, CA 91311
(818) 709-6000

Gateway Communications (C, H)
2941 Alton Ave.
Irvine, CA 92714
(800) 367-6555

General Technology (C, H)
415 Pineda Court
Melbourne, FL 32940
(800) 274-2733

Harris Adacom (C, H)
16001 Dallas Parkway
Dallas, TX 75248
(214) 386-2000

Hewlett-Packard
3000 Hannover St.
Palo Alto, CA 94304
(call local HP sales office)

h-three Systems
100 Park Drive, P.O. Box 12557
Research Triangle Park, NC 27709
(800) MAC-RING

Hughes Lan Systems
1225 Charleston Road
Mountain View, CA 94043
(415) 966-7300

IBM (C, H)
Armonk, NY 10504
(800) IBM-2468

Inmac (C, H)
2951 Zanker Road
San Jose, CA 95134
(408) 435-1700

Interphase
13800 Seniac
Dallas, TX 75234
(214) 919-9000

IQ Technologies
22032 23rd Dr. SE
Botheli, WA 98021
(800) 227-2817

Lanmaster (C, H)
1401 North 14th Street
Temple, TX 76501

Lantana Technology (C, H)
4393 Viewridge Ave., Suite A
San Diego, CA 92123
(619) 565-6400

Longshine
2013 North Capitol Ave.
San Jose, CA 95132
(408) 942-1746

Madge Networks (C, H)
1580 Oakland Road
San Jose, CA 95131
(800) 876-2343

NCR
1334 South Patterson
Dayton, OH 45479
(513) 445-5340

National Datacomm (C, H)
2/F 28 Industry East 9 Road

Science-Based
Hsinchu, Taiwan 30077
(886 035) 783-966

Netronix
1372 North McDowell Blvd.
Petaluma, CA 94954
(800) 282-2535

Olicom (C, H)
Overoedvej 5
Holte, Denmark 2840 +
(45) 42-33-88

Optical Data Systems (C, H)
1101 East Arapajo Road
Richardson, TX 75081
(214) 234-6400

Photoring
2060 Emery Ave., Suite 254
La Habra, CA 90631
(213) 694-1197

Plexcom (C, H)
65 Moreland Road
Simi Valley, CA 93065
(805) 522-3333

Proteon (C, H)
Two Technology Dr.
Westborough, MA 01581
(508) 898-2000

Puredata (C, H)
1740 South I-35
Carrollton, TX 75006
(214) 242-2040

Racore Computer Products (C, H)
170 Knowles Drive, Suite 170
Los Gatos, CA 95030
(800) 635-1274

RAD Data Communications (C, H)
151 W. Passaic St.
Rochelle Park, NJ 07662
(800) 969-4RAD

SBE
2400 Bisso Lane
Concord, CA 94520
(800) 347-COMM

Simware (offers single-port MAU)
(800) 451-3683

SynOptics (H)
501 East Middlefield Rd.
Mountain View, CA 94043
(800) PRO-8023

Thomas Conrad (C, H)
1908-R Kramer Lane
Austin, TX 78758
(800) 332-8683

3Com (C, H)
3165 Kifer Road
Santa Clara, CA 95052
(408) 562-6400

Tiara Computer Systems (C, H)
1091 Shoreline Blvd.
Mountain View, CA 94043
(800) NETIARA

Tri-Data System
1450 Kifer Road
Sunnyvale, CA 94086
(408) 746-2900

Ungermann-Bass, Inc., (Tandem)
(C, H)
3900 Freedon Circle
Santa Clara, CA 95054
(800) 999-3236

Unicom Electric (C, H)
11980 Telegraph Road, Suite 103
Santa Fe Springs, CA 90670
(800) 346-6668

Vaes Technology

Beemdenstraat 38
NL-6004 CT Weert, Netherlands
(31 4950) 77777

Wang Laboratories
(C, H)
1 Industrial Ave.
Lowell, MA 01851
(800) 225-0654

Western Digital (C, H)
2445 McCabe Way
Irvine, CA 92714
(714) 863-0102

Xircom
22231 Mulholland Hwy., Suite 114
Woodland Hills, CA 91364
(818) 884-8755

Yamatech Connectivity Solutions
(C, H)
1 Transborder Dr., P.O. Box 800
Champlain, NY 12919
(514) 737-5495

Zenith Electronics (C, H)
1000 Milwaukee Ave., Room 512
Glenview, IL 60025
(708) 391-8000

Zytec Systems
5323 Spring Valley Road
Dallas, TX 75240
(214) 991-9966

Bridge Vendors

Advance Computer
  Communications
720 Santa Barbara St.
Santa Barbara, CA 93101
(800) 444-7854

Alantec
101 Hammond Road
Fremont, CA 94539
(800) 727-1050

Allied Telesis
627 National Ave.
Mountain View, CA 94043
(415) 964-2771

Andrew Network
  Products
2771 Plaza del Amo
Torrance, CA 90503
(800) 733-0331

Applitek
100 Brickstone Square
Andover, MA 01810
(800) LAN-CITY

BICC Data Networks
1800 West Park Dr.
Westborough, MA 01581
(800) 4-ISOLAN

Cabletron Systems
35 Industrial Way
Rochester, NH 03867
(603) 332-9400

Canai
59 Iber Road
Stittsville, Ontario, K2S 1E7
(613) 831-8300

Castle Rock Computing
2841 Junction Ave., Suite 118
San Jose, CA 95134
(408) 434-6608

Chipcom
Southborough Office Park
118 Turnpike Road
Southborough, MA 01772
(800) 228-9930

Cisco Systems
1525 O'Brien Dr.
Menlo Park, CA 94025
(800) 553-NETS

Codex
20 Cabot Blvd.
Mansfield, MA 02048
(508) 261-4000

Concord Communications
753 Forest St.
Marlboro, MA 01752
(508) 460-4646

CrossComm
133 East Main St., P.O. Box 699
Marlboro, MA 01752
(800) 388-1200

Cryptall Communications
11110 Wellington Ave.
Cranston, RI 02910
(401) 941-7600

Dataco
Smedeholm, 12-14
Herley, Denmark DK-2730
(45 44) 53-01-00

Develcon Electronics
856 51st St.
Saskatoon, Sask. S7K 5C7
(306) 933-3300

DuPont Electo-Optics
P.O. Box 13625
Research Triangle Park, NC 27709
(800) 881-LAN1

Fairchild Data
250 North Hayden Road
Scottsdale, AZ 85257
(602) 949-1155

Fibercom
3353 Orange Ave. NE
Roanoke, VA 24012
(703) 342-6700

Fibermux
9310 Topanga Canyon Blvd.
Chatsworth, CA 91311
(818) 709-6000

Halley Systems
2730 Orchard Pkwy.
San Jose, CA 95134
(800) 432-2600

Hughes Lan Systems
1225 Charleston Rd.
Mountain View, CA 94043
(415) 966-7300

IBM
Armonk, NY 10504
(800) IBM-2468

ICL
9801 Muirlands Blvd.
Irvine, CA 92718
(714) 458-7282

Infotron Systems
9 North Olney Ave.
Cherry Hill Industrial
Center
Cherry Hill, NJ 08003
(800) 937-1010

Inmac
2951 Zanker Road
San Jose, CA 95134
(408) 435-1700

In-Net
15150 Ave. of Science
San Diego, CA 92128
(800) 283-FDDI

Interlink Computer Sciences
47370 Fremont Blvd.
Fremont, CA 94538
(800) 422-3711

Lanex
7120 Columbia Gateway Dr.
Columbia, MD 21046
(800) 638-5969

Larse
4600 Patrick Henry Dr.
Santa Clara, CA 95052
(408) 988-6600

Micro Bypass Systems
25 Braintree Hill Office Park
Braintree, MA 02184
(617) 843-8260

Microcom
500 River Ridge Road
Norwood, MA 02062
(800) 634-8786

National Datacomm
2/F 28 Industry East 9 Rd.
Science-Based
Hsinchu, Taiwan, 30077
(886 035) 783-966

Netcom Systems
21828 Lassen St., Unit G
Chatsworth, CA 91311
(818) 700-0111

Netronix
1372 North McDowell Blvd.
Oetaluma, CA 94954
(800) 282-2535

Network Application Technology
21040 Homestead Rd.
Cupertino, CA 95014
(408) 733-4530

Newbridge Networks
593 Herndon Parkway
Herndon, VA 22070-5421
(703) 843-5360

Olicom
Overoedvej 5
Holte, Denmark 2840 +
(45) 42-33-88

Plexcom
65 Moreland Road
Simi Valley, CA 93065
(805) 522-3333

Proteon
Two Technology Drive
Westborough, MA 01581
(508) 898-2000

Racal-Interlan
155 Swanson Road
Boxborough, MA 01719
(800) LAN-TALK

RAD DataCommunications
151 West Passaic St.
Rochelle Park, NJ 07662
(800) 969-4RAD

Raycom Systems
220 Gunpark Dr.
Boulder, CO 80301
(800) 288-1620

Retix
2644 30th Street
Santa Monica, CA 90405
(213) 399-2200

St. Clair Systems
2680 Marshfield Dr.
Pittsburgh, PA 15241
(412) 835-5000

SBE
2400 Bisso Lane
Concord, CA 94520
(800) 347-COMM

Symicron
23545 Crenshaw Blvd.
Torrance, CA 90505
(213) 530-2619

Synoptics
501 E. Middlefield Road
Mountain View, CA 94043
(800) PRO-8023

Tektronix/LPCOM
205 Ravendale Drive
Mountain View, CA 94043
(415) 967-5400

3Com
3165 Kifer Road
Santa Clara, CA 95052
(408) 562-6400

Ungermann-Bass, Inc. (Tandem)
3900 Freedom Circle
Santa Clara, CA 95054
(800) 999-3236

Vitalink Communications
6607 Kaiser Drive
Fremont, CA 94555
(800) 767-4533

Wellfleet Communications
18 Crosby Dr.
Bedford, MA 01730
(617) 275-2400

Xydex
330 Codman Hill Road
Boxborough, MA 01719
(800) 338-5316

Zenith Electronics
1000 Milwaukee Ave., Room 512
Glenview, IL 60025
(708) 391-8000

Routers

Advanced Computer
Communications
720 Santa Barbara St.
Santa Barbara, CA 93101
(800) 444-7854

Advanced Systems Concepts
2333 North Lake Ave.
Altadena, CA 91001
(818) 791-0983

Alantec
101 Hammond Ave.
Fremont, CA 94539
(800) 727-1050

Apple Computer
20525 Mariani Ave.
Cupertino, CA 95014
(408) 996-1010

Applitek
100 Brickstone Square
Andover, MA 01810
(800) LAN-CITY

APT Communications
9607 Dr. Perry Road
Ijamsville, MD 21754
(301) 831-1182

AT&T Computer Services
1 Speedwell Ave.
Morristown, NJ 07960
(800) 247-1212

Banyan Systems
120 Flanders Road
Westboro, MA 01581
(800) 2-BANYAN

cisco Systems
1525 O'Brien Dr.
Menlo Park, CA 94025
(800) 553-NETS

CMC (Computer Machinery Corp.)
125 Cremona Drive
Santa Barbara, CA 93117
(800) CMC-8023

Compatible Systems
P.O. Box 17220
Boulder, CO 80308
(800) 356-0283

Computer Network Technology
6655 Wedgewood Road
Maple Grove, MN 55369
(612) 420-4466

CrossComm
133 East Main St.,
P.O. Box 699
Marlboro, MA 01752
(800) 388-1200

Dataco
Smedeholm 12-14
Herley, Denmark DK-2730
(45 44) 53-01-00

Digital Equipment
146 Main St.
Maynard, MA 01754
(508) 493-5111

Eicon Technology
2196 32nd Ave.
Lachine, Quebec H8T 3H7
(514) 631-2592

Fibermux
9310 Orange Topanga Canyon
Blvd.
Chatsworth, CA 91311
(818) 709-6000

Fibronics
25 Communications Way
Independence Park
Hyannis, MA 02601
(800) 327-8526

Frontier Technologies
.3510 North Oakland Ave.
Milwaukee, WI 53211
(414) 964-8689

Gateway Communications
2941 Alton Ave.
Irvine, CA 92714
(800) 367-6555

Hewlett-Packard
3000 Hannover St.
Palo Alto, CA 94304
(call the local sales office)

Hughes Lan Systems
1225 Charleston Rd.
Mountain View, CA 94043
(415) 966-7300

ICL
9801 Muirlands Blvd.
Irvine, CA 92718
(714) 458-7282

Interlink Computer Sciences
47370 Fremont Blvd.
Fremont, CA 94538
(800) 422-3722

Jupiter Technologies
2402 West Beardsley Road
Phoenix, AZ 85027
(602) 869-4828

Lanex
7120 Columbia Gateway Drive
Columbia, MD 21046
(800) 312-2200

Network Resources
2450 Autumnvale Drive
San Jose, CA 95131
(408) 263-8100

Network Systems
7600 Boone Ave. North
Minneapolis, MN 55428
(612) 424-4888

Newbridge Networks
593 Herndon Parkway
Herndon, VA 22070-5421
(703) 843-5360

Niwot Networks
1930 Central Ave., Suite E
Boulder, CO 80301
(303) 444-7765

North Hills Electronics
1 Alexander Place
Glen Cove, NY 11542
(516) 671-5700

Novell
122 East 1700 South
Provo, UT 84606
(800) 453-1267

Open Networks Engineering
2521 Carpenter Road
Ann Arbor, MI 48108
(313) 677-2900

Promptus Communications
207 High Point Ave.
Portsmouth, RI 02871
(401) 683-6100

Proteon
Two Technology Drive
Westboro, MA 01581
(508) 898-2000

Racal-Milgo
1601 North Harrison Parkway
Sunrise, FL 33323
(800) RACAL-55

RAD Data Communications
151 East Passaic St.
Rochelle Park, NJ 07662
(800) 969-4RAD

SBE
2400 Bisso Lane
Concord, CA 94520
(800) 347-COMM

Shiva
155 Second St.
Cambridge, MA 02141

Sigma Network Systems
23 Walkers Brook Drive
Reading, MA 01867
(617) 942-0200

Sun Microsystems
2550 Farcia Ave.
Mountain View, CA 94043
(800) 334-7866

Symicron
23545 Crenshaw Blvd.
Torrance, CA 90505
(213) 530-2619

Telesystems SLW
85 Scarsdale Road, Suite 201
Don Mills, Ontario M3B 2R2
(416) 441-9966

3Com
3165 Kifer Road
Santa Clara, CA 95052
(408) 562-6400

Tri-Data System
1450 Kifer Road
Sunnyvale, CA 94086
(408) 740-2900

Ungermann-Bass, Inc.
3900 Freedom Circle
Santa Clara, CA 95054
(800) 999-3236

Vitalink Communications
6607 Kaiser Drive
Fremont, CA 94555
(800) 767-4533

Wellfleet Communications
15 Crosby Drive
Bedford, MA 01730
(617) 275-2400

Xylogics
53 Third Ave.
Burlington, MA 01719
(800) 225-3317

Zenith Electronics
1000 Milwaukee Ave., Room 512
Glenview, IL 60025
(708) 391-8000

C

IEEE Assigned Address Scheme

Network addresses of LAN vendors are as follows:

Address (first 3 bytes)	Vendor
00000C	Cisco
000020	DIAB (Data Industrier AB)
000022	Visual Technology
00002A	TRW
00005A	S & Koch
000065	Network General
000089	Cayman Systems Gatorbox
000093	Proteon
00009F	Ameristar Technology
0000A9	Network Systems
0000AA	Xerox (Xerox machines)
0000B3	CIMLinc
0000C0	Western Digital
0000DD	Gould
0000E2	Acer Counterpoint
000102	BBN
001700	Kabel
00608C	3Com (new)
00DD00	Ungermann-Bass
00DD01	Ungermann-Bass

020701	Interlan (Unibus, Qbus, Apollo)
020406	BBN (BBN Internal usage, i.e., not registered)
02608C	3Com (IBM PC, Image, Valid)
02CF1F	CMC (Masscomp, Silicon Graphics)
080002	Bridge Communications (3Com)
080003	ACC (Advanced Computer Communication)
080005	Symbolics (Symbolics LISP machines)
080008	BBN (Bolt Beranek and Neuman)
080009	Hewlett-Packard
08000A	Nestar Systems
08000B	Unisys
080010	AT&T
080014	Excelan (BBN Butterfly, Masscomp, Silicon Graphics)
080017	NSC (Network Systems)
08001A	Data General
08001B	Data General
08001E	Apollo
080020	SUN Microsystems
080022	NBI
080025	CDC (Control Data Corporation)
080028	TI (Texas Instruments)
08002b	DEC (Unibus, Q-bus, VAXen, LANbridges, DEUNA, DEQNA, DELUA)
080036	Intergraph (CAE stations)
080039	Spider Systems
080045	Xylogics (?)
080047	Sequent
080049	Univation
08004C	Encore
08004E	BICC
08005A	IBM
080067	Comdesign
080068	Ridge
080069	Silicon Graphics
08006E	Excelan
080075	DDE (Danish Data Elektronik A/S)
08007C	VitaLink (Translan III)
080080	XIOS
080089	Kinetics (Appletalk-Ethernet Interface)

08008B	Pyramid
08008D	XyVision (XyVision machines)
AA0000	Digital Equipment Corporation (obsoleted)
AA0002	Digital Equipment Corporation (obsoleted)
AA0003	DEC (global physical address for some DEC machines)
AA0004	Local logical address for systems running DECnet

The type field in an Ethernet packet (not IEEE 802.3) has a very special meaning (the Ethertype is only for Ethernet packets and not for IEEE 802.3 packets). This field contains entries that are registered with Xerox Corporation. Any company may register an Ethertype with Xerox.

The main purpose of the type field in the Ethernet packets is to allow the software to determine what type of protocol is being used inside the packet. Since packet formats are extremely different from protocol to protocol (e.g., the XNS packet is different from TCP/IP), this is a uniform way for telling the software how to decipher the packet. The type field describes the packet.

The type field starts at byte C right after the source address field in the packet reading from left to right (or 12 in decimal) and continues for 2 bytes. This is also a major difference between IEEE 802.3 and Ethernet packets. As noted in the first entry below, if the type field contains hexadecimal 0000 through 05DC, then the packet is determined to be a IEEE 802.3 packet (05DC in hexadecimal equals 1500 in decimal; 1500 is the largest data field allowed on CSMA/CD networks). Ethernet V2.0 type fields start at 0600 (hex).

Also, the Ethernet type field is a way for a network administrator to determine the protocols that are currently running on the net. Remember from the previous chapters that many protocols are allowed to run simultaneously on the same network. The networking software that runs in each node will determine whether it has the capability to process the packet or simply discard it.

The following table displays the registered Ethertypes, i.e., Ethernet type fields.

Hex	Description
0000–05DC	802.3 Length Field (0-1500)
0200	Xerox PUP (conflicts with IEEE 802.3 Length Field)
0201	Xerox PUP Address Translation (conflicts with IEEE 802.3 Length Field, see 0A01)
0600	Xerox NS IDP*

---

*These protocols use Ethernet broadcast where multicast would be preferable.

0800	DoD Internet Protocol (IP)*†
0801	X.75 Internet
0802	NBS Internet
0803	ECMA Internet
0804	ChaosNET
0805	X.25 Level 3
0806	Address Resolution Protocol (ARP) (for IP and CHAOS)
0807	XNS Compatibility
081C	Symbolics Private
0888	Xyplex
0900	Ungermann-Bass network debugger
0A00	Xerox IEEE 802.3 PUP
0A01	Xerox IEEE 802.3 PUP Address Translation
0BAD	Banyan Systems
1000	Berkeley Trailer Negotiation
1001–100F	Berkeley Trailer encapsulation for IP
1600	VALID system protocol *
5208	BBN Simnet Private ‡
6000	DEC unassigned
6001	DEC Maintenance Operation Protocol (MOP) Dump/Load Assistance
6002	DEC Maintenance Operation Protocol (MOP)
6003	DECNET Phase IV, DNA Routing
6004	DEC Local Area Transport (LAT)
6005	DEC diagnostic protocol
6006	DEC customer protocol
6007	DEC Local Area VaxCluster (LAVC)
6008	DEC unassigned
6009	DEC unassigned
6010–6014	3Com
7000	Ungermann-Bass download
7002	Ungermann-Bass diagnostic loopback
7020–7029	LRT
7030	Proteon
8003	Cronus VLN
8004	Cronus Direct

---

†BBN Buterful Gateway also use 0800 for non-IP, with IP version field = 3.
‡BBN Private Protocols, not registered.

8005	HP Probe protocol
8006	Nestar
8008	AT&T
8010	Excelan
8013	Silicon Graphics diagnostic
8014	Silicon Graphics network games
8015	Silicon Graphics reserved
8016	Silicon Graphics XNS NameServer, bounce server
8019	Apollo DOMAIN
802E	Tyrnshare
802F	Tigan
8035	Reverse Address Resolution Protocol (RARP)
8036	Aeonic Systems
8038	DEC LANBridge Management
8039	DEC unassigned
803A	DEC unassigned
803B	DEC unassigned
803C	DEC unassigned
803D	DEC Ethernet Encryption
803E	DEC unassigned
803F	DEC LAN Traffic Monitor Protocol
8040	DEC unassigned
8041	DEC unassigned
8042	DEC unassigned
8044	Planning Research Co.
8046	AT&T
8047	AT&T
8049	Experdata
805B	Stanford V kernel, experimental
805C	Stanford V kernet, production
805D	Evans and Sutherland
8060	Little Machines
8062	Counterpoint Computers
8065–8066	University of Massachusetts, Amherst
8067	Veeco Integrated Automation
8068	General Dynamics
8069	AT&T
806A	Autophon

806C	ComDesign
806D	Compugraphic
806E–8077	Landmark Graphics
807A	Matra
807B	Dansk Data Elektronik
807C	Merit Internodal
807D–807F	Vitalink
8080	Vitalink TransLAN III Management
8081–8083	Counterpoint Computers
809B	Ethertalk (Appletalk over Ethernet)
809C–809E	Datability
809F	Spider Systems
80A3	Nixdorf Computers
80A4–80B3	Siemens Gammasonics
80C0–80C3	DCA (Digital Communications Associates) Data Exchange Cluster
80C6	Pacer Software
80C7	Applitek
80C8–80CC	Intergraph
80CD–80CE	Harris
80CF–80D2	Taylor Instrument
80D3–80D4	Rosemount
80C3	DCA Data Exchange Cluster
80DD	Varian
80DE–80DF	TRFS (Integrated Solutions Transparent Remote File System)
80ED–80E3	Allen Bradley
80E4–80F0	Datability
80F2	Retix
80F3	Appletalk Address Resolution Protocol (AARP)
80F4	Kinetics
80F7	Apollo
80FF–8103	Wellfleet
8107	Symbolics Private
8108	Symbolics Private
8109	Symbolics Private
8130	Waterloo System
8131	VG Laboratory Systems
8137	Novell (old)
8138	Novell (new)

9000	Loopback (Configuration Test Protocol)
9001	Bridge Communications XNS Systems Management
9002	Bridge Communications TCP/IP Systems Management
FF00	BBN VITAL-LanBridge cace wakeup‡

Multicast addresses are as follows:

Ethernet Address	Type	Usage
01-80-02-00-00-00		Bridge CBPDα (spanning tree)
09-00-02-04-00-01	8080	Vitalink Printer
09-00-02-04-00-02	8080	Vitalink Management
09-00-09-00-00-01	8005	HP Probe
09-00-09-00-00-01	802.2 LLC	HP Probe
09-00-09-00-00-04	8005(?)	HP DTC
09-00-1E-00-00-00	8019(?)	Apollo Domain
09-00-2B-00-00-03	8038	DEC Lanbridge Traffic Monitor (LTM)
09-00-2B-00-00-0F	6004	DEC Local Area Transport (LAT)
09-00-2B-01-00-00	8038	DEC Lanbridge Copy packets
09-00-2B-01-00-01	8038	DEC Lanbridge Hello packets
		1 packet per second, sent by the designated LanBridge
09-00-4E-00-00-02	8137(?)	Novell IPX
09-00-7C-02-00-05	8080(?)	Vitalink Diagnostics
09-00-7C-05-00-01	8080(?)	Vitalink Gateway(?)
0D-1E-15-BA-DD-06	unknown	HP
AB-00-00-01-00-00	6001	DEC Maintenance Operation Protocol (MOP)
		Dump/Load Assistance
AB-00-00-02-00-00	6002	DEC Maintenance Operation Protocol (MOP)
		Remote Console
		1 system ID packet every 8–10 minutes by every:
		DEC LanBridge
		DEC DEUNA interface
		DEC DELUA interface
		DEC DEQNA interface (in certain mode)
AB-00-00-03-00-00	6003	DEC Phase IV end node Hello Packets
		1 packet every 15 seconds, sent by each DECNET host
AB-00-00-04-00-00	6003	DECNET Phase IV Router Hello packets
		1 packet every 15 s, sent by the DECNET router
AB-00-00-05-00-00 thru' AB-00-03-FF-FF-FF	unknown	Reserved DEC
AB-00-03-00-00-00	6004	DEC Local Area Transport (Old)
AB-00-04-01-xx-yy	6007	DEC Local Area VAX cluster groups
CF-00-00-00-00-00	9000	Ethernet Configuration Test protocol (Loopback)

Broadcast addresses are as follows:

Ethernet Address	Type	Usage

FF-FF-FF-FF-FF-FF	0600	XNS packets, Hello or gateway search
		6 packets every 15 seconds, per XNS station
	0800	IP
	0804	CHAOS
	0806	ARP (Address Resolution Protocol)
	OBAD	Banyan
	1600	VALID packet, Hello or gateway search
		1 packet every 30 seconds, per VALID station
	8035	RARP (Reverse ARP)
	807C	Merit Internodal (INP)
	809B	Ethertalk

Network Management

The following provides an introduction to a public domain network management standard (SNMP). Network management is a collection of tasks and responsibilities involved in maintaining a network.

Since this book is based on standards, it would be only proper to introduce a standard (or simple) network management protocol (SNMP) currently followed by over 44 networking vendors with many more indicating that they will also comply.

Network management should be broken down into five distinct categories:

1. *Account Management*—gathers information on which users or departments are employing which network resources.

2. *Fault management*—includes troubleshooting, finding and correcting failed or damaged components, monitoring equipment for early problem indicators, and tracking down distributed problems.

3. *Security*—includes authorization, access control, data encrypting, and management of encrypting keys.

4. *Configuration management*—tracks hardware and software information. Included with this is administration tasks, such as day-to-day monitoring and maintenance of the current physical and logical state of the network, as well as recognition and registration of applications and services on the network.

5. *Performance*—the monitoring of traffic on the network.

At this time, most installed network management platforms are completely proprietary, with each vendor stating that their platform is the best. While this may be true, most network equipment that is currently installed does not have only one vendor's name on it. Most users of today are using a computer supplied by one vendor, a cable plant that was installed by another vendor, LAN cards by another vendor, network operating systems (NOSs) by another vendor, and finally some mainframes by yet another company. If each of these vendors had a proprietary network management system in place, you would potentially not only have five network management platforms that you would have to run but would also be faced with an extreme and unnecessary expense of user training and equipment upkeep.

There is a network management standard today that most vendors are currently supporting. It is limited in functions but provides for vendor-independent expansion. It is called *Simple Network Management Protocol.*

Simple network management protocol (SNMP) was developed from the Department of Defense's Internet (formerly known as the ARPAnet). This Internet has grown to hundreds of networks that interconnect hundreds of thousands of hosts that are interconnected via an unknown number of gateways, routers, brouters, and equipment from a multitude of vendors.

Specifically, SNMP was developed by a group known as the Internet Engineering Task Force (IETF). This group is a large open community of individuals including network designers, operators, vendors, and researchers. This group is involved primarily with the evolution of the Internet Protocol Architecture (TCP/IP).

Some of these vendors who support SNMP are big names in the networking area: IBM, 3Com, Synoptics, and Ungermann-Bass. Even protocol analyzer companies are signing on: Network General (Sniffer) and Spider Systems (Spider Analyzer).

Key to its name is simplicity. SNMP has only three elements: The Manager, The Agent, and the Management Information Base (MIB). These are defined in the Request for Comments (RFCs) 1155, 1156, and 1157 or 1158 as follows (they may be ordered through the Network Information Center by calling 1-800-235-3155. There is a small charge for each of the RFC's.

RFC 1155 (formerly RFC 1065)—defines the structure of management information for SNMP implementations, including the naming and identification of managed objects.

RFC 1156 (formerly RFC 1066)—defines the groups of managed objects in the Management Information Base (MIB).

RFC 1157 (formerly RFC 1067)—defines the protocol used between SNMP application programs.

RFC 1158 (formerly 1066)—Management Information Base II. Expands the objects of MIB-1 from 140 to 171. This MIB is fully backward-compatible with the first MIB (MIB-1).

The SNMP is a simple request-response protocol which contains a manager and an agent. The agent is usually located on a network station. With one exception, the agent is passive and will perform operations only under the direction of a manager. The manager accomplishes this by polling the agent. With the exception of the trap state, the agent will respond only when the manager polls the device. This agent gathers and maintains certain information about its own internal workings and about the network.

This agent gathers and maintains certain information about its own internal workings and about the network. The type of information provided is contained in the MIB.

The information is acquired from this network node through the manager. The manager queries the network node for the information. The pools are submitted through a protocol known as User Datagram Protocol (UDP). This is a connectionless protocol, meaning that the manager and the agent do not have to first establish a reliable session before data is to be transmitted. Information is passed between the manager and agent via datagrams.

The manager performs only five operations:

1. The GetRequest PDU (protocol data units, a packet) requests an agent to return attribute values for a list of managed objects.

2. The GetNextRequest PDU is used to traverse a table of objects. Since the object attributes are stored in lexicographical order, the result of the previous GetNextRequest PDU can be used as an argument in a subsequent GetNextRequest. In this way a manager can go through a variable-length table until it has extracted all the information for the same types of objects.

3. The GetResponse PDU returns attribute values for the selected objects or error indications for such conditions as invalid object name or a nonexistent object.

4. The SetRequest is used to change the attribute values of selected objects.

5. The Trap PDU is used by the agent on its own. Traps are used to report certain conditions and changes of state to the managing process. The conditions are cold-start and warm-start ("cold-start" means a reinitialization where the configuration information is no longer valid. Link-up and link-down traps are used to indicate the status of attached communications facilities. The authentication failure trap is used when the system has detected an attempt to access resources by unauthorized parties. The EGP (exterior gateway

protocol) neighbor trap is used when external gateways detect the loss of a neighboring EGP system (routers). The enterprise-specific trap is left for enterprise-specific conditions and extensions. This simple protocol allows a wide range of management capabilities that can be scaled for both small- and large-scale Internet environments.

The operations performed are simple. The agent located on the network station continually gathers information and stores it in memory. To acquire the information, a management station simply queries the agent by sending a packet to it requesting specific information (GetRequestPDU). The agent will respond to this packet with a response packet (GetResponsePDU). The management station will take this information and store it; this information is used to display to the network manager the details of the network (the display will be vendor-independent). A general distinction is as follows:

Management station—executes the management applications that are used to poll agents on the network. The management station is tasked with providing the information in readable format.

Managed element—this is an intelligent device which contains an agent. The agents are tasked with performing any of the functions that the management station requests.

The objects which contain information that the management station may request is stored in the MIB. There is a standard set of inputs for this MIB. There is also something known as *MIB extensions*.

Since the architects of this standard could not build the standard for every vendor's implementation of network hardware and software, they provided a way for vendors to extend the MIB for their particular network devices. This enables vendors to be compatible with the standard and also publish their extensions to the MIB for their particular device.

The last implementation that SNMP provides is authentication. Since SNMP is an open standard, all information on this standard is publicly available. Authentication is used for security purposes. This prevents unauthorized access to the information contained in the agents or manager.

SNMP defines a community to be used. This community specifies the relationship between an SNMP agent and one or more SNMP managers. All members of a given community are given the same access privileges. The agent can be configured so that only managers that are members of this community can send requests and receive responses.

This security is extremely weak. For example, the community name is embedded in every SNMP packet that traverses the network. The community name is either encoded nor encrypted. Once the community name is known, object value may be read from or written to.

Despite its shortcoming, the best attribute for this management standard is compatibility. For example, if you have three vendors' network equipment installed at your site, you will not have to have three network management stations to manage the three devices. If all the devices follow the SNMP standard, you can purchase one network management station to manage all the devices. This allows companies to reduce the training and equipment costs.

For more information please refer to *The Simple Book* by Marshall T. Rose, Prentice-Hall, Englewood Cliffs, N.J., 1991 or *Internetworking with TCP/IP*, by Douglas Comer, vol. I, 2d ed., Prentice-Hall, Englewood Cliffs, N.J., 1991.

E

The Standards Committees

There are many standards represented today for data communications. But who are these parties that propose and recommend these standards? Surprisingly, there are only a few standards committees today that propose and recommend data communications standards. When reading the following paragraphs, please be reminded that these standards committees do not only recommend standards for the data communications industry but are also actively involved in producing many standards for many different environments.

Standards allow a specification to be brought to the public to allow a multivendor environment. Standards assist companies that purchase data communications equipment to realize the full potential of their investment. Companies today have different needs for their communication environment, which leads to a multivendor communication environment. Standards alleviate the problems companies find in a multivendor solution. These standards allow companies to communicate anything, anywhere, and anytime.

Purchasing proprietary (that based on no national or international standard) data communications equipment has grave complications for any company, large or small. A company may purchase this equipment and either have problems with it, or the equipment might not perform as stated, or worse, the company from which the equipment was purchased might no longer exist. In each case, a company will be forced to retrofit all the equipment—a costly and unnecessary expense.

With the maturing of the LAN environment, standards have set in, and most networking vendors are adhering to them. It was long believed that adherence to standards could and would eliminate companies. This has turned out to be a fallacy. In fact, standards have produced stiffer competition among LAN vendors, which has produced not only better equipment but more options for the customer. For example, 3Com is now offering a restricted lifetime warranty on their entire line of EtherLink network interface cards. Who has benefited the most from the adoption and adherence to standards? Everyone! Standards have generated competition, which has produced high-quality products, which has produced better manufacturing—and finally, but most importantly, standards have forced companies to reduce prices whenever possible!

How do you decipher the who, what, where, how, and so forth of standards? The following paragraphs attempt to enlighten you on how standards are developed, how to recognize a standard, and which to follow.

Four types of networking standards are in use today: emerging standards, industry standards, de facto standards, and committee standards. There are some standards that did not start out to be a standard, for example, Netbios.

Let's examine the standards bodies and how they interoperate. Hang on, this is no easy chore but is very worthwhile!!!! All ISO standards and other international standards come from the International Standards Organization (ISO), the Consultive Committee for International Telephone and Telegraph (CCITT), and the Institute for Electrical and Electronics Engineers (IEEE).

The ISO is headquartered in Geneva, Switzerland. This international standards organization coordinates the efforts of national standards organizations such as the American National Standards Institute (ANSI) and the British Standard Institute (BSI). The Institute of Electrical and Electronics Engineers (IEEE) is closely affiliated with ANSI and have made valuable contributions and recommendations in the development of LAN standards. These IEEE standards are developed by the 802 committees, and all LAN vendors support these standards. (These IEEE standards and their definitions are discussed in a moment.) The ISO has a broad responsibility for recommending standards for the international and national communications. These recommendations are standardized through the CCITT.

How do you determine which standards are specific for which organization or institute? The following will explain this. An ISO International Standard document is prefixed by the three letters ISO, followed by an index number depicting its origin (e.g., ISOx, where x is an integer number). There is an extensive proposal process which may take up to a few years to accomplish. The initial proposal is called a *Draft Proposal* (DP), then after a few committee meetings, the revised draft is called a *Draft International Standard* (DIS). As the DIS undergoes further revisions and addenda are added, prefixes are added, such as PDAD, DAD, and AD. No matter, these will always refer to the DIS and its number.

The CCITT is also headquartered in Geneva, Switzerland, and is a division of the International Telecommunications Union (ITU), which reports to the United Nations Organization (the CCITT was set up soon after the founding of the United Nations in 1945). The CCITT's primary design was to recommend standards for international adoption. The principal members of the CCITT are from the post, telegraph, and telephone authorities (PT&Ts) of member countries. Individual companies can belong to the CCITT, although they are cast as nonvoting members. The CCITT is responsible for the wide area aspects of national and international communications, publishing quadrennial recommendations. Each new book publishes recommendations for new facilities, and confirms or updates already existing recommendations. CCITT recommendations are distinguished by a prefix X to signify data communications services. The date that follows the specification [e.g., X.400 (1984) and X.400 (1988)] refers to the edition of the recommendation or update.

Well, that's the ISO and CCITT. How about the Institute for Electrical and Electronics Engineers (IEEE)? The following paragraphs will explain their role and association with the above-mentioned standards committees.

The standards that pertain to the Institute of Electrical and Electronics Engineers are developed groups within the IEEE Societies known as the Technical Committees and the Standards Coordinating Committees of the IEEE Standards Board. Who makes up all the members and nonmembers that institute the IEEE standards? Almost anyone. A standard that is developed from the IEEE represents a general consensus from not only members of the IEEE Society but also from those individuals and companies who have expressed an interest in participating. Participating in the IEEE is strictly voluntary. Members and nonmembers are not compensated for their participation.

The IEEE standards are preceded with IEEE and a number. The number that follows this is the working group within the IEEE, for example, IEEE 802. There can also be another number attached, for example, IEEE 802.3, which specifies a subgroup under the working group.

The IEEE 802 committee has the task of defining standards for LANs. The subcommittee x is defined with each individual standard. For example, the IEEE 802.3 committee is tasked with creating the IEEE version of the Ethernet standard.

IEEE Standards are reviewed at least once every 5 years. Additional comments for revisions may be addressed to the IEEE by anyone who is willing to submit one. Of course, this response must be in the appropriate format stated by the IEEE.

IEEE Standards working groups are listed by number as follows.

IEEE 802.0	Executive Committee
IEEE 802.1	High-Level Interface (HLI) Working Group
IEEE 802.1a, b	Network Management Working Group
IEEE 802.1d	Bridging Working Group
IEEE 802.2	Logical Link Control Working Group
IEEE 802.3	CSMA/CD Working Group
IEEE 802.4	Token Bus Working Group
IEEE 802.5	Token Ring Working Group
IEEE 802.6	Metropolitan Area Network (MAN) Working Group
IEEE 802.7	Broadband Technical Advisory Group
IEEE 802.8	Fiber-Optic Technical Advisory Group
IEEE 802.9	Integrated Voice and Data LAN Working Group
IEEE 802.10	Standard for Interoperable LAN Security Working Group

Hexadecimal and Binary Number Systems

The purpose of this appendix is to introduce you to different numbering systems that are in use with LANs. The numbering system of hexadecimal is used for Token Ring and Ethernet addresses. Since most people understand the decimal numbering system, the purpose of this appendix is to show you that a hexadecimal number may be translated to decimal.

There are two types of numbering systems in use for computer systems today: binary and hexadecimal. Binary is the numbering system that computers use. When information is transferred or a CPU reads its instructions, it is all accomplished with the binary numbering system. Hexadecimal is the numbering system that enables the binary numbering system to be easily readable. The purpose of this chapter is to enable you to understand that an Ethernet or Token Ring address can be translated into the decimal numbering system. This will show you an Ethernet address and translate it to the decimal numbering system.

But to understand how to translate between all those numbering systems, we must have a good understanding of how the decimal numbering system works. All of us should know the decimal numbering system, but let's take a quick review and actually decipher the decimal numbering system.

The decimal numbering system is based on 10 numbers: 0, 1, 2, 3, 4, 5, 6, 7, 8, and 9. Each position in a decimal number actually represents a power 10. The value of the first place is 1 or 10^0, the value for the second position is 10 or 10^1, the value for the third position is 100 or 10^2, the value for the fourth position is 10^3 or 1000, and so on. So the decimal number 4096 is actually 4 times 1000, plus

0 times 100, plus 9 times 10, plus 6 times 1. Multiplying and adding the numbers together represent the decimal number 4096. The following table further illustrates this process:

Decimal	4	0	9	6
Values	1000	100	10	1
Powers	10^3	10^2	10^1	10^0
	$10 \times 10 \times 10$	10×10	10×1	1
	4×1000 +	0×100 +	9×10 +	$6 \times 1 = 4096$

Binary Numbering System

The binary number system is not based on 10 numbers, only 2: specifically, 0 and 1. In the binary (meaning 2) number system the same rules apply with the exception that powers of two are represented for the position and there are only two numbers, 0 and 1. You can read a binary number as well as a decimal number (once you are used to the conversion).

We use the base of 2 for the multiplier. For example, now the value of the first position is 2^0 or 2^1, the value of a second position is 2^1 or 2^2, the value of the third position is 2^2 or 2^4, the value of the fourth position is 2^3 or 2^8, and so on. So the number 1001 is actually 1 times 8, plus 0 times 4, plus 2 times 0, plus 1 times 1, giving the decimal number of 9. The result of 9 is found by simply multiplying the digits by the values and adding the results as follows:

Binary	1	0	0	1
Values	8	4	2	1
Powers	2^3	2^2	2^1	2^0
	$2 \times 2 \times 2$	2×2	2	1
	1×8 +	0×4 +	0×2 +	$1 \times 1 = $ decimal 9

Simple enough. Using this simple method, we can see that with four binary positions we can represent a decimal number as high as 15. How? If every position is filled by the highest allowable number 1 and converting the binary number 1111 is 8 + 4 + 2 + 1 = 15.

As you should be able to see, reading a large binary number could be a very tedious job. Numbers in binary are usually read only by the computer. Humans can read the binary numbers that a computer reads in hexadecimal. Hexadecimal is the numbering system used for Ethernet and Token Ring addressing.

Hexadecimal Numbering System

Hexadecimal can represent 16 numbers the same way decimal can represent 10 numbers (0-9) and binary can represent 2 (0 and 1) numbers per position.

When we count in hex, the numbers start at 0 and continue to F: 0, 1, 2, 3, 4, 5, 6, 7, 8, 9, A, B, C, D, E, F. Numbers 0 to 9 should seem obvious enough, but what do the letters A-F represent? In hexadecimal to decimal: A represents 10, B represents 11, C represents 12, D represents 13, E represents 14, and F represents 15. Let's take a hexadecimal number and break it down. Let's break down the hex number FF:

HEX	F	F
Values	16	1
Powers	16^1	16^0
	16×1	1
	$F \times 16$ + $F \times 1 = 255$ decimal	

Let's try another one: FFD

HEX	F	F	D
Values	256	16	1
Powers	16^2	16^1	16^0
	16×16	16	1
	$F \times 256$ +	$F \times 16$ +	$D \times 1 = 4093$ decimal

We should be able to see now that the Ethernet and Token Ring address is one giant decimal number compressed into an easily readable formal known as hexadecimal. To place decimal numbers in a packet would be futile, especially since most computers can understand only binary. So, instead of reading binary, we use hexadecimal, which is why you will always see Ethernet and Token Ring addressing in hexadecimal.

For obvious reasons, representing LAN addresses using decimal is not implemented. You should also see that allowing 48 bits (6 bytes, as there are 8 bits per byte, yielding 6 bytes) for the source and destination addresses allow for a seemingly endless possibility of LAN addressing. Let's take a closer look.

First, for bits and bytes, we know that the first 3 bytes are always the same on a per vendor basis. This allows the last 3 bytes for the vendor's unique station addresses. The largest number that these 3 bytes can represent is FF FF FF, or:

	Byte 2		Byte 1		Byte 0
HEX	F	F	F	F	F	F
Powers	16^5	16^4	16^3	16^2	16^1	16^0
Value	1,048,576	65,536	4096	256	16	1
	$F \times 1,048,576 + F \times 65,536 + F \times 4096 + F \times 256 + F \times 15 + F = 16,777,215$ decimal					

The following table should be used as a reference to help you translate the different numbering systems up to 255 decimal.

Decimal	Hexadecimal	Binary
0	0	0
1	1	0001
2	2	0010
3	3	0011
4	4	0100
5	5	0101
6	6	0110
7	7	0111
8	8	1000
9	9	1001
10	A	1010
11	B	1011
12	C	1100
13	D	1101
14	E	1110
15	F	1111
16	10	0001 0000
17	11	0001 0001
18	12	0001 0010
19	13	0001 0011
20	14	0001 0100
21	15	0001 0101
22	16	0001 0110
23	17	0001 0111
24	18	0001 1000
25	19	0001 1001
26	1A	0001 1010
27	1B	0001 1011
28	1C	0001 1100
29	1D	0001 1101

(Continued)

Decimal	Hexadecimal	Binary
30	1E	0001 1110
31	1F	0001 1111
32	20	0010 0000
33	21	0010 0001
34	22	0010 0010
35	23	0010 0011
36	24	0010 0100
37	25	0010 0101
38	26	0010 0110
39	27	0010 0111
40	28	0010 1000
41	29	0010 1001
42	2A	0010 1010
43	2B	0010 1011
44	2C	0010 1100
45	2D	0010 1101
46	2E	0010 1110
47	2F	0010 1111
48	30	0011 0000
49	31	0011 0001
50	32	0011 0010
51	33	0011 0011
52	34	0011 0100
53	35	0011 0101
54	36	0011 0110
55	37	0011 0111
56	38	0011 1000
57	39	0011 1001
58	3A	0011 1010
59	3B	0011 1011
60	3C	0011 1100
61	3D	0011 1101
62	3E	0011 1110
63	3F	0011 1111
64	40	0100 0000
65	41	0100 0001
66	42	0100 0010
67	43	0100 0011
68	44	0100 0100
69	45	0100 0101
70	46	0100 0110
71	47	0100 0111
72	48	0100 1000
73	49	0100 1001
74	4A	0100 1010
75	4B	0100 1011
76	4C	0100 1100
77	4D	0100 1101
78	4E	0100 1110
79	4F	0100 1111
80	50	0101 0000
81	51	0101 0001

Decimal	Hexadecimal	Binary
82	52	0101 0010
83	53	0101 0011
84	54	0101 0100
85	55	0101 0101
86	56	0101 0110
87	57	0101 0111
88	58	0101 1000
89	59	0101 1001
90	5A	0101 1010
91	5B	0101 1011
92	5C	0101 1100
93	5D	0101 1101
94	5E	0101 1110
95	5F	0101 1111
96	60	0110 0000
97	61	0110 0001
98	62	0110 0010
99	63	0110 0011
100	64	0110 0100
101	65	0110 0101
102	66	0110 0110
103	67	0110 0111
104	68	0110 1000
105	69	0110 1001
106	6A	0110 1010
107	6B	0110 1011
108	6C	0110 1100
109	6D	0110 1101
110	6E	0110 1110
111	6F	0110 1111
112	70	0111 0000
113	71	0111 0001
114	72	0111 0010
115	73	0111 0011
116	74	0111 0100
117	75	0111 0101
118	76	0111 0110
119	77	0111 0111
120	78	0111 1000
121	79	0111 1001
122	7A	0111 1010
123	7B	0111 1011
124	7C	0111 1100
125	7D	0111 1101
126	7E	0111 1110
127	7F	0111 1111
128	80	1000 0000
129	81	1000 0001
130	82	1000 0010
131	83	1000 0011
132	84	1000 0100

(Continued)

Decimal	Hexadecimal	Binary
133	85	1000 0101
134	86	1000 0110
135	87	1000 0111
136	88	1000 1000
137	89	1000 1001
138	8A	1000 1010
139	8B	1000 1011
140	8C	1000 1100
141	8D	1000 1101
142	8E	1000 1110
143	8F	1000 1111
144	90	1001 0000
145	91	1001 0001
146	92	1001 0010
147	93	1001 0011
148	94	1001 0100
149	95	1001 0101
150	96	1001 0110
151	97	1001 0111
152	98	1001 1000
153	99	1001 1001
154	9A	1001 1010
155	9B	1001 1011
156	9C	1001 1100
157	9D	1001 1101
158	9E	1001 1110
159	9F	1001 1111
160	A0	1010 0000
161	A1	1010 0001
162	A2	1010 0010
163	A3	1010 0011
164	A4	1010 0100
165	A5	1010 0101
166	A6	1010 0110
167	A7	1010 0111
168	A8	1010 1000
169	A9	1010 1001
170	AA	1010 1010
171	AB	1010 1011
172	AC	1010 1100
173	AD	1010 1101
174	AE	1010 1110
175	AF	1010 1111
176	B0	1011 0000
177	B1	1011 0001
178	B2	1011 0010
179	B3	1011 0011
180	B4	1011 0100
181	B5	1011 0101
182	B6	1011 0110
183	B7	1011 0111

Decimal	Hexadecimal	Binary
184	B8	1011 1000
185	B9	1011 1001
186	BA	1011 1010
187	BB	1011 1011
188	BC	1011 1100
189	BD	1011 1101
190	BE	1011 1110
191	BF	1011 1111
192	C0	1100 0000
193	C1	1100 0001
194	C2	1100 0010
195	C3	1100 0011
196	C4	1100 0100
197	C5	1100 0101
198	C6	1100 0110
199	C7	1100 0111
200	C8	1100 1000
201	C9	1100 1001
202	CA	1100 1010
203	CB	1100 1011
204	CC	1100 1100
205	CD	1100 1101
206	CE	1100 1110
207	CF	1100 1111
208	D0	1101 0000
209	D1	1101 0001
210	D2	1101 0010
211	D3	1101 0011
212	D4	1101 0100
213	D5	1101 0101
214	D6	1101 0110
215	D7	1101 0111
216	D8	1101 1000
217	D9	1101 1001
218	DA	1101 1010
219	DB	1101 1011
220	DC	1101 1100
221	DD	1101 1101
222	DE	1101 1110
223	DF	1101 1111
224	E0	1110 0000
225	E1	1110 0001
226	E2	1110 0010
227	E3	1110 0011
228	E4	1110 0100
229	E5	1110 0101
230	E6	1110 0110
231	E7	1110 0111
232	E8	1110 1000
233	E9	1110 1001

(Continued)

Decimal	Hexadecimal	Binary
234	EA	1110 1010
235	EB	1110 1011
236	EC	1110 1100
237	ED	1110 1101
238	EE	1110 1110
239	EF	1110 1111
240	F0	1111 0000
241	F1	1111 0001
242	F2	1111 0010
243	F3	1111 0011
244	F4	1111 0100
245	F5	1111 0101
246	F6	1111 0110
247	F7	1111 0111
248	F8	1111 1000
249	F9	1111 1001
250	FA	1111 1010
251	FB	1111 1011
252	FC	1111 1100
253	FD	1111 1101
254	FE	1111 1110
255	FF	1111 1111

G

Communication Servers

Most of this book has covered the direct attachment of devices (personal computers, hosts, etc.) to Ethernet and Token Ring networks. A problem arises when a device does not support a direct network attachment. Asynchronous terminals such as VT100s®, 200s, and 300s, asynchronous modems and serial printers, all do not support an attachment to any kind of network. During the

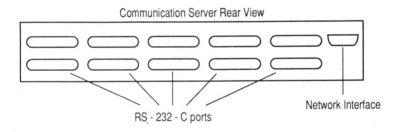

Communication Server Rear View

RS - 232 - C ports

Network Interface

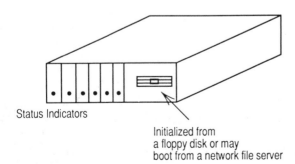

Status Indicators

Initialized from
a floppy disk or may
boot from a network file server

Figure G.1 Anatomy of a communication server.

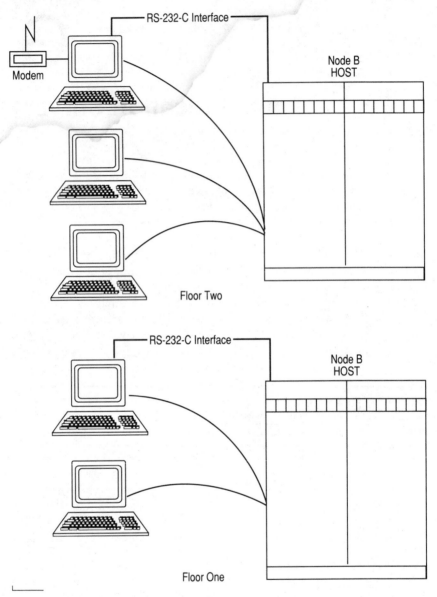

Figure G.2   Terminal-host connection without comm servers.

early 1980s when LANs were entering the commercial world, most computer devices did not directly support networks.

Throughout the 1960s and 1970s, as businesses expanded, the computer became a necessity in most businesses. For the data communications department of any business (with the exception of IBM cus-

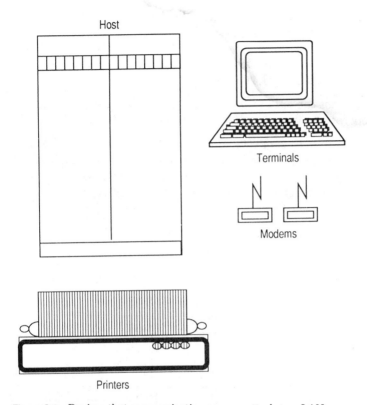

Host

Terminals

Modems

Printers

Figure G.3   Devices that communication servers attach to a LAN.

tomers), most employed one of the oldest and most prevalent standards known as the RS-232-C specification for connection of serial devices. This specification is a standard from the Electronic Industries Association (EIA). Terminals were directly connected to hosts using this standard. RS-232-C devices, such as terminals, modems, and printers, constituted a major part of the investment that businesses had made in data processing equipment. Most businesses, large and small, have spent billions of dollars acquiring equipment with this type of interface. Refer to Fig. G.2.

During this time, each connection to the host required a cable to be run to each terminal. This represented two problems:

1. *Cost:*   This tends to be a major consideration in installing and maintaining a computer system. A large percentage of the cost of installing a large network can be expenditure for labor for cable companies pulling cable.

2. *Multiple-host access:*   What if the user wanted to access multiple hosts or decided to move the business office from one floor to another? Before communication servers and LANs, new cable was

generally pulled to the new location. For accessing multiple hosts, a business would commonly use A-B switches, or pull multiple cables to the same terminal (a very high cost) or might use a digital private branch exchange (DPBX, to be explained at the end of this appendix; see also Fig. G.4).

Cable cost was not the only reason for businesses to incorporate LANs into their operation. Two other factors are also involved:

1. Modems used to be connected directly to the user's terminal or PC. Or even worse, the company would not buy all their personnel a modem, and special terminals were set up so that users had to walk over to the terminal to use the modem. This represented a major expense for com-

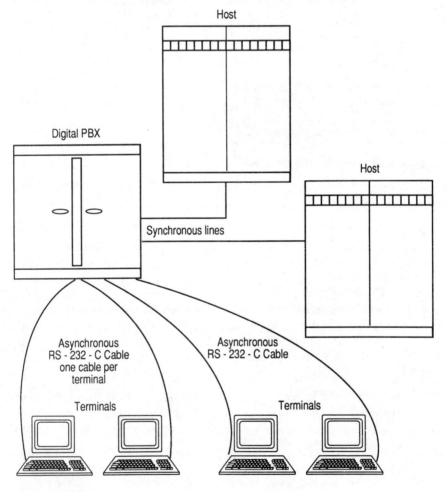

Figure G.4 DPBX connections.

panies in that only one user had access to the modem at a time and a company with many employees had to buy many modems.

2. Printers were usually located within 50 ft of the host. (This is because the specification for connection of asynchronous devices states that a connection run between the two devices shall be no more than 50 ft end to end; parallel printers were located within 25 ft.) This presented many problems for users. A user would submit a print job to the host, then would have to leave the office, walk down to the computer room, and pick up the printout. While the low cost of dot-matrix printers have eliminated some of these problems, a majority of the printers are still connected directly to the host computer.

Commercial businesses were enthused by LANs, but all the equipment mentioned above had to be able to connect to the LAN. Hence, there was a special device developed for those pieces of equipment that allowed a connection to a network. It is known as a *communication server* (also known as terminal server or comm server). Communication servers probably represent one of the oldest techniques used to connect any device to a network. Their original purpose was to connect asynchronous hosts and terminals across a LAN.

A communication server can be regarded as an asynchronous multiplexor. On one end of the communication server are RS-232-C ports that connect to asynchronous devices such as terminals, modems, printers, hosts, and even a personal computer's comm ports. On the other end is the attachment interface to the network (Ethernet or Token Ring). Refer to Fig. G.1.

Some still consider this device as a gateway. Communication servers are not gateways, for gateways take input from one protocol and convert the input into another form for output. Conversely, a communication server takes the input data, encapsulates (does not convert) it into a network packet, and then sends that packet to the network. When the packet arrives at the destination device, the destination device strips the network information off the packet and submits the data to the receiving device in its original form.

In the early 1980s, communication servers were also known as "milking machines." Looking at Fig. G.5, we see that the connection from the host to the comm server does resemble a milking machine. While a connection to a host such as this had many advantages early on, today it represents many disadvantages, particularly hardware interrupts on the host device. RS-232-C devices interrupt the host processor via a hardware interrupt. Many hardware interrupts on a mini or mainframe host will slowly consume many of the host's processing cycles, thereby reducing the efficiency of the host.

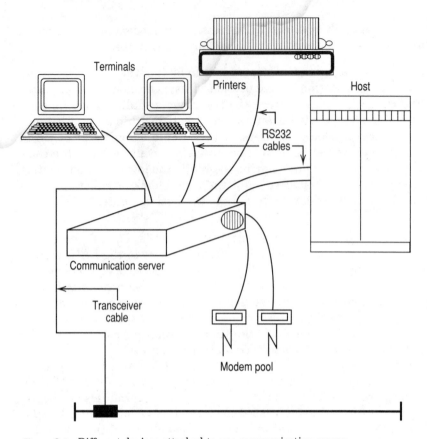

Figure G.5   Different devices attached to one communication server.

Communication servers today are still attaching to hosts, terminals, printers, and other serial devices, but their use is taking a different turn. With most terminals being replaced by personal computers, and mini and mainframe computers having built-in network controllers, communication servers are providing communications connectivity in a different manner. They are being used in three basic areas. One predominant use for them is for modem and printer pools.

Modem pools are groups of modems clustered together for use by anyone who has access to the comm server. By connecting modems directly to a communication server, any user with access to the network may have access to one of the modems (provided that no user has already established a connection to that modem port on the communication server). Instead of a company buying one modem for each user on the network, they can buy a few modems, connect them to a communication server, and then have the users access the modems through the network. This is extremely efficient, for few modems were used 100 percent of the time. With a connection to the comm server, modems are now accessed by multiple users, thereby increasing the use of the modem. Even if the modem port on the communication server is busy, most networking companies have developed their servers to queue requests to a particular communication server port (see Fig. G.6).

For printers, communication servers can provide remote printing capabilities. For example, (referring to Fig. G.7) a communication server may be connected to the host computer. Another communication server may be placed somewhere on the network. This communication server may have a printer attached to it. A virtual circuit (session) will be established between the two servers. The print job that is submitted on the host is printed to the communication server and that server will send the data over the network to the communication server with the printer attached.

Some hosts with an internal network controller (direct attachment

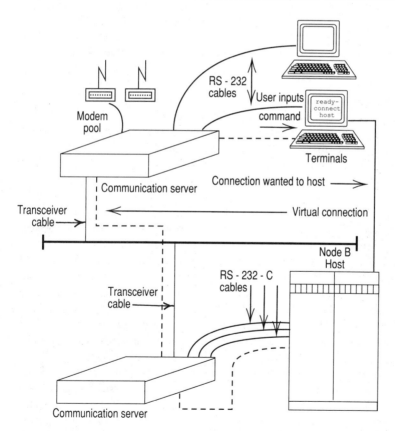

Figure G.6   Terminal-host session establishment.

to the LAN) have the capability to send the data over the network without the communication server attached to it.

Let's explore exactly how communication servers work. Communication servers are devices that allow any piece of data communications equipment supporting the RS-232-C standard (terminals, modems, printers, hosts, and personal computers) to attach to a network.

Let's say you are sitting at a terminal device (also known as your local device) and you wish to connect to some resource out on the network, say, a host (also known as the remote device). It does not matter what the operating system of the remote host is running. Communication servers have their own internal operating system that enables the data that you transfer from your local device to the remote device to look the same. Referring to Figs. G.6 and G.7, you first issue some type of connect command. This command enables the communication server to connect to a remote device.

Once the connection is made between the local and remote devices, the user will never know that they are running through a communication server. The communication server from that point on is used only as a vehicle to transport the user's data to the host or remote device and to accept data from the host or the remote device. It will appear as if the users are directly connected to the host computer modem, etc.

Depending on the protocol suite, communication servers can establish connections to other communication servers or communication servers can establish connections directly to a host, provided the host has some type of internal networking capabilities.

Communication servers cannot only establish connections to devices on the local LAN but also traverse through bridges, routers, and other network-extending devices.

Therefore, if your site in New Orleans wishes to connect to a host in Washington, DC, the same "connect" command issued for connection to a local device will establish a connection to the remote device. Some communication servers support scripting so that menu systems can be built so that users can pick a menu item and the connection will be established for them. 3Com communication servers offer an extensive customizable script menu system. They also support multiple protocol suites such as TCP, XNS, OSI, and LAT. Remember communication servers are independent devices, and it does not matter what the operating environment (vendor independent) they are placed in.

Communication servers have two connection points. One is the connection to the network. The other are the ports that are connected to the serial device. The number of ports available is dependent on the networking vendor. The number of ports ranges from 2 to 128, depend-

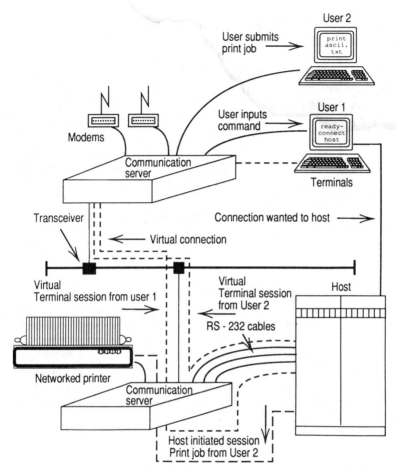

Figure G.7 Multiple communication server sessions.

ing on the user's individual needs and what their networking vendor can provide. Refer to Fig. G.1.

Configuring a communication server port so that it communicates correctly with a terminal, modem, or printer is the same as configuring the port as if it were to be connected directly to the host. All we are doing with a communication server is functionally bringing the host's ports to the user instead of running a terminal cable to the host. The communication server acts as an interface between two devices and a LAN.

During the configuration process, some type of script will ask a series of questions enabling you to configure a port for the particular device that you wish to connect to it. Whatever the asynchronous device is configured for, the port on the terminal server must exactly match it.

The network port cannot be configured. It will attach to the network cable plant that you have installed. Each asynchronous port is usually individually configured. Some configuration parameters you should be familiar with are baud rate, parity, data bits, and flow control.

In the asynchronous world, you will hear terms such as baud rate (for the purposes of this book, baud and bits per second (bps) will mean the same thing), male-female connectors, data communications-terminating equipment (DCE), data terminal equipment (DTE), hardware-software flow control, and communication server aggregate throughput. All of these terms are used to define each port on the communication server.

The baud rate is the speed of the port. Most ports on a communication server support 75 to 38.4 kbps. This is on a per port basis. One port may be configured to handle 9600 baud for terminal connection, while another port can be configured to handle 2400 baud for a modem attachment.

One point to emphasize here is that the baud rate does not have to be the same on each end of the connection. For example, if your terminal is running at 9600 baud and you want to connect to a comm server that has a modem attached to it, the modem does not have to be at the same baud rate. The modem could be running at 2400 baud. The communication server will take care of the speed mismatch. The parameters at each port must match the device that is to be directly attached to it. Most comm servers now support something called *autobaud*. If the comm server supports autobaud, it will figure out the speed at which you are running. The advantages to this are many. For example, every time you move a terminal, the user will not have to reconfigure the port. Some comm servers can be configured only by someone who has the privilege to change the parameters.

The data bits indicate how many bits will be used to represent a character. This field ranges from 5 to 8 bits per character. Five bits per character were used in very old teletype systems. Most characters are now represented by 7 or 8 bits.

Characters are represented as a series of 7 bits. For the extended character set, 8 bits is used. A parity bit is added to the data to ensure the integrity of the data. The parity is used for checking errors on the asynchronous bits. Parity types are odd, even, mark, space, and none (no parity added). The most common type is 8 data bits with no parity. Some comm servers have a capability known as autobaud (mentioned above) and *autoparity*. This allows a comm server port to determine the baud and parity setting without the administrator specifying it.

Another common configuration is the null-modem cable. Asynchronous devices are known as either data terminal equipment (DTE) or data circuit-terminating equipment (DCE). This terminology specifies the interface of the equipment. For example, an asynchronous terminal is defined as DTE. By specifying this, we know that the equipment transmits on a certain wire and receives data on another wire. It will also determine what special signals this equipment will set up. DTE devices usually initiate sessions, and DCE devices usually accept connections.

A modem is known as a DCE-type device. This specifies that it, too, will transmit on a certain wire and receive on another. According to the way it is set up, a DCE device will transmit on the same wire that a DTE device will receive on. The DCE device will receive on the same wire that a DTE device will transmit on. DCE devices will also have certain signals to present to the DTE device about its status.

This DCE-DTE connection is specified to allow devices to talk to each other. If a DCE device were connected to a modem (which is a DCE-type device), neither device would be able to communicate with one another (both will try to transmit and receive on the same wires). When would this type of connection exist? The ports on the comm server are DCE-type devices. Instead of changing the connector interface for the device to be attached to the comm server, a special cable is used to connect these devices together. It is called a null-modem cable. This cable will reverse its signals by simply moving the wires around to their respective positions. This is the most common problem found when hooking a modem up to a comm server. This cable fools each device into thinking that it is connected to a DTE device. A terminal is a DTE device and is connected to a comm server using a straight through cable. Hosts can either be a DCE or DTE.

Each communication server port has the capability of handling multiple sessions from the same physical port. This enables the user to establish one remote connection, put that connection on hold, establish a connection to another remote device, and so forth. 3Com terminal servers allow up to eight sessions per physical port. An analogy would once again be the phone system. The common office phone has the capability to make one call, put that call on hold, and make another phone call. The comm server acts the same way.

A communication server port may be in one of three states: command mode, data transfer mode, or listen mode. *Command mode* indicates that a device is attached and is not connected to any other device. If this device is a terminal, the command processor of the terminal server will prompt the user for input. These commands may be to connect to a remote device, change some of the parameters on the port, or show some status configuration. The command mode state means that the port is alive and is waiting for input from the user.

Data transfer or *connected mode* indicates that a connection has been established between two devices and data may be transferred from one device to the other. *Listen mode* indicates that the port is available, as is waiting connection from a remote device, for example a modem port waiting for a connection from a terminal.

One other point to note is the type of terminal emulation that is required. Network designers should be aware that most comm servers emulate simple ASCII terminals such as the VT100 series if they emulate at all. Some comm servers do have the capability to attach to specific host interfaces. The network designer should investigate thoroughly the host connection and ensure that the comm server has the capability to emulate that type of terminal.

We know that communication servers can support terminals, modems, hosts, printers, and virtually any RS-232-C device (refer to Figs. G.3, G.5), but the unique quality of these servers is that they can support all these devices on a single communication server. In other words, you do not have to buy one communication server for printers, another for modems, another for the hosts, and so forth. All the devices mentioned above can be connected on one communication server as shown in Fig. G.5. On larger networks, most network designers will separate their communication servers as to the application; one for the host, one for the terminals, and one for the modems. This is for convenience management only and is not a characteristic of the communication server.

If you want to extend the connection between the local device and the communication server, there is a standard to support this: the RS-422/449 connection. This standard was intended to supersede the RS-232-C standard but to date has failed to do so. This standard supports connections between devices of up to 1000 ft. Some comm servers support this standard. 3Com CS/1's support it.

And that is what communication servers provide. They are inexpensive and provide a great service for those devices that cannot connect directly to a network.

Communication servers are used to connect asynchronous devices to a LAN. This does not mean that a LAN may only control communication servers or that they should be separated from those devices that can attach directly to the LAN. With the correct network operating system (TCP/IP), for example, communication servers and the directly attached network stations may communicate with each other. In any case both reside on the same LAN harmoniously.

Since communication servers are commonly compared to digital private branch exchanges (DPBXs), a comparison between the two is in order. It is commonly thought that digital private branch exchanges are primarily used for telephone systems, but that isn't necessarily true. Digital private branch exchanges offered many of the same functional characteristics of terminal servers in the data communications environment in the 1970s, 1980s, and even today.

Private branch exchanges (PBXs) were first developed to connect calls between parties on the same premises and to switch calls to facilities outside the premises through the public telephone network. Prior to the PBX, every telephone call that was placed resulted in the call being placed through the outside telephone system by using a local switching office of the public telephone system. An increased demand on the telephone system soon produced a burden on the public telephone system, and PBXs were developed.

Prior to 1968, the only attachment to the public telephone system had to be accomplished through AT&T. The Carterfone decision of 1968 from the FCC changed all that. The PBX system grew rapidly as more vendors entered the market. The PBX was redesigned to accept not only the analog devices of telephone systems but also, eventually, to accept digital data, and the digital PBX was invented.

Prior to the evolution of LANs in the early 1980s, DPBXs offered many attractive benefits for terminals desiring access or connection to a local host processor and the ability to switch between host processor and other devices such as modems (see Fig. G.4).

As Fig. G.4 shows, a connection to a DPBX is accomplished by running a cable between the device and the DPBX. Another connection is made to one or more hosts. (Sounds similar to the communication server technology, doesn't it?) The DPBX multiplexed connections from the terminals to the host(s).

DPBXs are centralized switches that allow multiple-host connections and terminal connections. A connection was made between a terminal and host by electrically switching the circuit to reach the host port. This is known as circuit switching. Networks are packet switching. This allowed the user access to one host and multiple hosts. Connections from the DPBX to the hosts were usually made via a synchronous connection at speeds of 64 kbps. Because of this link, digital DPBXs are always located near the host processor to which they are connected. Unlike a communication server attached to LAN, there is no distribution of PBXs throughout a site. DPBX capabilities are limited though when compared to a terminal server.

These disadvantages include a slow-speed link between the DPBX and the host processor. Terminal cables still had to be run for long distances, for the DPBX was still located near the host processor.

DPBXs represent a centralized switch. If the DPBX went down, many users on the DPBX would be idle until the DPBX came back on line. However, the whole DPBX seldom failed. Usually the individual cards in the DPBX would fail, causing only those users connected to that card to become idle.

Even with the limitations of the DPBXs, this was impressive during the 1970s and early 1980s. With the emergence of new technology in the 1980s (Ethernet), having a speed of 10 Mbps and enhancing the same features of a DPBX, while distributing the servers over the network, resulted in the demise of the digital PBX, at least for the purposes of interconnecting computers.

Glossary

access method A means of determining which workstation or PC will be the next to use the LAN; a set of rules used by the network software and hardware that direct traffic over the network. Examples of access methods are token passing and collision detection.

address The location of a terminal, a peripheral device, a node, or any other unit or component in a network. Also a set of numbers identifying the location of a node on the network. Each node must have a unique address on the network.

amplifier A device used to boost the strength of an electronic signal.

ANSI American National Standards Institute.

application program interface (API) An interface that allows programmers to call certain functions of a protocol without changing the interface itself. This interface allows a window into a software module without having to know any underlying protocols.

Asynchronous Transmission Transmission in which each information character is individually synchronized, usually by means of start and stop elements. Also called "start-stop" transmission.

attenuation The difference (loss) between transmitted and received power due to transmission loss through equipment, lines, or other communications devices.

audit trail A function of a network management system that provides a list of information about connections and disconnections and the reasons for them. It also explains excessive errors on the network.

bandwidth The range of frequencies that can pass over a given circuit. Generally, the greater the bandwidth, the more information that can be sent through the circuit in a given amount of time.

baseband An electrical signaling technique used to transmit information. Baseband signaling uses unmodulated signals. The carrier is present only when data is being transmitted. The entire frequency range of the channel is used during this transmission. In baseband signaling the signal is transmitted in its original form and not changed by modulation.

baseband LAN A LAN employing baseband signaling. An example of a baseband LAN is Ethernet—a bus topology with a CSMA/CD access control technique.

A Local Area Network based on the technique of transmitting digital signals without the need for a carrier signal.

binary synchronous communication (BSC/BISYNC)   A half-duplex, character-oriented synchronous data communications protocol originated by IBM in 1964.

bridge   Equipment which allows the interconnection of LANs, allowing communication between devices on separate networks using similar protocols.

broadband   An electrical signaling technique used to transmit information. Broadband signaling involves modulation of the signal before transmission. Broadband networks typically divide the total bandwidth of the communication's channel into multiple subchannels so that different types of information can be transmitted simultaneously using different frequencies. Broadband signaling is used when mixing multiple types of information such as video, voice, and data on a single cable or multiple cables.

broadband LAN   LAN which uses FDM (frequency-division multiplexing) to divide a single physical channel into a number of smaller independent frequency channels. The different channels created by FDM can be used to transfer different forms of information—voice, data, and video.

broadcast   The act of sending a signal from one station of a LAN to all other stations, all of which are capable of receiving that signal.

BSI   British Standards Institute.

bus   A network topology which functions like a single line which is shared by a number of nodes.

cable loss   The amount of RF (radio frequency) signal attenuated by coaxial-cable transmission. The cable attenuation is a function of frequency, media type, and cable distance. For coaxial cable, higher frequencies have greater loss than do lower frequencies and follow a logarithmic function. Cable losses are usually calculated for the highest frequency carried on the cable.

CASE   Common application service elements standard.

CATV   Community antenna television; the use of a coaxial cable logical loop to transmit television or other signals to subscribers from a single head-end location.

CCITT   Consultive Committee International for Telephony and Telegraphy; an international organization (part of ITU) concerned with devising and proposing recommendations for international telecommunications.

channel   (1) A path for electrical transmission—also called a circuit, facility, line link, or path; (2) a specific and discrete bandwidth allocation in the RF spectrum (e.g., in a broadband LAN) utilized to transmit one information signal at a time.

channel translator   Device used in broadband LANs to increase carrier frequency, converting upstream (toward the head-end) signals into downstream signals (away from the head-end).

circuit   A communication path between two points.

circuit switching   A switching technique in which an information path (i.e., circuit) between calling and called stations is established on demand, for exclusive use by the connected parties until the connection is released.

CMIP   Common Management Information Protocol; the protocol used to provide the CMIS services.

CMIS   Common Management Information Specification; a network management scheme for networks using the OSI protocols. CMIS provides for event notification, information transfer, and control.

coaxial cable   A physical transmission medium with two conductors. The center conductor carries the information signals; the outer conductor (electrostatic shielding) acts as a ground. Also a physical network medium which offers large bandwidth and the ability to support high data rates with high immunity to electrical interference and a low incidence of errors.

CODEC   An assembly consisting of an encoder and a decoder in the same equipment.

collision   Overlapping transmissions which occur when two or more nodes attempt to transmit at or about the same instant. Their interference is a collision.

collision detection (CD)   The ability of a transmitting node to detect simultaneous transmission attempts on a shared medium. See also **CSMA/CD**.

communication server   A combined hardware-software medium that allows a device such as a terminal, a host computer, or a printer to access a network without having to implement the communications protocol in the device itself. The communication server communicates with the device using standard protocols built into the device.

connection   A communications path between two devices that allows the exchange of information. Other terms used to refer to a connection are session or circuit.

connectionless mode   The transmission of data without having established a circuit to the addressed station.

connection-oriented mode   The transmission of data is allowed only after a connection is set up between the source and destination stations.

contention   a "dispute" between two or more devices over the use of a common channel at the same time.

COS   Corporation for Open Systems.

CRC   Abbreviation for cyclical redundancy check. This is a method of detecting errors in a message by performing a mathematical calculation on the bits in the message and then sending the results of the calculation along with the message. The receiving network station performs the same calculation on the message data as it receives it and then checks the results against those transmitted at the end of the message. If the results do not match, the receiving end asks the sending end to send the entire message again. In other words, the CRC is an error-checking algorithm which is included in a packet before transmission. The receiver checks the CRC on each packet it receives and strips it off before giving the packet to the station. If the CRC is incorrect, there are two options: either discard the packet or deliver the damaged packet with an appropriate status indicating a CRC error.

CSMA   Acronym for carrier sense multiple access. A contention technique which allows multiple stations to gain access to a single channel (cable).

CSMA/CD   Acronym for carrier sense multiple access with collision detection. It is an access method that allows many nodes to share a single channel of a communications medium. If more than one signal is transmitted at the same time, the signals collide and are retransmitted at a later, randomly calculated time. CSMA/CD is a contention technique which allows multiple stations to successfully share a broadcast channel (cable) by avoiding contention via carrier sense and deference, and managing collisions via collision detection and packet retransmissions.

datagram   A transmission method in which sections of a message are transmitted in random order and the correct order is reestablished by the receiving workstation. Also, a packet that includes a complete destination address specification (provided by the user, not the network) along with whatever data it carries. There are no acknowledgments to a datagram; therefore, very little overhead processing is provided on the network. It is a one-way construct much like a telegram.

data-link service   A service which guarantees transmission between two stations sharing the same physical medium.

data rate   A measure of the signaling rate of a data link.

datastream   A series of bits appearing on a communications link structured according to some agreed-on rules. These rules may consist of character codes, control characters, header and trailer information, or field lengths.

DECconnect   Also known as DECnet; Digital Equipment Corporation's proprietary cabling system for LANs, i.e., proprietary communications protocol.

dB (decibel)   The standard unit used to express the relative strength of two signals. When referring to a single signal measured at two places in a transmission system, it expresses either a gain or a loss in power between the input and output devices. The reference level must always be indicated, such as I1 mW for power ratio.

dBmV (decibel millivolt)   A measurement of signal strength.

DCE   Acronym for data circuit terminating equipment; carrier equipment—equipment installed at the user's premises which provides all the functions required to establish, maintain, and terminate a connection, and provides the signal conversion, and coding between the data terminal equipment and the common carrier's line; e.g., data set, modem.

DDCMP   Acronym for Digital Data Communications Message Protocol. A byte-oriented synchronous protocol developed by Digital Equipment Corporation that supports half- or full-duplex modes, and either point-to-point or multipoint lines in a DNA (digital network architecture) network.

DECnet   Digital Equipment Corporation's line of communications software products that implement DNA.

destination   Receiver of data.

directional coupler   A passive device used in a cable system to divide or combine unidirectional RF power sources.

DNA   Acronym for digital network architecture. Digital Equipment Corporation's proprietary overall specification for networking with DEC computers.

download   The process of loading software into the nodes of a network from one node or device over the network media.

drop cable   The cable which allows connection and access to and from the distribution and trunk cables of a cable network.

DTE   Acronym for data terminal equipment. User equipment. The end-user machine (terminal, computer, controller, etc.) which plugs into a unit which is the termination point of the communications circuit (DCE).

dual cable   A two-cable system in broadband LANs in which the coaxial cable provides two physical paths for transmission, one for transmit and one for receive, instead of dividing the capacity of a single cable. ECMA (European Computer Manufacturers Association) Standards organization dedicated to the development of data processing standards; not a trade organization. ECMA was the first group to define the OSI Transport Layer Protocol.

EIA (Electronics Industries Association)   The U.S. national organization of electronic manufacturers. It is responsible for the development and maintenance of industry standards for the interface between data processing machines and data communications equipment.

error detection   Code in which each data signal conforms to specific rules of construction so that departures from this construction in the received signals can be automatically detected. Any data detected as being in error is either deleted from the data delivered to the destination, with or without an indication that such deletion has taken place, or delivered to the destination together with an indication that it has been detected as being in error.

Ethernet   A LAN that utilizes baseband signaling at 10 Mbps; developed jointly by Xerox Corporation, Intel Corporation, and Digital Equipment Corporation to interconnect computer equipment using coaxial cable and "transceivers." Ethernet is the predominant LAN standard.

F-type connector   A low-cost connector used by the television industry to connect coaxial cable to equipment.

FDDI   Abbreviation for Fiber Distributed Data Interface (ANSI X3T9.5 specification). FDDI is an emerging standard for a 100-Mbps fiber-optic LAN. It uses a counterrotating Token Ring topology. It is compatible with the standards for the physical layer of the ISO model.

FDM   Acronym for frequency-division multiplexing. Method by which the available transmission frequency range is divided into narrower bands, each used for a separate channel. As utilized by broadband technology, the frequency spectrum is divided up among discrete channels to allow one user or a set of users access to single channels.

fiber optics   A technology that uses light as an information carrier. Fiber-optic cable (light guides) are a direct replacement for conventional coaxial cable and wire pairs. The glass-based transmission facility occupies far less physical volume for an equivalent transmission capacity; the fibers are impervious to electrical interference.

flow control   The hardware or software mechanisms employed in data communications to turn off transmission when the receiving workstation is unable to store the data it is receiving. Software flow control can be in the form of ENQ/ACK or Xon/Xoff. Hardware flow control can be (RTS-232) RTS-CTS or DTR-DSR, i.e., the capability of network nodes to manage buffering schemes in order to allow devices of differing data transmission speeds to communicate with each other.

forward direction   The direction of signal flow away from the head-end in a broadband LAN. High frequencies travel in this direction.

forward error correction   Code incorporating sufficient additional elements to enable the nature of some or all errors to be indicated and corrected entirely at the receiving end.

frame   A group of bits sent over a communications channel, usually containing its own control information, including address and error detection. The exact size and format of a frame depends on the protocol used.

frequency   The number of cycles per second at which an analog signal occurs, usually expressed in hertz (Hz). One hertz is one cycle per second.

frequency plan   Specification of how the various frequencies of a broadband cable system are allocated for use.

frequency translator   See **channel translator.**

gateway   A special node that interfaces two or more dissimilar networks, providing protocol translation between the networks.

HDLC   High-Level Data-Link Control; the International Standards Organization data-link protocol. Various manufacturers have their own derivative of HDLC, the most common of which is IBM's SDLC (Synchronous Data-Link Control). HDLC uses a specific series of bits rather than control characters for transmitting and receiving data.

head-end   A central point in broadband networks that receives signals on one set of frequency bands and retransmits them on another set of frequencies. Viewed as a central hub.

high-split   A broadband cable system in which the bandwidth utilized to send toward the head-end (reverse direction) is approximately 6 to 180 MHz, and the bandwidth utilized to send away from the head-end (forward direction) is approximately 220–400 MHz. The guard band between the forward and reverse directions (180 to 220 MHz) provides isolation from interference.

IEEE   Institute for Electrical and Electronics Engineers.

IEEE 488   Institute of Electrical and Electronics Engineers 488. An IEEE-standard parallel interface bus consisting of eight bidirectional data lines, eight control lines, and eight signal grounds, which provide for connection to an IEEE 488 device networking computer equipment. The IEEE 802 standard deals with the physical and data-link layers of the ISO Reference Model for OSI.

IEEE 802.2   A data-link layer standard used with the IEEE 802.3, 802.4, and 802.5 standards.

IEEE 802.3   A physical layer standard specifying a LAN with a CSMA/CD access method on a bus topology. Ethernet follows the 802.3 standard.

IEEE 802.4   A physical layer standard specifying a LAN with a token-passing access method on a bus topology. Used with manufacturing automation protocol (MAP) LANs.

IEEE 802.5   A physical layer standard specifying a LAN with a token-passing access method on a ring topology. Used with IBM's Token Ring hardware.

impedence   A measure of the electrical property of resistance, expressed in ohms (Ω). Different cable systems have different resistance levels: broadband utilizes CATV standard 75-Ω cable, and baseband Ethernet utilizes 50 Ω while WANGnet utilizes 93-Ω cable. The impedance range for unshielded twisted-pair (UTP) cable is 75 to 125 Ω.

in-band signaling   The transmission of signaling information at some frequency or frequencies that lie within a carrier channel normally used for information transmission.

internetwork   A term used to indicate two distinct networks that are usually logically and geographically separated; i.e., an interconnected network.

intranetwork   The means of communication from within one network. In other words, not extending between logically separate networks.

ISO Reference Model for OSI   International Standards Organization Reference Model for Open-Systems Interconnection. A standard approach to network design which introduces modularity by dividing the complex set of functions into more manageable, self-contained, functional slices. These layers, from the innermost layer, are as follows: (1) physical layer—concerned with the mechanical and electrical means by which devices are physically connected and data is transmitted; (2) data-link layer—concerned with how to move data reliably across the physical data link; (3) network layer—provides the means to establish, maintain, and terminate connections between systems; concerned with switching and routing of information; (4) transport layer—concerned with end-to-end data integrity and quality of service; (5) session layer—standardizes the task of setting up a session and terminating it; coordination of interaction between end-application processes; (6) presentation layer—relates to the character set and data code which is used, and to the way data is displayed on a screen or printer; (7) application layer—concerned with the higher-level functions which provide support to the application or system activities.

ITU International Telecommunications Union. This organization is the one that reports directly to the United Nations.

jam A short encoded sequence transmitted by a node to ensure that all other nodes have detected a collision.

local area network (LAN) A communications network that provides high-speed data transmission over a small geographic area. The LAN is most frequently used to transfer data over distances of several thousand feet to several thousand miles. These networks can use the international telephone network to transport messages over most or part of these distances.

logical link control (LLC) Upper sublayer of the ISO model data-link layer.

MAC Abbreviation for media access control. Lower sublayer of the data-link layer of the ISO model. The MAC layer supports medium-dependent functions and controls framing of a packet.

MHS Message Handlink System (electronic mail).

midsplit A broadband cable system in which the cable bandwidth is divided between transmit and receive frequencies. The bandwidth utilized to send toward the head-end (reverse direction) is approximately 5 to 100 MHz; and away from the head-end (forward direction), approximately 160 to 300 MHz. The guard band between the forward and reverse directions (100 to 160 MHz) provides isolation from interference.

modem A contraction of modulate and demodulate; a conversion device installed in pairs at each end of an analog communications line. The modem at the transmitting end modulates digital signals received locally from a computer or terminal; the modem at the receiving end demodulates the incoming analog signal, converting it back to its original (i.e., digital) destination device.

multicast The ability to broadcast messages to one node (station) or a select group of nodes (stations).

multidrop See multipoint circuit.

multiplex The use of a common physical channel in order to make two or more logical channels, either by splitting of the frequency band transmitted by the common channel into narrower band—each of which is used to constitute a distinct channel (frequency-division multiplex)—or by allotting this common channel, in turn, to constitute different intermittent channels (time-division multiplex).

multiplexor Equipment that permits simultaneous transmission of multiple signals over one physical circuit.

Netbios Network basic input/output system. A collection of interfaces and protocols designed to support many of the functions of session management as defined by the OSI reference model. This interface also includes datagram support.

network   A series of nodes connected by communications channels.

network interface controller (NIC)   A communications device that allows the connection of devices to a network.

network management   The overseeing and maintenance of a network; i.e., administrative services performed in managing a network, such as network topology, software installation and configuration, downloading of software, monitoring network performance, maintaining network operations and keeping an operation log, diagnosing and troubleshooting problems, and statistics.

network service   An application available on a network, e.g., file transfer.

network topology   Geography of a network or a set of networks.

node   A station; i.e., a point in a network where service is provided, service is used, or communications channels are interconnected. The term *node* is sometimes used interchangeably with *station*.

out-of-band signaling   A method of signaling which uses a frequency that is within the passband of the transmission facility, but outside a carrier channel normally used for information transmission.

PABX   Acronym for Private Automatic Branch Exchange. Equipment originally used as a means of switching telephone calls within a business site and from the site to outside lines. Can also be used for low-speed transmission of data, in addition to voice.

packet   A block of data handled by a network in a well-defined format; a collection of bits that contain both control information and data. The basic unit of transmission in a packet-switched network. Control information is carried in the packet, along with the data, to provide for such functions as addressing, sequencing, flow control, and error control at each of several protocol levels. A packet can be of either fixed or variable length, but generally has a specified maximum length.

packet format   The exact order and size of the various control and information fields of a packet, including header, address, and data fields.

packet switching   The internal operation of a communications network in which data is transmitted by means of addressed packets and a transmission channel is occupied for the duration of transmission of the packet only; i.e., software is used to dynamically route packets from a source to a destination. The channel is then available for use by other stations on the channel; thus, packet switching allows the sharing of a single communications channel among several connections.

PAD   Acronym for packet assembler-disassembler. An interface device which buffers data sent to or from character mode devices and assembles and disassembles the packets needed for X.25 operation; and extension of CCITT X.25. A PAD allows asynchronous terminals to have access to a public data network.

parallel interface   An interface which permits parallel transmission, or simultaneous transmission of the bits making up a character or byte, either over separate channels or on different carrier frequencies of the same channel.

PBX   Acronym for Private Branch Exchange. See **PABX.**

PEER   Used for distributed systems and intelligent workstations to denote a balanced relationship in their communication. There is no master-slave or primary-secondary relationship.

point-to-point   (1) Point-to-point transmission—transmission of data between only two stations or nodes, i.e., one sender and one receiver; (2) point-to-point link—a circuit which connects two (and only two) nodes without passing through an intermediate node.

polling   A method of controlling the sequence of transmission by devices on a multipoint line by requiring each device to wait until the controlling processor requests it to transmit.

port   The entrance or physical access point to a computer, multiplexor, device, or network where signals may be supplied, extracted, or observed (e.g., RS-232-C).

preamble   A sequence of encoded bits which is transmitted before each frame to allow synchronization of clocks and other circuitry at other stations on the channel. In the Ethernet specification, the preamble is 64 bits.

protocol   A strictly defined procedure and message format that allows two or more systems to communicate over a physical transmission medium. Because of the complexity of communications between systems and the need for different communications requirements, protocols are divided into layers. Each layer of a protocol performs a specific function, such as routing, end-to-end reliability, and connection. More broadly defined, protocol is a set of rules and conventions governing the exchange of information between or among communicating stations. Both hardware protocols and software protocols can be defined.

protocol converter   A device for translating the data transmission code and/ or protocol of one network or device to the corresponding code or protocol of another network or device, enabling equipment with different conventions to communicate with one another.

public data network (PDN)   A packet-switched or circuit switched network available for use by many customers; i.e., a network that provides data transmission to the public. PDNs may offer value-added services at a reduced cost because of communications resource sharing, and usually provide increased reliability due to built-in redundancy. Typically, a PDN uses packet switching technology.

remote station   Data terminal equipment for communication with a data processing system in a distant location.

repeater   For LANs, a device which increases the length of a single LAN segment by joining it to another, so that packets sent on one segment can be "repeated" or copied onto the other.

retransmit   To send a packet again if the original packet is not acknowledged, if it is received in error, or if a collision is detected.

reverse direction The direction of signal flow toward the head-end in a broadband LAN. Low frequencies travel in this direction.

RF radio frequency; a generic term referring to the technology employed in the CATV industry and broadband LANs. Uses electromagnetic waveforms for transmission, usually in the megahertz (MHz) range.

RF modem Device used to convert digital data signals to analog signals (and from analog to digital), then modulate and/or demodulate them to or from their assigned frequencies.

ring A network topology in which stations are connected to one another in a closed logical circle. Typically, access to the media passes sequentially from one station to the next by means of polling from a master station, or by passing an access token from one station to another.

RS-232-C Recommended Standard 232, Revision C. A technical specification published by the EIA (Electronic Industries Association) that specifies the mechanical and electrical characteristics of the interface for connecting DTE and DCE. It defines interface circuit functions and their corresponding connector pin assignments. The standard applies to both asynchronous and synchronous serial, binary data transmission at speeds of up to 20 Kbps in full- or half-duplex mode. RS-232-C defines 20 specific functions. The physical connection between DTE and DCE is made through plug-in, 25-pin connectors.

RS-422 A standard operating in conjunction with RS-449 that specifies electrical characteristics for balanced circuits (circuits with their own ground leads).

RS-423 A standard operating in conjunction with RS-449 that specifies electrical characteristics for unbalanced circuits (circuits using a common ground or shared grounding techniques). Another EIA standard for DTE/DCE connection which specifies interface requirements for expanded transmission speeds ($\leq$ 2 Mbps), longer cable lengths and 10 additional functions. RS-449 applies to binary, serial synchronous, or asynchronous communications. Half- and full-duplex modes are accommodated, and transmission can be over 2- or 4-wire facilities such as point-to-point or multipoint lines. The physical connection between DTE and DCE is made through a 37-contact connector; a separate 9-contact connector is specified to service secondary channel interchange circuits, when used.

SDLC Synchronous Data-Link Control. An IBM communications line discipline or protocol associated with SNA, SDLC provides for control of a single communications link or line, accommodates for a number of networks, and arrangements, and operates in half- or full-duplex over private or switched facilities.

serial interface An interface which requires serial transmission, or the transfer of information in which the bits composing a character are sent sequentially. Implies the use of only a single transmission channel.

server A processor which provides a specific service to the network. Examples of servers are as follows: routing server—connects nodes and networks of like architectures; gateway server—connects nodes and networks of different architectures by performing protocol conversion; terminal, print, or file server—provides an interface between compatible peripheral devices on a LAN.

session   A logical connection between two entities on the network. A session may be established on a LAN or a wide area network.

single cable   A one-cable system in broadband LANs in which a portion of the bandwidth is allocated for send signals, and a portion for receive signals, with a guard band in between to provide isolation from interference.

SNA   Acronym for systems network architecture. The network architecture developed by IBM.

source   Originator of data.

splitter   A passive device used in a cable system to divide the power of a single input into two or more outputs of lesser power. Can also be used as a combiner when two or more inputs are combined into a single output.

star   A network topology consisting of one central node with point-to-point links to several other nodes. Control of the network is usually located in the central node or switch, with all routing of network message traffic performed by the central node. Each station communicates with all other stations through the central node, potentially creating a central point of failure.

station   A network node.

subchannel   A frequency subdivision created from the capacity of one physical channel by broadband LAN technology. Bands of frequencies of the same or different sizes are assigned to transmission of voice, data, or video signals. Actual transmission paths are created when each assigned band is divided, using FDM, into a number of subchannels. The bandwidth of the subchannels is determined by the form of information to be transmitted.

subnet   A portion of a network that is partitioned by a router.

subsplit   The most common form of transmission in the CATV industry. In the subsplit scheme, the bandwidth utilized to send toward the head-end (reverse direction) is much smaller, approximately 5 to 30 MHz, and the bandwidth utilized to send away from the dead-end (forward direction) is very large, approximately 55 to 300 MHz. The guard band between forward and reverse directions (30 to 55 MHz) provides isolation from interference.

T-1 Carrier   A digital transmission system developed by AT&T that sends information at 1.544 Mbps. T-1 links can transmit voice or data.

tap   (1) Baseband—the component or connector that attaches a transceiver to a cable; (2) broadband (also called a directional tap or multitap)—a passive device used to remove a portion of the signal power from the distribution line and deliver it onto the drop line.

TCP/IP   Abbreviation for Transmission Control Protocol/Internet Protocol. A set of de facto networking standards commonly used over Ethernet or X.25

networks. It was sponsored by the U.S. Government [Department of Defense ARPANET (DARPA) standard] and is now supported by many equipment manufacturers. It defines high-level protocols such as Telnet (terminal connection), FTP (file transfer), and SMTP (electronic mail). The TCP/IP protocol module corresponds to layers 3 and 4 of the ISO protocol model.

TDM Acronym for time-division multiplexing. A method of utilizing channel capacity efficiently in which each node is allotted a small time interval, in turns, during which it may transmit a message or a portion of a message (e.g., a data packet). Nodes are given unique time slots during which they have exclusive command of the channel. The messages of many nodes are interleaved for transmission and then demultiplexed into their proper order at the receiving end.

terminator A resistive connector used to terminate the end of a cable or an unused tap into its characteristic impedance. The terminator prevents interference-causing signal reflections.

thin Ethernet A lighter (0.2-in-diameter, black coating) variation of Ethernet cable that saves cable and installation costs, but is restricted in effective distance. This type of cabling is specified under the IEEE 802.3 10BASE2 standard.

throughput The total useful information processed or communicated during a specified time period. Expressed in bits per second or packets per second.

token bus A token access procedure used with a broadcast topology or network.

token passing A mechanism whereby each device receives and passes the right to use the channel. Tokens are special bit patterns or packets, usually several bits in length that circulate from node to node when there is no message traffic. Possession of the token gives a node exclusive access to the network for transmitting its message, thus avoiding conflict with other nodes that wish to transmit.

Token Ring A ring access procedure developed by IBM whereby a token is used to direct traffic on the network. There is only one token on the ring (the network) at a time. It is either free or busy. A node must wait for a free token to transmit data; it marks the token as busy, then transmits a frame of data onto the ring. Data collisions cannot occur as only one node can transmit at any one time. Token Ring is used on a network with a sequential or ring topology.

topology (1) Physical topology—the configuration of network nodes and links. Description of the physical geometric arrangement of the links and nodes that make up a network, as determined by their physical connections. (2) Logical topology—description of the possible logical connections between network nodes, indicating which pairs or nodes are able to communicate, and whether they have a direct physical connection. Examples of network topologies are bus, ring, star, and tree.

transceiver   A device required in baseband networks which takes the digital signal from a computer or terminal and imposes it on the baseband medium.

transceiver cable   Cable connecting the transceiver to the network interface controller, allowing nodes to be placed away from the baseband medium.

trunk cable   Coaxial cable used for distribution of RF signals over long distances throughout a cable system.

twisted pair   A form of wiring commonly used for telephone installations. Standard networks such as Ethernet can operate over such wiring. The method is economical because it imposes distance limitation, unlike coaxial cable.

VAX   The tradename for a family of computers manufactured by Digital Equipment Corporation.

vendor independence   The ability to allow devices manufactured by different vendors, often using different protocols, to communicate with each other.

virtual circuit   Provision of a circuitlike service by the software protocols of a network, enabling two endpoints to communicate as though via a physical circuit; a logical transmission path. The network nodes provide the addressing information needed in the packets that carry the source data to the destination. Advantages of virtual circuits over physical circuits include the resolution of speed mismatch between the data-generating and data-consuming endpoint (send and receiver of data), data retransmissions in case of transient communication errors, and transformation of the information that traverses the circuits. More generally defined, a virtual circuit is a facility in a packet-switching network in which packets passing between a pair of devices are kept in sequence. This is a "virtual" circuit because it appears that there is an actual point-to-point connection.

wide area network   A data communications network designed to serve an area of hundreds or thousands of miles. A wide area network can be either public or private.

X Series   The CCITT recommendations that relate to data communications.

X.21   The CCITT standard for accessing circuit-switched networks.

X.21   An intermediate standard which enables RS-232-C terminals to access a digital network over voice lines.

X.25   A CCITT standard that defines the standard communications protocol by which mainframes access a public or private packet-switching network often referred to as X.25 networks), i.e., defines the interface between a PDN and a packet-mode user device (DTE); also defines the services that these user devices can expect from the X.25 PDN, including the ability to establish virtual circuits through a PDN to another user device, to move data from one user device to another, and to destroy the virtual circuit when finished.

X.28   Defines the interface between PADs and non-packet-mode DTEs (hosts).

X.29   Defines the interface between PADs and packet-mode DTEs.

X.400   The CCITT recommendation for the family of Message-Handling Systems, e.g., an international standard for electronic mail.

X.401   A CCITT standard for handling the service features of the X.400 standard.

X.409   The international standard for cleaning solutions. In reality, the CCITT standard for transfer syntax notation for the X.400 standard.

XNS   Abbreviation for Xerox Network Systems. A protocol family specifically designed to run on Ethernet. It contains the Internetwork Datagram Protocol (IDP) (level 3) and the Sequenced Packet Protocol (SPP) (level 4).

Bibliography

Bridges, Routers, and Brouters: An Internetworking Tutorial, 3Com Corp., Santa Clara, Calif., 1990.

Brouter Operation Guide, 3Com Corp., Santa Clara, Calif., March 1990.

EtherLink Product Line Guide, 3Com Corp., Santa Clara, Calif., 1989.

The Ethernet Version 2.0, 2d ed., Xerox Corp., Intel Corp., Digital Equipment Corp., Maynard, Mass., 1984.

Greenfield, David: "Into the Ring," *LAN Magazine*, Miller Freeman Publications, San Francisco, Calif., Sept. 1989.

Haugdahl, J. Scott: *Inside Netbios*, 2d ed., Architecture Technology Corp., Minneapolis, Minn., March 1988.

Haugdahl, J. Scott: *Inside the Token Ring*, Architecture Technology Corp., Minneapolis, Minn., 1988.

Internetworking Bridge Operation Guide, 3Com Corp., Santa Clara, Calif., March 1990.

Kessler, Gary C: "Tokenism," *LAN Magazine*, Miller Freeman Publications, San Francisco, Calif., Sept. 1989.

LAN Magazine staff, *LAN Magazine Buyers' Guide*, Miller Freeman Publications, San Francisco, Calif., August 1990.

LAN Planning Guide, 3Com Corp., Santa Clara, Calif., 1989.

Multiconnect Repeater Guide, 3Com Corp., Santa Clara, Calif., 1989.

Netbios Programmers Reference Guide, 3Com Corp., Santa Clara, Calif., 1987.

Roman, Bob: "Making the Big Connection: Implementing Internetworks with Bridges, Routers, and Brouters," *3Tech: The 3Com Technical Journal*, 3Com Corp., Santa Clara, Calif., 1990.

Shock, John F., Dalal, Yogen K., Redel, David D., and Ronald C. Crane: "Evolution of the Ethernet Local Computer Network, *Computer Magazine*, IEEE Computer Society, Los Alamitos, Calif., 1982.

Token Ring Network Architecture Reference Manual, 3d ed., IBM Corp. Research, Triangle Park, N.C., 1989.

White, David: "By This Token," *LAN Magazine*, Miller Freeman Publications, San Francisco, Calif., September 1988.

Index

ABOUT THE AUTHOR

Matthew G. Naugle is currently a systems engineer for
3Com Corporation (Virginia), a global data networking
company. He is involved in the design of large- to
medium-scale networks, installation of software, and
network training for customers. He also teaches a course in
local area networking at Northern Virginia Community
College. His varied background includes work for Digital
Equipment Corporation, Proteon, Inc., Ungermann-Bass,
Inc., and Burroughs Computer Corporation.